Mediated Mormons

MEDIATED MORMONS

Shifting Religious Identities in the Digital Age

ROSEMARY AVANCE

The University of Utah Press
Salt Lake City

THE JUANITA BROOKS SERIES IN MORMON HISTORY AND CULTURE
SERIES EDITOR: Amanda Hendrix-Komoto

This series welcomes exciting new academic monographs and contributed volumes of previously unpublished essays that break new ground in the study and understanding of Mormon history and culture.

The Defiance House Man colophon is a registered trademark of the University of Utah Press. It is based on a four-foot-tall Ancient Puebloan pictograph (late PIII) near Glen Canyon, Utah.

LIBRARY OF CONGRESS CATALOGING-IN-PUBLICATION DATA
Names: Avance, Rosemary, author.
Title: Mediated Mormons : shifting religious identities in the digital age / Rosemary Avance.
Description: Salt Lake City : The University of Utah Press, [2025] | Series: The Juanita Brooks series in Mormon history and culture | Includes bibliographical references and index.
Identifiers: LCCN 2024016370 | ISBN 9781647692056 (cloth) | ISBN 9781647692063 (paperback) | ISBN 9781647692070 (ebook)
Subjects: LCSH: Church of Jesus Christ of Latter-day Saints--Public opinion--History--21st century. | Latter Day Saints in mass media--Case studies. | Mass media--Religious aspects--Church of Jesus Christ of Latter-day Saints--Case studies. | Internet--Religious aspects--Church of Jesus Christ of Latter-day Saints--Case studies. | Identity (Psychology)--Religious aspects--Church of Jesus Christ of Latter-day Saints--Case studies. | Latter Day Saints--Public opinion--History--21st century.
Classification: LCC P94.5.M67 A93 2024 | DDC 306.6/86373--dc23/eng/20240920
LC record available at https://lccn.loc.gov/2024016370

Errata and further information on this and other titles available at UofUpress.com

For Carolyn, for everything

Contents

Preface

Social belonging is among our most central needs. Our longing for community is as old as communication itself. Throughout history, human societies have relied on religion and other social institutions to structure and restrict a community into a usable, functioning system. The digital age has confounded notions of community as embodied, temporally and spatially limited, and narratively closed. But the expansiveness of life online, while threatening hegemony, offers new generations a new place and new ways to do religion.

This book is an exploration of the human struggle for belonging, set in a particular time and a particular place and with a focus on a small subset of a particular faith. In these pages, I explore how unprecedented media attention on Mormonism and the Church of Jesus Christ of Latter-day Saints during the "Mormon moment" of 2012–13 contributed to changing discourses in Mormon communities about what it means to be Mormon. While I do not attempt to embed this one moment in an exhaustive study of religion, I do suggest that this brief moment in recent history can provide important insight into the messy, contradictory, and very human ways we do life in the twenty-first century.

I began the academic study of the Church of Jesus Christ of Latter-day Saints in 2009 during doctoral training at the University of Pennsylvania's Annenberg School for Communication. This book builds especially on my dissertation research from 2011 to 2014, primarily consisting of on- and offline ethnography and rhetorical analysis, and a subsequent decade of citizen sampling of Mormon news, social media, and institutional goings-on.

Mormon identities change. They move with the currents of their institution, their social settings, and their historical moments. Pinning down what it means to be Mormon is no small feat, and although I cannot say I have done so exhaustively, any success to that end is a result of the time and generosity of dozens of Mormons who, over the years, graciously shared their experiences and visions for their church with this curious outsider. This analysis of one moment in Mormon history is my humble attempt to repay a portion of the insight these generous Mormons have shared with me.

This work occurred in three states and across a decade of my life. I could not begin to thank everyone who had a hand in its completion: every Mormon who shared their story, every family member who expressed support or picked up my slack while I was neck-deep in my research, every colleague who provided mentorship and advice, and the thorough and insightful reviewers who helped me polish my ideas into something intelligible.

My most heartfelt thanks to Carolyn Marvin, my mentor and friend, who taught me that we Southern girls can change the world. Here's the book!

My warmest thanks to my wonderful family: to my husband, Andrew, who put his plans on hold to support mine, sojourned with me on three cross-country moves, cared for our children, and pulled me through the darkest days. To Casper, Cortez, and Evelyn, our three beautiful children, this project is as old as you are. You helped me become the person who could write it. Thanks for putting up with Academic Mom.

Finally, my most bittersweet thanks to my grandparents Jerry and Dora Lee, who did not live to see this book's publication but who nurtured my soul throughout my childhood and adolescence. Thank you for helping me believe that my ideas were worth speaking.

Introduction

Viewing Mormonism through a Media Lens

> Most certainly, religion conserves and legitimates, and these are indispensable social and psychological functions, but by its very nature more is involved than this singular abstraction would imply: religion is also process, movement, aspiration, quest. These liminal qualities point to its effusive and creative potential, its recurrent capacity to combine elements into new forms, its bumptiousness, or ability to reinvent itself on occasion. To overlook religion's transforming force, in both personal and social life, is to lose sight of a fundamental feature of human quest, the hope that lies in an indeterminate and unrealized future.
>
> —Wade Clark Roof, *Spiritual Marketplace: Baby Boomers and the Remaking of American Religion*

What does it mean to be part of a religious community? Is it the same as claiming a religion? These two questions define religious politics. Their answers illuminate the power structures that matter most within a given organization or community. To answer the first, we must further ask, Who decides? Does a religious organization or leader determine the demarcations for who belongs and who does not? Do you need an officially sanctioned membership? To engage in ritual actions like attendance, tithing, or volunteer work? Must you believe in a sacred text and history? Is the process based on a social contract passed down through official and unofficial norms, rules, policies, and practices?

To be sure, organizational factors matter. Consider "belonging" in an orthoprax, or practice-focused, system—think of most American Jewish or Hindu congregations—where community is primarily defined by members who trace a similar history and engage in the right ritual actions. This type of belonging is different than, for example, in the belief-based, Evangelical Christian community, which values orthodoxy first and foremost, emphasizing central tenets of faith and right belief. Belonging is different still for those in belief- *and* practice-emphasizing communities, like Orthodox Judaism and Roman Catholicism and any number of fundamentalist iterations of the world's various faiths, and all of these are different from belonging in loosely organized spiritual belief systems such as Wicca or Spiritualism, where neither belief nor practice is strictly policed.

To answer the second question, we must determine whether and how individual actors in these communities may claim an identity as an exercise in self-determination (my academic mind wants to call this agency, but that word has a differently nuanced connotation in Mormonism). If you think of yourself as X or Y faith, does that make you X or Y? And further, if an organization's structures determine whether an individual may exercise that self-determination, is it self-determination at all? When we affiliate with an intentional community—that is, one that we must choose and pursue rather than an identity characteristic we're born with, like sex or race—we enter a social contract. Group expectations and shared definitions make community life possible. So where identity is personal and individual, communities choose us as much as we choose them.

Still, a community is not so easily defined, whether by the organization's priorities or by the whims of individuals. We become what we can see. Since the slow birth of the digital age in the 1970s, media have increasingly created and reflected a vast landscape of possibilities for avant-garde identity exploration. Those who push the boundaries of belonging in religious organizations often receive critical attention, and when these stories are publicized via social media, television, or other media, community stakeholders often pay the closest attention. Questions like "What are they saying about us?" and "How are we being represented?" are often at the forefront of group members' minds. Moreover, when media and religion converge, not only do in-group members surveil their own group's representation, but the public simultaneously glimpses the tensions undergirding others' religious lives. Only with the hindsight of history can we start to unpack the broad-ranging effects of these moments of heightened visibility.

Diverse understandings and practices have always differentiated religious identities, but never more so than today. In the twenty-first century, religious identity as a social and personal category is both confounded by new challenges to orthodoxy and orthopraxy and afforded unmatched opportunities for expression and expansion. While types and expressions of American faith continue to diversify at an unprecedented rate,[1] this has not come without a cost: the mediation technologies that make the personalization of faith both possible and visible challenge institutional power and control within the nation's various faith communities. Groups whose members have been historically understood as streamlined or even uniform in belief, practice, and rote conformity to moral codes have gained increasing visibility via new media.

With this growing visibility comes new recognition that an individual's membership in a faith community cannot be simply understood as their full acceptance of that community's codes. Instead, as members of faith communities engage with these mediation platforms, identities are negotiated, and diverse voices are heard, complicating easy social categories for membership and belonging. The simple question of whether an individual is part of a religious group tells you very little about them; rather, we must ask how that individual navigates membership and belonging, what strategies the individual employs to craft their own religious identity, and how these choices interact with (or counteract) the rest of the community, the organization, and broader society.

In this brave new religious world, the mediated visibility of the Church of Jesus Christ of Latter-day Saints provides an important and compelling case study for the challenges and opportunities confronting religious identity construction and maintenance in the digital age. This book is a snapshot of a not-so-distant moment in history, what many media outlets called the "Mormon moment," when American popular culture and politics set the stage for a brief but important national conversation on what it means to be Mormon today. HBO's *Big Love*, a drama about a polygamist Mormon family living in Utah, had just drawn to a close; TLC's *Sister Wives* reality show had just gotten off the ground;[2] and *The Book of Mormon* musical launched on Broadway to massive critical acclaim. The nomination of 2012 Republican presidential candidate Mitt Romney, the first Mormon to be tapped to run by a major party, sealed the nation's focus on the LDS church. In these pages, I look back on the Mormon moment with an eye for the impact of those two years of intense scrutiny on identity and community in the Church of Jesus Christ of Latter-day Saints.

Normative Mormon identity has traditionally been constrained by both strict orthodoxy and orthopraxy, idealized in the active, temple-worthy member who must both affirm belief in institutionally sanctioned teachings and leaders and embody (and avoid) particular behaviors. The church's traditional top-down communication and modern "correlation"—LDS institutional efforts beginning in the 1960s to streamline all church materials with normative, single-purpose messaging—contribute to this construction of Mormons as homogeneous. During the Mormon moment, the powerful and wealthy church pushed back against public scrutiny and worked to mainstream its image through public relations efforts like the "I'm a Mormon" campaign.

Simultaneously, popular culture representations continued to reinforce Mormonism's paradoxical public image as, according to a 2011 Pew Research poll, a "cult" simultaneously associated with "family/family values" and "good people" while still "strict/restrictive" and linked to "polygamy/bigamy."[3]

With the organization struggling to control public perception and the public eye so tightly focused on this often-controversial organization, I observed in real time as church members themselves squirmed uncomfortably under the scrutiny and vied for a say in their own representation. For American Mormons, it was a "white-knuckle moment—a moment of self-searching [and] of wondering, 'What will they say about us next?'"[4]

For this reason, in the following pages, I do not merely present the institutional perspective of what it means to be a Mormon; identity is never quite so tidy. Instead, I explore how Mormons themselves negotiated identity, practice, and doubt during the Mormon moment. The digital age has provided unprecedented platforms for new and rarely heard voices, including heterodox and dissenting members, to contribute to the social construction of Mormon identity. The Mormon moment sparked a perfect conflagration: amid contending representations from the church and the mainstream media, new opportunities emerged for everyday Mormons to join the conversation.

Building on a lengthy ethnographic study of the institution and its diverse members, in this book I use a case study approach to consider various iterations of Mormon identity as presented by normative authorities, faithful members, the secular media, and heterodox and former members. These often-conflicting perspectives challenge traditional models of authority in the LDS context, dismantling views of Mormons as monolithic and offering a window into processes of social activism and institutional change in this very top-down, bureaucratic American faith. Highlighting moments of tension and change, I unpack the discursive construction of identity among members of the Church of Jesus Christ of Latter-day Saints during the Mormon moment, particularly as these constructions challenged traditional notions of what it means to be Mormon. In exploring these themes, I hope to contribute to the ongoing and often baffling conversation about what it means to be part of a religious group as a citizen of the world in this twenty-first century.

Approaching Identity

Do we choose who we are, or are our choices limited to such an extent that power structures choose for us? Any study of identity is necessarily an inquiry into this often-debated space where institutional, hegemonic structure meets and collides with individual agency or choice. The structuralist approach to identity construction suggests that the hegemonic state creates subjects without their necessary assent. Following in the tradition of Karl Marx, Louis Althusser, Jacques Derrida, and Michel

Foucault, this view sees the individual as relatively powerless in the construction of the self. Identity is a subject position constructed through ideology and constituted by discourse, which reflects inherent power differentials. Identity itself is defined by what it is not—what Derrida called a "deferred presence"[5] wherein "every concept is inscribed in a chain or a system within which it refers to the other, to other concepts, by means of the systematic play of differences."[6] Religious identity, then, is defined or "constituted 'historically' as a weave of differences."[7] As with other aspects of identity, it is defined socially against what it is not; functionally, religious identities are boundary markers, categories for exclusion or inclusion.

It is not simply an individual's self-concept that matters in defining their identity; it is how they are socially categorized. The Swiss linguist Ferdinand de Saussure wrote in the late nineteenth century that words themselves are not inherently meaningful but simply signifiers that must be mentally associated with the signified, or the thing itself, to then become a sign imbued with meaning.[8] Signs in a particular community emerge through both collective and individual mental conceptions of what those signs essentially capture. In religion, this categorization often hinges on institutional affiliation. Meaning can then be altered, depending on the context, to reinforce the institutional status quo.[9] In this way, membership in minority religions is defined in relation to the roles established for them by their institution and often as a foil to their culture's religious majority (a sort of social status quo).

Likewise, ideological power structures enable concepts of the self and Others. Identity is developed through a process French philosopher Althusser referred to as interpellation,[10] whereby ideologies of the ruling elite create identities or roles for individuals to inhabit. Interpellation creates subjects who are sutured to these identities subconsciously. Moreover, ideological identity roles become naturalized and reflected in an individual's utterances so that the individual is passive and nonagential in their own identity construction.[11] For Althusser and other Marxist thinkers, constructs like religious identity are always already ways of inhabiting domination and subjugation; they cannot be neutral constructs in a democratic state. Religious identities are constrained or even entirely determined by hegemonic ideals; religious authorities define and monitor appropriate participation in a community.

However, many postmodern thinkers have challenged this strict structuralist reading of identity, instead suggesting that individuals can "script" their own identities according to their own reflexive sense of self. While past conceptions of identity were limited by religion, socioeconomic status, race, or other characteristics that were viewed as immutable, modern identities are open to customization.[12] Because late modernity is "post-traditional," individuals are free to choose their identities with few or no constraints.[13] Individuals are agents who imagine, negotiate, and construct their senses of self in reflexive, self-conscious, and individuated ways.

While both structuralist and postmodern approaches offer insight into how identity is constructed, their explanatory reach is limited, particularly regarding religious identities today, as both fail to simultaneously account for belief, community, and practice. In particular, the ideological emphasis ignores individuals' complicity through choice and participation in the ritual community (e.g., if choices are so constrained, how do we account for conversion? For spiritual experiences?) and the ways they may use narrative and other strategies to resist or nuance their relationships to their faiths. The postmodern frame, on the other hand, misses important implications of religious identity as historically contingent, ideological, institutionalized, highly canonic, and a construct that—because of its normative implications—automatically legitimizes and delegitimizes various other identity constructs.

Religious identity is complicated, and I am feeling for the middle ground. My approach to religious identity both eschews theoretical extremes and attempts a more careful balance between the two imagined poles. Normative Mormon identity is not interpellated by unconscious, unwilling actors; nor is it chosen by agents free to negotiate and adapt it to their liking. Instead, it involves negotiation, submission, interpretation, and subjugation of given narratives to personal circumstances and idiosyncrasies. These complex negotiations involve the interplay of competing norms and values. To the extent that they are performed externally, they form a ritual public sphere wherein Mormon identity is publicly constructed and performed amid various pressures and constraints.

The idea that identity is constructed via social, communicative processes is not a new one: as American philosopher and psychologist John Dewey stated, "Society not only continues to exist *by* transmission, *by* communication, but it may fairly be said to exist *in* transmission, *in* communication. There is more than a verbal tie between the words common, community, and communication. Men live in a community in virtue of the things which they have in common; and communication is the way in which they come to possess things in common."[14] Communities and the identities they support are created through social processes; this is the social construction of reality.[15] Interactions create and maintain ourselves and our world as we know it such that communication itself can be seen as the basis for identity. Communication "is directed not toward the extension of messages in space but toward the maintenance of society in time; not the act of imparting information but the representation of shared beliefs," as American media theorist James Carey observed.[16] Social interactions are performances that construct identity along agreed-upon narrative lines, and these interactions shape (and even determine) individual identity.[17] Our sacred selves appear only as we relate with others.[18]

In this way, conceptual dichotomies between public and private selves can be misleading. Private identity cannot exist without the public sphere giving it shape and content, since, as Jürgen Habermas paradoxically observes, "subjectivity, as the innermost core of the private, was always already oriented to an audience."[19] So religious identity as an aspect of a person's private interiority results from interactions in the public sphere.

If identity is established through social interaction, what happens when conflict arises in social institutions? When individuals disagree with the direction of an organization they belong to, they are, practically speaking, limited to three options: maintain the status quo, vocally dissent, or leave.[20] These categories provide a framework for understanding Mormon affiliation and the dynamics of attempting to speak out within an authoritarian system.

Religious Identity and Community

Religion and religious identity, like all expressions of culture, are not inherent qualities of the individual; nor are they merely expressions of individual belief, faith, opinion, or preference. Religion and religious identity are social constructions, derived by communicating and negotiating meaning, that situate the individual in a cultural collective. An understanding of the constructed nature of religious identity helps us clear away some of the semantic debris that threatens to mark some versions of said identity as more or less authentic. In my view, the range of interpretations of what it means to be Mormon are not just competing perspectives that should be analyzed for their doctrinal proximity to some imagined standard but rather instantiations of power that can be analyzed for their social effects in real time. As pioneering sociologists W. I. and Dorothy Thomas noted in 1929, "It is not important whether the interpretations are correct—if men define situations as real, they are real in their consequences."[21]

Before we can talk about the social manifestations of lived religion, then, we must begin with an outline of the boundaries of religion itself. Cultural anthropologist Clifford Geertz famously defined religion as "a system of symbols which acts to establish powerful, pervasive, and long-lasting moods and motivations in men by formulating conceptions of a general order of existence and clothing these conceptions with such an aura of factuality that the moods and motivations seem uniquely realistic."[22] As a symbolic system, religion creates for its adherents both a *model of* and a *model for* the world itself. Religions' symbolic systems situate the individual in the group by allowing them to partake in shared symbols through language. In confessional faiths, the act of confessing (that is, saying aloud) literally communicates an assertion of identity. Christianity, in its varied forms, emphasizes this act as vital to participation in the faith community. St. Paul the Apostle, revered as the first Christian missionary and author of much of the New Testament, highlights this impetus when he promises, "If thou shalt confess with thy mouth the Lord Jesus, and shalt believe in thine heart that God hath raised him from the dead, thou shalt be saved. For with the heart man believeth unto righteousness; and with the mouth confession is made unto salvation."[23] One is not a partaker in the faith, not *a Christian*, until one has communicated one's Christianity socially. This urgency is evident in ubiquitous religious words like *witness*, *testify*, *share*, and *confess*: confessional religion is lived, religious identity established, through voice. Just as one "puts on" culture, religion must be put on in the public sphere.

Thus, individuals establish their religious identities through narrative cohesion. In a nod to the centrality of narrative in religious identity construction, conversion itself can be understood primarily as "a process of acquiring a specific religious language or dialect" that starts "when an unsaved listener begins to appropriate in their inner speech the saved speaker's language and its attendant view of the world," as anthropologist Susan Friend Harding brilliantly put it.[24] Conversion is a rebirth, the creation of a new identity, that "aims to separate novice listeners from their prior, given reality, to constitute a new, previously unperceived or indistinct reality, and to impress that reality upon them, make it felt, heard, seen, known, undeniably real."[25] In Mormonism, this change is manifest through religious testimonies that bind the actor to the group through narrative cohesion.

Religious narratives take different forms across various traditions, but in all cases, these narratives serve a vital function in constructing identity by locating an individual as a member of the group. In other words, the type of story you tell about yourself positions you within your community, where others also tell locating stories about themselves. Formal identity rituals utilize a "more limited and rigidly organized set of expressions and gestures, a 'restricted code' of communication or behavior in contrast to a more open or 'elaborated code'" so that "formal speech tends to be more conventional and less idiosyncratic or personally expressive."[26] For Mormons, bearing testimony is a formal, ritualized process that relies on codes and scripts specified by the group's shared history. Indeed, one main function of ritual is the performance of the group's formative myths.[27] The individual sharing testimony writes themselves into their group's mythic script through a process called triadic co-definition, wherein "a social group, a set of ritual performance, and a set of mythic narratives produce one another."[28] These interaction rituals allow religious people to "perform" identity using a social "script," which is established through ritual conventions.[29] In this way, religious identity can be parsed through rhetorical analysis of religious narratives. In Mormonism, identity is indeed normatively scripted but also allows for cultural resistance as individual members self-construct their own narratives and thus their Mormon identities.

As with any other institution subject to the forces of political economy, religious groups must deal with threats and pressures from outside and inside forces. Unlike some organizations with more tangible products to sell, religion offers an identity and a community. Religious groups must provide both continuity and tension with the broader society: they must be different enough that they have something to offer potential converts but similar enough that joining does not cost the convert too much in social capital.[30] Continuity and tension, rather than some tangible actuality of identity, can be established as products of specific stories told within and without the group about the meaning of belonging. In Mormonism, then, the success or failure of the church hinges on its own narrative strategies. Moreover, and more relevant to this study, individual Mormons must also navigate these tensions and continuities between their Mormon identities and other aspects of their identities (e.g., gender, race, socioeconomic status / class, political leanings, sexual orientation), sometimes resulting in intense social and personal dissonance. Resolution of these tensions becomes necessary to ensure continued feelings of belonging in the religious community. Such resolution is only possible by either negotiating identity or rewriting the narrative about what it means to belong in the first place.

Identity in the Digital Realm

Today, our on- and offline selves converge and diverge, complicating even further our conceptualizations of who we are. Online identities, in particular, appear more porous and allow for more play, which early scholars of online identity viewed as inauthentic, both privileging an individual's offline self over online constructions of self as somehow more "real" and assuming that the relative anonymity afforded by online spaces would promote insincerity and duplicity.[31] However, ethnographies of internet communities have largely refuted these assumptions and illustrated that both off- and online identities are legitimate, though differently nuanced, constructions and performances of self.[32] Mirroring famed Canadian sociologist Erving Goffman's insights into the ways in which individuals perform various aspects of self in different offline milieus like work, church, and home, individuals today also craft meaningful and socially relevant selves situated in online environments. These selves are constructed and performed vis-à-vis expectations and narratives in various online communities, just as Goffman might have predicted.

This implies, of course, that the online self is not always contiguous to the offline self. The availability of so many types of online communities, combined with the seeming anonymity of some forms of online participation, gives individuals the opportunity to construct alternative or idealized identities online that they hesitate to enact in their embodied lives.[33] Still, due to the nature of symbolic mediation on the internet, online identities are often more *deliberately* constructed than offline ones—but no less authentic. Mormons performing Mormonism online often perform a different version of self at church, at home, or at work (but then, don't we all?).

In my analysis, I noted one clear exception to the general rule of a kind of performed online authenticity: so-called internet trolls who deliberately misled others about their identities or posted inflammatory comments on message boards or other social networking sites to incite controversy (today, this is referred to as rage-baiting and is often done for clicks and likes to feed social media algorithms). While these types of users were certainly present on the sites I analyzed throughout this research, they were generally recognized and flagged as trolls by board moderators, and except to the extent that they evoked genuine responses from other participants, their impact is disregarded as data in my research.

Features of internet culture and digital life continue to facilitate this modern renegotiation of what it means to be Mormon. First, unprecedented (but still by no means universal) access to the internet contributes to the balkanization of LDS identity as nontraditional members and those entirely antagonistic to the church problematize traditional conceptions of legitimate Mormon identity. Indeed, Mormon identity no longer rests solely on acceptance by the traditional Mormon community. Instead, "cultural Mormonism," an understanding of Mormonism more akin to a tribal affiliation than a belief system, proliferates as an identity construct. Similarly, the semblance of privacy and anonymity online frees members to express unconventional and even heretical ideas about Mormonism and its proper expression. Despite these challenges to institutional control, the digital sphere also offers a unique opportunity for church leadership to stay abreast of the perceptions of members and the broader society and respond immediately to threats to institutional hegemony. These three features of digital culture—access, anonymity, and surveillance—together contribute to shifts in modern LDS identity and expression.

Unprecedented high internet penetration rates in the United States mean that the majority of American Mormons have access to the technology and thus can choose to participate in online conversations and communities centered on religious identity navigation. The digital divide, or the discrepancy in social capital between those with and those without internet access, is particularly salient among those of differing languages, nationalities, socioeconomic backgrounds, and generational placement.[34] Internet culture, including Mormon internet culture, tends to reflect a white, Western, upper-middle-class, educated, and relatively young population.

Still, high penetration means that niche communities have developed online for nearly every conceivable interest group, providing opportunities for community building among groups that otherwise would not have access to other like-minded individuals. In the context of this study, for example, feminist Mormons who reported knowing few or no other feminist Mormons in their offline lives found themselves able to interact daily in online spaces with feminist Mormons from around the world, reinforcing and strengthening their own identities as such. Access to the internet challenges the hegemonic, institutional image of Mormon identity presented by the church by providing a platform for the voices and experiences of the heterodox.

Another feature of Web 2.0 participation involves users' perceptions or assumptions of anonymity. Closed (membership-restricted) groups and the ability to post using pseudonyms may provide a semblance of safety to users and allow them to act in ways they wouldn't in their offline life. The perception that a given online space is unmonitored by those they know "in real life" can influence users' willingness to self-disclose. The more an individual believes a particular online space is anonymous, the more likely they are to divulge personal information they would otherwise keep private.[35]

Some early observers of internet culture feared that anonymity online would lead to duplicity (e.g., individuals would pretend to be someone they are not), but again, this assumes that the online life is less important or central to a person's self-conceptions than the offline. Many regular participants on social media groups, chatrooms, blogs, and listservs are highly invested in their online communities and devote large amounts of time to sharing content, reading, and engaging with others in those spaces. In Mormon online communities, many regulars have met other participants offline. Still, the question of duplicity is not straightforward; the identities individuals craft online are not reducible to their offline selves but are instead performances specific to the online milieu.

In a seeming contradiction of the feature of anonymity, a third feature emphasizes the ability of those with social and/or institutional power to employ the internet as a surveillance tool and the users' awareness that they may be monitored online. Many scholars have considered the role and function of the internet as a modern-day panopticon, allowing government, corporations, and other institutions the ability to monitor users' behaviors and opinions to variously control, police, or market to them.[36] Internet users tack back and forth between comfortable assurance that they are anonymous and safe and a fear of surveillance by those in power. While online actors enjoy a semblance of privacy, especially when acting in closed or private groups or when operating under a pseudonymous username, they do so with an on-again, off-again cognizance that "nothing is ever really private online." This recognition manifests in inconsistent yet frequent attempts to self-censor and police online expression and action. Mormons seem especially aware of the potential for online surveillance, given the history of such community policing within the church. In interviews, many heterodox LDS expressed fears that their bishops, members of their local church, or LDS family members may be monitoring their online activities. These fears were not always unfounded: members regularly reported being called to disciplinary councils (a term, but not a practice, that the church officially curtailed in 2020) because of something they posted online. As a result of this type of policing, many individuals are reluctant to fully disclose their opinions, even in seemingly private online communities.

*

In this book, I investigate these various contestations of the meaning of religious identity and belonging as a way of considering, in our digital and diverse age, what narratives are privileged in the definition of religious identity. I hope to provide a window into the ways that individuals use their personal agency to negotiate structural constraints in the ongoing task of crafting their religious identities. Since the LDS church is a rigidly structured, bureaucratic organization, leaders with more bureaucratic authority also have more authority when they speak. Normative, public Mormon voices offer constructions of Mormonism that conflict with lived Mormon identities in stark and explicit ways. The vision of Mormon identity cast by those with the power to speak normatively sometimes conflicts with how individuals in the church see themselves. Moreover, some of the church's teachings about morality, modern-day revelation, and divine order, silence and delegitimize certain identity constructs altogether.[37]

These tensions between institutional and individual discourses often result in mediated and publicly visible internecine conflicts that offer real-time instantiations of the negotiation of power inherent in religious belonging. While much has been written on the marginalization of minority groups within the broader American culture, little research has been done on the ways that minority groups themselves marginalize certain members or particular identity constructs. In the case of the Mormon faith, an array of actors—normative Mormon authorities, orthodox practitioners, heterodox members, dissidents, former members, and the non-Mormon public—converge in a discursive interplay aimed at crafting the very definition of Mormonism. This interplay is competitive in nature, with each voice contending for the role of identity gatekeeper; and the stakes are high for American culture, the Mormon institution, and Mormons themselves.

To understand these tensions in Mormon identity in their experiential context, I foreground the conceptual categories of structure versus agency as orienting categories, relevant here both for their salience to Mormon history and doctrine, a connection that will be parsed out in the following chapter, and for their role as orienting categories in the academic discipline of cultural studies more broadly. These categories stem from a long tradition of cultural studies research, with a particular connection to sociologist Anthony Giddens's concept of identity as a project that tacks back and forth between expectations, constraints, and norms created and enforced by social institutions of power (what he calls and I adopt as *structure*) and an individual's desire and capacity to independently pick and choose among available options for their own behavior and identity (an ability I conceptualize as *agency*).[38] And yet these categories, while useful, are simplifications that suggest by their duality that there is no overlap between social institutions of power and the options that agents may choose.

I draw on fieldwork among Mormons to foreground the importance of internecine conflict in these negotiations, which I define as *discursive contestations involving two or more community subgroups and focusing on the groups' irreconcilable ideological stances on appropriate interpretation and enactment of identity*. While conflicts of various intensities exist in any organization, I restrict my inquiry to internecine conflicts that threaten the cohesion of the broader Mormon community. My research found that internecine conflicts in Mormonism are ongoing, often volatile, and divisive. Informants indicated that their experiences of acceptance or rejection in Mormon communities were frequently shaped by these conflicts. In this way, internecine Mormon conflicts function as largely grassroots efforts to police the borders of the community, often forcing out certain heterodox perspectives.

To understand the function of intragroup conflict in Mormon identity construction, I employ the concept of "voice." If Mormon identity is dialogically constructed, then its meaning is socially constituted by the interplay of competing voices engaged in internecine conflict. Voice as a theoretical category implies a construction of identity that is active, intentional, and social. Rather than considering the narratives of various Mormon voices in isolation, I use Michael Holquist's dialogic analysis to locate key voices in the construction of interanimated Mormon identity and consider these often competing voices *in conversation with one another*.[39] As a dialogic analysis of the concept of Mormon identity, this project juxtaposes categories of various relevant voices competing to define LDS identity, which I draw from my own previous fieldwork and research on Mormon identity, to locate emerging Mormon identities as they are constructed.

To that end, I begin with a place-setting chapter, "Identity in the Church of Jesus Christ of Latter-day Saints," which I hope will orient the reader to various important tensions that have competed to shape Mormon identity from the founding of the church to the present day. This chapter does not pretend to offer a complete history of Mormonism or its public image; instead, it provides a shared language through which we can explore specific, often rather esoteric, details from the remaining chapters' curated selection of mediated Mormon moments.

Subsequent chapters examine these case studies as competing efforts to define Mormon identity. They open with a focusing narrative—each a widely circulated, mediated example of internecine conflict that took place during my main research period (2012 through early 2013). These events, true Mormon moments, are case studies that introduce, contextualize, and challenge ways of being Mormon in line with the practice of incident analysis within the field of history. As cultural historian Robert Darnton explains, incident analysis "deals with the concatenation of events rather than merely the events themselves. It attempts to find their meanings—what they meant to the people who experienced them and to those who learned about them later. It therefore concentrates on reports of incidents and how they echoed through various modes of communication."[40]

I chose each of these mediated moments because of their importance and high circulation within Mormon communities and because the conflicts largely mattered most to Mormons, not to the broader American public. The conflicts disrupted the community, and the narratives deployed to negotiate these conflicts highlight the structural constraints on Mormon identity across particular contexts. These events offer a glimpse of the tensions at work in Mormon identity construction, and responses to these events help pinpoint the limits of Mormon agency. My aim is not to play the role of the empirical historian in parsing out exactly what happened in each internecine conflict (although I go to some trouble to do so accurately and thoroughly). Instead, I'm interested in tracking how the *narratives* of these events circulated and transformed as they moved through the media and through Mormon communities and exploring these movements as evidence for identifying the structural and agential elements of Mormon identities. In other words, while what *happened matters*, the *interpretations and effects* of what happened matter more. Also, because this book zooms in tightly on a two-year period in Mormon history, I do not attempt to overextend my analysis much beyond my research period, although I note several instances where reverberations of the events from 2012–13 may still be felt today.

Chapter 2, "Caffeine and Agency in Mormon Boundary Work," examines the relationship between LDS bureaucracy and the quotidian lives of Mormons through internal debates over whether Mormons should consume caffeine, a relatively minor issue with far-reaching implications in certain circles. Think of this chapter as an investigation of the distinctions between institutional and lived religion or between doctrine and culture, illustrating that while the two constructions may differ in type, they do not differ in kind: both are social contracts, normalized to carry the weight of authority and to bound off the ritual community. Culture becomes structure in Mormon practice; discourses within the community that draw a line between "doctrine" and "culture" on any number of issues are emic strategies for negotiating identity. The placement of that line (or the extent to which issues are parsed in keeping with the institutional party line) discursively locates individuals within fragmented Mormon communities—ever more ubiquitous due to increasing access to and participation in online forums—and signals fault lines within Mormonism as a whole. Moreover, ways of parsing identity serve as surveillance technologies for members of the community to monitor other members' identities, particularly when these are broadcast via mediating technologies.

In chapter 3, "Mitt Romney and Bifurcated Mormon Representation," I rely on the previous chapter's explanation of group monitoring and normativity to explore the discourse surrounding Mitt Romney's 2012 presidential run, reading these discourses through the perspectives of three primary interpretive communities: First, the press, with its own tensions between the duty to inform and the need to entertain, wavered between respectful avoidance and salacious digging, hinting at Mormonism's precarious standing in the national conversation between mainstream and decidedly weird. Second, Romney himself and his conservative Mormon supporters obscured his Mormonism, depicting him as a patriotic, blue-blooded American for whom Mormonism was an important yet tangential aspect. This perspective parallels the modern LDS church's public relations strategy with its attempt to downplay significant differences. Third, progressive Mormons supportive of Barack Obama's incumbency used the political moment to depict Romney as a poor example of lived Mormonism—indeed, as a *bad Mormon*—simultaneously advancing their own vision of proper Mormon identity. These narratives represent diverse camps in Mormon identity and ideology, and the conflicts and tensions between these groups came to a head on the internet, where their narratives were circulated and reproduced. In addition to shedding light on in-group social cues as a mechanism for determining someone else's standing in the faith, these narratives highlight the tensions between structure (e.g., roles and norms) and agency (individualization and interpretation) in Mormon identity construction today.

Chapter 4, "Wars and Rumors of Wars: Apologetic and Dissent Communities," examines the limits of Mormon belonging by considering two largely internet-based communities on the periphery. If Mormon identities fall on a spectrum from conservative and orthodox to progressive and heterodox, apologetic and dissent communities online map out the margins of belonging. In a rather bizarre instance of internecine conflict between two primarily male LDS communities on either periphery of Mormon identity, institutional forces policed and contained unacceptable discourse. I generate a two-part analysis of this conflict. First, I focus on normative expectations, built on gendered notions of group cohesion and deferral to authority, for proper interpersonal exchange. I show how volatile conflicts between apologetic and dissent groups violate these norms, marking moments of agential renegotiation of group boundaries. I argue that the disruption of fundamental Mormon traits in these groups' performance of a kind of Mormon machismo places them outside the limits of Mormon belonging. In the second part of the chapter, I analyze the mechanisms used by the church to police these boundaries to show how the institution's public censuring polices the boundaries of Mormon identity.

Chapter 5, "Patriarchy, Feminisms, and Digital Discourse," examines how Mormon women negotiate belonging within this both theologically and institutionally patriarchal church. Examining the institutional rhetoric around womanhood, I present the church's discursive and idealized feminine archetype that Mormon women then adopt, negotiate, or resist in their own identity articulation. Again focusing largely on peripheral identities and grounding my analysis in a case study of a prominent Mormon feminist mass action, I show how feminist Mormons during the Mormon moment used the mediated spotlight to undercut the church's gender essentialism yet still rhetorically grounded their identities in Mormonism's essential reliance on community.

Finally, chapter 6, "Identity Shifts in a Mormon Moment," examines this period more broadly as one of historic shifts in Mormon identity facilitated by the internet as an agent of change. While the church has a long history of policing media content through "correlation," a strict process of monitoring church-related materials for content cohesion, the open text of Web 2.0 introduced new threats to institutional control and created openings for new negotiations of what it means to be Mormon. In this chapter, I juxtapose two institutional efforts to confront the reality of the digital age: (1) efforts toward greater institutional transparency and accountability, exemplified in the Gospel Topics essay initiative, and (2) a nearly simultaneous rash of excommunications aimed at those who campaigned for greater institutional transparency and accountability. I argue that these contravening efforts are two sides of the same coin, both evidence of an institution grappling with the reality of shifting cultural norms. I conclude with a revisitation of the role of the internet in Mormon identity construction, considering the evidence for a shift in both the cultural and sacred meanings of Mormon identity and the implications of change within an institution whose raison d'être is its contradictory supposed sacred immutability and its reverence of continual revelation. Beyond Mormonism, I suggest that analyses of religious identities and the internet, when located within dynamic fields of historical and political contingencies, irrefutably point toward a revolution in what we mean by religion in the digital era.

Notes on Terminology

Throughout this book, I use the term *LDS church* or simply *the church* to refer to the Church of Jesus Christ of Latter-day Saints and *Mormon* to refer to members. That decision is for simplicity of writing and ease of reading, but it is also my way of highlighting the fraught nature of identity in the Mormon context. As I will discuss more in the following chapter, the church has vacillated in its preferences for terminology regarding the institution and its members. As of this writing, the church's style guide asks the media to avoid using the term *LDS* or *Mormon* to describe members and to call the organization by its full name, the Church of Jesus Christ of Latter-day Saints, allowing for *the Church* or *the Church of Jesus Christ* on subsequent mentions. This has not always been the case: in 2002, the church trademarked the term *Mormon* and dozens of phrases that use the word, later initiating legal challenges against businesses attempting to use it.[41] In 2012, as I conducted much of my research for this project, the church embraced the term *Mormon*, widely broadcasting its "I'm a Mormon" advertising campaign and directing investigators to mormon.org for more information. As an outsider bent on getting to the crux of identity in the Church of Jesus Christ of Latter-day Saints and recognizing that church leaders' preferences may change at any time, I play with all monikers throughout this text but lean most heavily on those used most frequently within the communities I've studied. Unquestionably in my research, the terms *Mormon* and *LDS* are emic ones, and I treat them as such here.

Additionally, throughout the book, I make mention of various groups and their relationships with the LDS church. Creating a complex taxonomy of all possible Mormon identities is not my task here, except to say that there are innumerable ways to signal Mormon-ish identities through labels, and none of them capture the full complexity of this religious tradition. You'll see that I sometimes refer to orthodox or faithful Mormons on the one hand and heterodox and/or progressive Mormons on the other. These are oversimplifications, but they are important for analysis and discussion for two reasons: first, they delineate the imagined poles at either end of the Mormon identity spectrum, between which fall innumerable iterations of what it means to be Mormon today; and second, the oversimplifications themselves are useful to group members, who often narratively place themselves somewhere along these continua.

I define faithful Mormons as those who are both orthodox and orthoprax in their approach to their religion. This is a construction of the ideal Mormon as presented by the church itself. Orthodoxy refers to right belief, meaning these members believe the church's teachings as the church presents them (that is, they accept LDS scripture as literally and historically true, believe that the church is led by God's Prophet on Earth, and believe the church is the one true, restored church today). Orthopraxy, or right actions, is also central to faithful Mormon identity; members must fulfill the ritual, bodily obligations of their faith: to the extent they are able, they serve missions for the church, marry in the temple, faithfully attend services and fulfill their callings (volunteer positions in their local wards), tithe 10 percent of their income, and more. Orthodox Mormons often use the internet as a platform for proselytization, for fulfilling church directives to love and minister to their neighbors, and sometimes to engage in debate or damage control to defend and protect the church and its reputation. Scriptures, official talks, publications, and other approved material from the church and its PR department create the bulk of the content faithful Mormons reproduce and circulate on- and offline.

Heterodox, as the moniker implies, is shorthand for all the other ways of being Mormon. Heterodox Mormons fall into lots of nuanced categories: those who practice their faith and value their culture but don't believe literally in all LDS teachings (sometimes called cultural Mormons); those who consider themselves Mormon but don't attend or practice, sometimes called "Jack Mormons"; former Mormons who identify culturally with Mormonism but have left the church and/or officially resigned; and politically liberal and/or feminist Mormons who hold LDS teachings dear and value their place in Mormon communities but whose views on issues like historicity or gender roles contradict official church teachings. Generally, former Mormons who feel no kinship or association with the broader LDS church are not part of this analysis, as they do not generally engage with issues and discussions related to Mormon identity construction. While heterodox Mormons differ vastly in practice and interpretation, those I discuss throughout these pages generally populate the more extreme margins of Mormon identity and use social media and other online spaces to bring attention to issues they see as dangerous or outdated in church teachings or practice, to create community with other like-minded people, and to advocate for change.

The term *faithful* may feel charged, perhaps implying that orthodox Mormons are doing it right and heterodox Mormons are, by extension, "unfaithful." Some unorthodox Mormons told me that they considered themselves more truly faithful than orthodox members, since they saw their conceptualization of Mormonism as a better, more nuanced, and more egalitarian way of being Mormon. I use the term anyway, and intentionally, to emphasize faithfulness to LDS bureaucracy and existing structures. I hope to underscore that while an individual or group may contravene the norms of an organization, the organization itself predates and exists outside of that self-construction. While heterodox Mormons may be faithful to their own interpretations of their faith, by my definition, they are not faithful to the Church of Jesus Christ of Latter-day Saints as it stands.

Despite these particularities, the loudest Mormon voices (and therefore the ones I've charted most closely) represent the vocal minority extremes of the Mormon spectrum, with orthodox voices on the one hand and progressive voices on the other. These categories largely epitomize the extreme ends of the Mormon continuum, and I often found the most vocal members of these opposing groups at the center of the types of conflict and tensions I explore in this book. Throughout the following chapters, I hope the details of each case study begin to problematize easy simplifications and illustrate the role of the internet in shifting social and religious identities in the Church of Jesus Christ of Latter-day Saints.

A final note: This book is, in large part, an exploration of identity on the internet. As anyone who has spent time on social media can attest, traditional grammar rules often go out the window when communicating online. So rather than make cumbersome notations of spelling and grammar errors and/or the stylistic choices of internet commentators, I note here that all original language idiosyncrasies are retained throughout.

1

Identity in the Church of Jesus Christ of Latter-day Saints

Modernity fragments; it also unites. On the level of the individual right up to that of planetary systems as a whole, tendencies towards dispersal vie with those promoting integration. So far as the self is concerned, the problem of unification concerns protecting and reconstructing the narrative of self-identity in the face of the massive intensional and extensional changes which modernity sets into being.

—Anthony Giddens, *Modernity and Self-Identity: Self and Society in the Late Modern Age*

What does it mean to be Mormon? To answer that question, we must start at the beginning.

Mormonism's history starts in 1820 during the height of America's Second Great Awakening, when a teenage Joseph Smith prayed to know which of the many New England churches was true. In response to his prayers, he experienced a series of supernatural visions from which he learned that all churches were corrupt and that he would be responsible for restoring Christ's true church, thereby ushering in the latter days before Christ's return. Soon Smith was divinely led to the Hill Cumorah in Manchester, New York, where he unearthed a buried ancient record written on metal plates. Smith translated the record, which was in an unknown language he called "reformed Egyptian," with the help of special glasses, a hat, and a seer stone.[1]

His translation became the Book of Mormon, a collection of purportedly ancient prophetic writings that tell the story of a lost Israelite tribe that fled Jerusalem to the Americas by boat more than five hundred years before Christ. Written in narrative prose akin to the Old Testament, the Book of Mormon climaxes with Christ's post-Resurrection visit to the tribe's descendants and culminates with the death of these early Western Christians in warfare with a wicked splinter group (this latter group is considered a now-extinct Native American tribe). Upon his death, the last surviving ancient prophet and one of the book's authors, Moroni, buried the record of his people in the Hill Cumorah.

After a series of fits and starts, Smith completed his translation, filed for copyright, and began selling *The Book of Mormon: An Account Written by the Hand of Mormon, upon Plates Taken from the Plates of Nephi* in March 1830.[2] The next month, having amassed several dozen followers, he officially founded the Church of Christ (renamed a few years later the Church of the Latter Day Saints, renamed again in 1838 as the Church of Jesus Christ of Latter Day Saints, and officially branded the Church of Jesus Christ of Latter-day Saints [LDS] in the 1960s). Over the following months, Smith and his followers converted family members and friends; by autumn, they had deployed the first Mormon missionaries.[3]

The burgeoning new faith did not escape scrutiny from the rest of the nation. To be sure, a major element of Mormon history, spilling over into current manifestations of LDS identity, involves accounts of persistent hostility and violence perpetrated against early church members. These narratives include an 1838 government-sanctioned "extermination order" in Missouri, which resulted in forced migration westward, and Smith's 1844 death due to jailhouse mob violence.[4] This early persecution is at least in part attributable to unfavorable media depictions: newspaper treatment of the Saints emphasized controversial elements of Mormonism like esoteric temple rites and the early practice of polygamy as divinely sanctioned and integral to the gospel plan.[5] Even popular novels included "anti-Mormon" sentiment: Mark Twain's 1872 *Roughing It* famously derided the Book of Mormon as "chloroform in print" and Sir Arthur Conan Doyle's 1887 *A Study in Scarlet* depicted Mormons as brainwashed, corrupt, and murderous.[6]

After Mormon settlers fled to Utah Territory to escape persecution and ultimately disavowed polygamy, they evaded public scrutiny for a while, but at a cost: their seclusion in the Great Basin led to increasing suspicion among the non-Mormon public, who feared the Mormons' opacity and secretiveness.[7] Yet despite continuing popular perceptions of Mormons as dangerous Others, Mormons have gradually gained a measure of favor as one of America's "model minority" groups, like Asians and Jews, lauded for their hard work and traditional values.[8] Of course, the model minority concept is its own kind of prejudice, suggesting that members of a group are homogenous and that they are acceptable because of the way they relate to the broader community. Americans' ambivalence toward Mormons continues, reflected in the top two terms Americans in 2010 associated with Mormons: the suspicion-loaded *cult* and the all-American *family / family values*.[9]

Correlation and LDS Imagined Community

Mormonism rapidly expanded globally in the mid-twentieth century thanks to its large-scale missionary program. This growth created a challenge: how best to control the message of a worldwide church and maintain cohesion among thousands of worldwide congregations. By 1950, the church's membership tallied 1.1 million. Religious historian Matthew Bowman explains that by that time, "fragmentation, overlap, and dysfunction had grown almost unmanageable. The curricula of the various auxiliaries overlapped and sometimes contradicted one another; they claimed different influences and priorities, and bureaucratic turf battles were common.... The problem remained: if they attended all their meetings, church members would be instructed from three or four different curricula, each at best vaguely aware of the others."[10]

In the early 1900s, then president Joseph F. Smith began serious efforts known as "correlation" to streamline the organization and its auxiliary programs with the goal of developing a consistent curriculum for the men of the church.[11] Various efforts to navigate correlation persisted for the next half century and came to a head under the leadership of President David O. McKay. Traveling the globe more than any previous church leader, McKay visited Europe, South Africa, South America, the South Pacific, and New Zealand, where he noted the extent of fragmentation and waning institutional control across the global membership. As a remedy, in 1960 McKay began to formalize church-wide correlation efforts to streamline all church-produced materials—curricula, magazines, handbooks, videos—with single-purpose messaging (even the name of the church was correlated in this period, standardized in the modern format).[12] The newly formed All-Church Coordinating Council, which came to be known as the Correlation Committee, was largely under the direction of Harold B. Lee, who served as an apostle, as counselor to Joseph Fielding Smith, and briefly as president. Lee's work ensured that all church media were noncontradictory and consistent. Anything unapproved by the Correlation Committee was and continues to be referred to as "uncorrelated," implying it is unofficial and thus untrustworthy, sometimes even anti-Mormon.

After correlation, the LDS church enjoyed a period of retrenchment and ensuing communal solidarity,[13] a moment that mirrors historian Benedict Anderson's observations on the early days of print media (primarily newspapers and novels). Anderson argues that homogenized media led to the homogenization of culture across geographically dispersed European regions; individuals who would never know one another could imagine themselves unified as members of an "imagined community," holding important things in common.[14] The years of strict LDS correlation before the internet provide a convincing test case of this idea of media-induced homogenization; official scriptures, teaching and training manuals, magazines, pamphlets, and videos ensured that Mormons across the globe were exposed to the same messages, often at the same time. Despite geographic peculiarities or cultural disparities, Mormon imagined community meant that belonging to the same church was quite easily mistaken for homogeneity of belief and practice. Christ's church seemed unified.

That unity was short-lived. Today, despite the LDS church's continued attempts to correlate its message, the polyphony of the internet makes it clear that actual members of the church are anything but unified in their interpretations and embodiments of LDS teachings, though the church still attempts to correlate its message. These challenges to LDS hegemony are policed within the church through the ongoing efforts of its Correlation Committee, through attempts to police and discipline voices in the mainstream media, and through efforts to mold and prescribe acceptable talk (both on- and offline) among members. This discipline, which can be likened to both a form of "impression management" or "brand imaging" and a form of institutional policing, manifests in reactive strategies for communicating with the world inside and outside of the church.

Contesting Modern Mormon Identity

Just as in the early days of Mormonism, almost two centuries after its inception, the church still struggles to maintain control over its representation in the public sphere. Digital media compound the issue like never before, allowing unprecedented access to controversial and damaging information and the impossibility of evading scrutiny in the age of instant sharing across social networks. But far from being just the problem, the church also uses media as the solution: for decades the church has shown media savvy. Through Deseret Management Corporation, the church's for-profit arm, it operates media and marketing firms including media conglomerate Bonneville International and Bonneville Communication, which includes a full-service advertising agency and a nonprofit foundation that conducts opinion polling and tactical message framing. The foundation especially functions to both proselytize and influence social discourse and public opinion on the church.

The church's public relations and marketing efforts in recent decades reflect the paradox of LDS institutional efforts to be accepted as mainstream while simultaneously differentiating themselves from the rest of the largely Christian American culture.[15] From the late 1970s to the 1990s, the church made its way into American households through a well-known series of televised advertisements featuring prosocial vignettes that presented wholesome, family-centered Mormon values while rarely mentioning faith or doctrine. Often, the only indication these messages were sponsored by the church, or any religious organization at all, was a comforting male voice at the end of the commercial saying, "From the Church of Jesus Christ of Latter-day Saints" along with the church's logo appearing on the screen's lower third. This campaign, which avoided all mention of anything unique to Mormonism and instead focused exclusively on noncontroversial positive messaging, went a long way in normalizing Mormonism in the broader American social context.

Church branding in the 1990s also reflects this mainstreaming strategy. In response to popular opinion that held that Mormons were not Christian, the church recruited graphic designers and marketing experts to reimagine its brand image to be more palatable to the general public. Its previous logo put equal emphasis on the words *church*, *Jesus Christ*, and *Latter-day Saints*. The new logo, premiering in 1995, literally put *Jesus Christ* at the forefront, centering and enlarging those words and framing them with smaller words above and below. It was meant to feel "non-designed" rather than modern and to be "less corporate-looking" with a "warm, friendly, inviting feel."[16] For the next twenty-five years, the logo's ubiquity paralleled institutional efforts to mainstream Mormonism.

In the first decade of the new century, the church shifted tack in its advertising. A successor to its attempts at mainstreaming, the 2008 multimedia "Truth Restored" ad campaign integrated billboards and television, radio, and internet advertising with innovative "pass-along cards" that members were encouraged to carry with them in case a nonmember asked about their faith.[17] Consisting of emotional interviews with members shot in black-and-white and interspersed with images of family photographs and dramatic vignettes, these ads focused on Christian teachings but did not go so far as to identify or delve into teachings particular to Mormonism.[18] These two approaches, the first all but ignoring religious content and the second focusing almost exclusively on it while still avoiding some more esoteric topics, underscore the paradox of a church at once attempting to position itself as a viable Christian option in the American marketplace of religion while recognizing its murky status as a distrusted outsider.

In 2008, internal LDS research indicated that the church still held a largely conflicted public image in America. This research came on the heels of a 2002 Olympics bid scandal in which prominent Mormon businessmen were accused of bribing the International Olympic Committee to secure the Winter Olympics in Salt Lake City. It also came during the height of a massive April 2008 federal raid at the Fundamentalist Church of Jesus Christ of Latter-day Saints' (FLDS) Yearning for Zion Ranch, where some media reporting obscured distinctions between the practices and beliefs of the polygamous FLDS and the mainstream LDS. The internal research found that American ambivalence toward Mormonism stemmed from "confusion" and "misunderstanding" about the church's history, practice, and unique vocabulary. The report concluded that there were six main factors in American's perceptions of the church: ignorance of the church's teachings, misunderstandings around the history of polygamy, fear of the church's extensive power and wealth, assumptions that Mormons and their beliefs were "weird," fear of the unknown, and the feeling that Mormonism was exclusive and self-important. The researchers noted that Americans who did not personally know any Mormons were more likely to have negative impressions of the church.[19]

Partially in response to this research, in 2010 the church began new efforts to repackage and rebrand the faith, launching a public relations campaign entitled "I'm a Mormon" in nine U.S. markets.[20] The campaign began with televised and YouTube videos designed to normalize Mormon identity by equating it with constructions of idealized American life. In these upbeat and colorful ads, individual Mormons described their secular jobs, hobbies, and interests, which tended to be remarkable rather than average: an internationally recognized musician, a world champion surfer, a wheelchair-bound homeland security consultant, a female Haitian American mayor in Utah, and a mustachioed sculptor for Harley Davidson. Each ad was interspersed with B-roll footage of the subject's family, home, and work and, harking back to the church's ads from the 1970s to 1990s, did not mention faith or religion until the subject ended the ad by adding simply "I am a Mormon"—implying, of course, that Mormonism is not contraindicated for ideal, successful, and happy American lives.[21]

In addition to the video ads, the church's official missionary website, mormon.org, was redesigned as an extension of the campaign, complete with a searchable database of individual Mormons' biographies.[22] Mormon leaders urged members to submit personal profiles to the site to help correct misconceptions about Mormons and what they believe, and members responded in droves. The site eventually featured thousands of profiles searchable by gender, age, ethnicity, and previous religion; site visitors were invited to "Discover Mormons who share your personal experience." Importantly, every submission to this site was moderated or "screened" for content by a team of young missionaries at the Missionary Training Center in Utah. If the submission was found to be too long, confusing, or doctrinally unsound—subjective terms that were never explained—the submitter was invited to revise and resubmit their profile.[23]

Beyond the "I'm a Mormon" campaign, the pendulum of control over the image of Mormonism continued to swing in popular culture and beyond. In March 2011, the satirical musical *The Book of Mormon*, written by the creators of the often raunchy and impious adult cartoon *South Park*, launched on Broadway, much to the dismay of many Mormons who felt ill-represented by the play's construction of Mormons as uniform, naive, and unthinking. Just three months later, the "I'm a Mormon" campaign expanded into the coveted New York City market, with two forty-foot, million-dollar digital billboards in Times Square along with hundreds of smaller ads placed on taxis and in subway stations throughout the city. Ads were even placed in the *Book of Mormon* playbill itself, offering an alternate reading of Mormonism to playgoers: "You've seen the play... now read the book!"[24] Some missionaries even stood outside the theater, introducing themselves to audience members after the show so that they could meet a "real" Mormon missionary.[25]

Again and again, the institutional church talks back to the public realm, wrangling for control over who can say what about Mormons, and negotiating which construction of belonging will be accepted by the American populace as the "right" or "true" image of Mormonism. Moreover, this dialogue is complicated by the proselytizing emphasis of the church: the stakes are high for a group that not only seeks control over its own oft-maligned image but also seeks to recruit new members to share in that identity.

*

But let's rewind; these shifts did not occur in a vacuum. While we could zoom in on many moments that have shaped Mormon identity over the past century, popular interest in Mormonism came to a head in 2011 and 2012; American media declared this period the "Mormon moment" (although the "moment" arguably began but failed to launch ten years earlier during the Salt Lake City Olympics).[26] With a Mormon as a viable contender for the most powerful political office in the land and popular cultural depictions of Mormons garnering major media attention, many Mormons and onlookers used this period to seriously consider what it meant to be Mormon, a meaning that continues to evolve through dialectic processes involving those who are Mormon and those who are not.

As the contest for control over Mormonism's public image raged, an internal struggle within the church went mostly unnoticed by those on the outside. In a church with an increasingly large and diverse membership and with growing opportunities for both gathering and disseminating uncorrelated information online, institutional control over individual piety and practice was increasingly stifled. More visibly than ever before, individual Mormons began to defy institutional norms in practice and belief or in the extent to which they embody Mormon orthopraxy (right actions) and orthodoxy (right thinking). These negotiations ranged from practice-based resistance like pushing back against Mormon sartorial injunctions or not following norms concerning dietary restrictions to belief negotiations or doubts involving the historicity of the Book of Mormon or the inspired nature of an all-male priesthood. In addition to individuals with isolated issues with the church, a large movement of "cultural Mormonism" gained traction among those who identify as Mormon for the cultural and emotional benefits of affiliation but who do not believe literally in the church's teachings or inspired nature.

It bears mentioning that Mormonism has always been home to many heterodox members—some of whom, like the September Six, have been notoriously punished for voicing their heterodoxy.[27] As with members of all faiths, individual Mormons embody varying degrees of assent and reservation both in belief and in action. Lingering fears about social and institutional sanctions for outspoken heterodoxy still prevent many Mormons from going public with their heterodox status. But digital media changed the game by offering a platform for voiced dissent and creating a pronounced wedge in Mormon identity, normalizing heterodoxy for some and reinforcing traditional boundaries for others. The church, for its part, continues to struggle against the vastness of the internet, which is by its very nature "uncorrelated."

Unpacking Mormon Identity

Unpacking research on Mormon identity is a practical challenge, not least because prior to sometime around 2010, much of it promoted a homogenous and nearly monolithic view of what it means to belong to the LDS church. This work largely emphasizes normative identities, idealizing the active, temple-worthy member as representative of what it means to *be* Mormon and leaving other manifestations of Mormonism unexplored.[28]

Perhaps the two most prominent scholars of Mormonism both within and outside of church circles are Richard L. Bushman, a professor of history at Columbia University, and Terryl L. Givens, a professor of literature and religion at the University of Richmond. Both Bushman and Givens are generally considered faithful church members, and both have been cited numerous times by church authorities and in church publications to give academic credence to the church and its history and/or practices.[29] In conversations and interviews with me, several LDS bishops and faithful members have cited Bushman and Givens as sources that I might find relevant to my study of Mormon identity. Bushman's 2005 biography of Joseph Smith, *Rough Stone Rolling*, was even recommended to me by Mormon missionaries, who do not generally recommend noncorrelated materials. Though some very staunch apologists may take issue with what they see as a tendency to rationalize and equivocate on disputed matters of history or doctrine,[30] Bushman's and Givens's works, while academic in tone and content, are widely considered "faith-promoting" and safe.

Another reason for the scholarly proliferation of a monolithic view on Mormon identity, which I experienced firsthand, is the difficulty of studying heterodoxy in a controlling religious space like Mormonism. To gain access to study Mormon communities openly and ethically, researchers must often follow an authoritarian chain of command that necessitates gaining clearance from local bishops, stake presidents (who oversee congregations in particular geographic regions), and church leaders at higher levels. Researchers may lose access to useful sources, like spokespeople and church leaders, if they study alternate Mormon narratives. A researcher may even be suspected of being "anti-Mormon" simply for investigating nonnormative Mormon sources or lifestyles. In many ways, researchers must choose whether to tell stories of orthodoxy or heterodoxy. Telling both becomes fraught with methodological constraints.

A notable exception, sociologist of religion Armand Mauss parses distinctions between institutional and what he calls "grassroots" approaches to LDS identity. In his influential 1994 volume on Mormon identity, Mauss describes the tensions between Mormons and broader American culture.[31] He traces the historical development of what was once a small sect into a mainstream church, locating where tensions with the broader society served to reinforce Mormon identity and commitment and thus became key elements of Mormon identity today, manifesting in narratives of persecuting and misunderstanding (e.g., Mormons as a "peculiar people" forever outside the mainstream). Throughout its history, the church moved in and out of discernible phases of mainstreaming and retrenchment, assimilation, and exceptionalism; by the 1960s, the Mormons were largely assimilated into mainstream American culture. Mauss's data leaves off in the 1980s, offering evidence to suggest that the period was one of retrenchment and differentiation from broader society. Applying Mauss's model today might suggest that efforts like the "I'm a Mormon" campaign, which seeks to make Mormonism a viable option in the Christian marketplace, indicate an institutional move toward assimilation once more (a strategic shift that seemed to occur just in time for the Romney candidacy).

In a classic study of nineteenth-century utopian communities (of which the original Mormon Church was one), Rosabeth M. Kanter famously identified traits of successful groups that she described as "commitment mechanisms."[32] These mechanisms function by dissociating the individual from the rest of society while associating them with the group. Robert R. King and Kay A. King extended Kanter's analysis to show how formal elements of Mormonism function as commitment mechanisms, reinforcing organizational boundaries by affirming individual commitment to the group.[33] Among these mechanisms are expectations and rules for behavior and belief, which I adopt and adapt as central structural constraints in LDS identity construction.

More recent scholars of Mormon identity see inherent tensions at the center of LDS identity—both historical and modern—and note the peculiarities of a faith that at once embraces and distances the broader American culture through, among other things, a desire to be seen as mainstream and Christian coinciding with a contradictory impulse to maintain exclusivity and chosenness. The previously mentioned Terryl L. Givens has gone so far as to assert that paradox itself is at the root of Mormon identity and manifests variously as an emphasis on the preeminence of bureaucratic authority while also privileging personal freedom and revelation; the primacy of knowledge and certainty pitted against the need for constant searching and self-improvement; and the chosen, elect status of Mormons contrasted with their cultural marginalization and even persecution.[34] These tensions manifest in unique rhetorical strategies for navigating identity and managing norms for who is on the inside and who is on the outside of legitimate Mormonism.

Between 1847 and 1947, Mormons were largely secluded behind their western "mountain curtain" in the Salt Lake Basin and were only known by outsiders through print media and hearsay,[35] which almost universally portrayed the Mormons as secretive, cultlike, ignorant, and dangerous. After World War II, the church's public image began to improve as many members moved to other parts of the country in a Mormon diaspora; Americans could finally meet members of the church rather than simply read or hear about them through sensational accounts. Through the 1970s and '80s, Mormons continued to build a mainstream reputation as virtuous model citizens, partially thanks to public relations efforts in then new media, especially television. The church continued to evolve throughout the rest of the twentieth century, changing from "an institution and a people embedded in a particular [western American] culture to being a church, belief system, and worshipping body able to thrive in many cultures."[36]

The church's move toward universality and what some have called "big-tent" Mormonism became even more pronounced in the early years of the twenty-first century. The global spread of Mormonism through missionary efforts has proven a major impetus for this shift. LDS church membership is no longer predominantly American, with the church reporting about 6.8 U.S. and 10.2 million international members in 2023.[37] Still, despite its global impact and international growth, Mormonism remains entrenched in American particularities. The culture of the church, if not the identity of most members, still largely reflects its white, upper-middle-class, and conservative roots, symbolized in the Utah milieu in which it is headquartered.

Still, to become increasingly mainstream, the public face of the church has emphasized what Jan Shipps calls "LDS atonement discourse," focusing on the role of Christ's redemption because it is held in common with mainstream Christianity and blunting elements of Mormon doctrine that are anathema to the mainstream, such as the idea that faithful Mormons progress toward eventual godhood. As the church expands, it receives increasing scrutiny from the media, and the diversity of stories and experiences found in a worldwide church challenges its overall image as a model minority.

*

In this book, I'm asking what it means to belong to a religious community in America today. American values of self-determination and agency, as well as the arguable hegemony of confessional faiths, contribute to a socially normative view of individual religiosity as predicated on a series of binaries: membership in a group or lack thereof, belief or disbelief in a doctrinal canon, acceptance or rejection of an identity. Affiliation with a particular religious group is taken as evidence of an individual's adoption of an entire canon of belief and practice. Indeed, many religious groups rely on these categories for boundary maintenance. In most organized religions, cultural gatekeepers determine who is in and who is out by bounding off salient identity constructs: insiders and outsiders, saved and unsaved, member and nonmember, the church and the world.

The Church of Jesus Christ of Latter-day Saints, a religion that requires both belief and participation as markers of appropriate belonging, provides a compelling setting to study religious identity in the digital age. The institutional church recognizes specific categories of belonging that loosely represent a hierarchy of communal legitimacy: from active, temple-worthy members at one extreme to nonmembers and the excommunicated at the other, each category is marked by its own behavioral and belief expectations. Beyond these institutional categories, how do conceptions of appropriate and legitimate identity change both during moments of heightened media attention and, more broadly, in this age of internet community? As Mormonism comes increasingly under public scrutiny in highly visible, mediated environments, how do Mormons themselves make sense of what it means to belong?

While popular media depictions and Mormon institutional categories idealize and normalize the active Mormon and promote an image of homogeneity in both Mormon belief and practice, my inquiries into Mormon identity show that individual Mormons nuance their faith and practice, crafting negotiated versions of what it means to be Mormon. Some do so in ways that challenge the culture or doctrine of the church; to the extent that their beliefs or behavior threaten the authority of orthodox teachings and practice, they may be marginalized, ostracized, sanctioned, or even excommunicated.

2

Caffeine and Agency in Mormon Boundary Work

Wherefore, men . . . are free to choose liberty and eternal life, through the great Mediator of all men, or to choose captivity and death.

—2 Nephi 2:27, Book of Mormon

Whatever the unifying nature of religion . . . the history of religions has been the history of great discord. It would seem that nothing can more effectively set people at odds than the demand that they think alike. For, given our many disparate ways of life, we couldn't really think alike, even if we wanted to. Though we repeated exactly the same articles of faith, we'd understand them differently to the extent that our relations to them differed.

—Kenneth Burke, *The Rhetoric of Religion: Studies in Logology*

Throughout 2012, critical national attention on the Church of Jesus Christ of Latter-day Saints seemed at an all-time high as the media worked to translate Mormonism for public consumption. In one wide-reaching instance of this attention, on August 23, NBC featured a special Mormon-themed edition of its primetime television news show *Rock Center with Brian Williams*. Titled "Mormon in America," the hour-long episode explored various aspects of Mormon life. The ostensible aim of the special—airing as it did just four days before the start of the Republican National Convention at which Mitt Romney would become the first Mormon ever nominated for president by a major party—was to educate the American public on little-known aspects of Romney's faith. During the hour-long report, one topic mentioned only in passing set off a whirl of discussion across Mormon communities: the often-cited but poorly explained relationship between the Mormon faith and caffeine consumption.

Amid representations of diversity in Mormon identity, such as noted feminist Joanna Brooks, gay progressive Mitch Mayne, and former Mormon Abby Huntsman (daughter of one-time presidential hopeful Jon Huntsman), the report highlighted one suburban Utah family as archetypal Mormons, fulfilling cultural stereotypes (prevalent both within and without the church) of Mormons as traditional and orthodox practitioners.

On *Rock Center*, the Jacksons were models of normativity and assent to the institutional church, illustrating idealized Mormon belonging underscored by film footage and discussion of their dedication to family and congregation, daily family prayer, faithful service to church callings, and devotion to even the minutiae of LDS belief and lifestyle expectations. In one brief moment, stay-at-home mother of five Juleen Jackson was asked by the interviewer whether she drinks caffeine; with a slight smile, she responded, "No." Then, when pressed on whether she had ever had a cup of coffee, she said "No" but laughed and added apologetically that she did *once* consume a Coke. These questions were followed by other inquiries into her Mormon bona fides—whether she consumes alcohol and wears her temple garments. Later in the program, her husband, a convert to the church, joked that he struggled with his Coke habit, a reference not to the illicit drug but to the soft drink.

These casual inquiries into Mormon caffeine consumption on a primetime news special sounded no alarms in the secular media (except as a way of marking Mormons as different) but set off a discursive firestorm within Mormon communities about the contested role of caffeine in the LDS lifestyle: whether or not it is against LDS doctrine and/or policy to avoid it and what it says about a Mormon who chooses to forgo (or not) its consumption. Many Mormons believe that avoiding caffeine is a "higher law," and their avoidance of it serves as a status symbol or mark of commitment to righteous living, or orthopraxy. Other Mormons routinely drink caffeinated soft drinks or even energy drinks, avoiding coffee and tea but not caffeine per se, and believe the avoidance of caffeine to be a legalistic and ignorant misinterpretation and a failure to properly divide culture from doctrine.

The debate, of course, was never just about caffeine; it was about the porosity or density of boundaries for being Mormon, about the role of rules in religious life, and about the nature of authority and revelation in the context of Mormon praxis. Using this mediated moment as a launching point to dissect questions of authority and normativity, this chapter examines the construction of Mormon identity through discourses of boundary delineation and negotiation. As Michel Foucault reminds us,[1] how we experience reality is mediated by how we describe it. These descriptions are never neutral, being overdetermined by structures of power; and yet they are also never static, being negotiated and reimagined through an individual's own agency. Institutionally, the Church of Jesus Christ of Latter-day Saints provides an ideological structure through which faithful Mormons interpret its edicts, transforming these spoken and unspoken rules into cultural norms.

In lived Mormonism, discourses differentiating between culture and doctrine serve as ways to police belonging but, because of their ambiguity, allow for renegotiation of Mormon norms by practitioners. The polyphony of the internet brings these numerous renegotiations to the fore for analysis, while the transparency of the internet allows us to capture the process of identity construction in real time. Using data from discourse analysis and interviews, I will show how institutional, church-sponsored representations of Mormon identity become constructions of normativity that presuppose a form of power and authority apart from theological ideas about doctrine, which are in turn negotiated by members in a cultural dance of meaning-making. This is the interplay of structure and agency, the intermingling of constraint with choice and play.

First, I briefly outline some structural considerations that may seem ancillary to our main points of discussion but provide an important framework for understanding identity negotiation within the Mormon context. I then describe the history and role of dietary rules in Mormon identity as an entryway into a discussion of two important nodes of LDS institutional control, authority, and normativity; these nodes form the structure against which Mormons enact their religious identities. This is followed by an exploration of orthopraxy, or right living, as a cultural linchpin for being Mormon and a prime example of the role of agency in negotiating identity within the bounds of structure. I conclude with a discussion of Mormon imagined community and the threats posed to it by digital interactions.

Contextualizing Mormon Identity: A Structural Sketch of the LDS Church

As an entrée into a discussion of the roles of structure and agency in Mormon identity, we first must go into some detail about the institutional church. The history, governing structure, rules, policies, and teachings of the institution, as well as the cultural disciplinary mechanisms that maintain those norms, form the structure against which agency is exercised in the LDS context. These structural elements are interwoven, albeit often loosely, forming a complex cultural system in which norms often go unspoken.

Points of Departure from Mainstream Christianity

The organization that would become the Church of Jesus Christ of Latter-day Saints was founded in 1830 not as a new religion but as a restoration of Christ's original church and the true Christian gospel that, according to Joseph Smith, had been corrupted and ultimately lost from the earth after Jesus's death. These two competing impulses—that of a new religious movement versus an ancient faith restored—manifest in a modern tension between progressivism and change on the one hand and conservatism and tradition on the other. Moreover, the church-as-restoration paradigm has, since the church's inception, defined Mormon identity by simultaneously equating and differentiating it with mainstream notions of Christianity, as the power of Mormonism is found in both its claim to continuity with Christ's gospel and its selfsame avowed difference from the corruption of that very gospel. The church has grown from its original six members to its current worldwide estimate of seventeen million. In the United States, Mormons comprise somewhere between 1.6 to 2.3 percent of the population, or between the CIA's estimated 5.4 million and the church's estimate of 6.8 million members.[2] For comparison, the number of Mormons in the United States as well as worldwide is almost identical to prominent estimates of the number of Jews, a detail that is one of many parallels between LDS and Jewish identity. In many ways, the LDS church positions itself as a restoration of both true Christianity and true Judaism, teaching that nearly all Mormons are literal genetic descendants of a lost tribe of Israel.[3] But perhaps more interesting for our purposes, both groups' population counts are loose estimates and highly controversial,[4] signaling difficulty within and without the groups in accounting for who belongs—and who does not.

Despite their reliance on Jesus Christ in theology and worship, other distinctive and central beliefs and practices place Mormons squarely outside the American mainstream, a difference that has historically led to the perception among many mainstream Christians that Mormonism is a dangerous cult rather than a legitimate Christian denomination.[5] This aversion is centered in many major doctrinal and practical departures from historical Christian norms, not the least of which is that while mainstream Christian churches teach that the canon of scripture is closed, the LDS church emphasizes "continuing revelation."[6] In theory, if not in frequent practice, the canon of scripture is never closed in Mormonism, and not only can new revelations be received, but prior ones can be revealed to be outmoded (e.g., the once "new and everlasting covenant" of plural marriage was later declared to have only been required by God for a particular historical season[7]) or even wrongly ascribed revelatory status (e.g., the priesthood ban on men of African descent is now said to have never been an actual doctrine, just a mere cultural practice wrongly afforded doctrinal status).

The doctrine of continuing revelation specifies that new truths are revealed as God communicates directly with modern-day prophets, of whom Joseph Smith was the first; he has been succeeded by subsequent presidents of the church who are sustained as "prophets, seers, and revelators."[8]

Because of continuing revelation, then, the question of doctrinality is always open. Missionaries and other LDS proselytizers often challenge the Western hegemonic conception of a closed canon by asking mainstream Christian investigators, "Why would God stop speaking to his children?"[9] But continuing revelation means that Mormon doctrine is always a moving target; continuing revelation is not only a system for integrating new, unprecedented information and circumstances into Mormon belief and practice. It is also retroactively applied to norms previously accepted by the church that have since fallen out of favor. In theory, then, continuing revelation could upend Mormon beliefs and practices in any area at any time.

The Canonization Process

Because of Mormonism's open scriptural canon, the sacred text known as Doctrine and Covenants is viewed as a living document, a record of revelations received by the church's founding prophet Joseph Smith and, to a much lesser degree, by his successors.[10] Despite the importance of the open canon in Mormonism, while new revelations were prolific in the church's early years, the most recent addition to the Doctrine and Covenants is Official Declaration 2, which in 1978 extended the LDS priesthood to men of African descent; before that, the Vision of the Redemption of the Dead, recorded in section 138, was accepted as doctrine in 1976, although it had been received and taught by President Joseph F. Smith in 1918.[11]

In a church founded and dependent on this idea of an open canon, new doctrines must go through a ritualized canonization process to attain the weight of authority necessary to become naturalized in members' beliefs and behaviors.[12] The ritual processes surrounding the acceptance and institutionalization of doctrine function sociologically to reaffirm group cohesion and commitment among Mormons. Only four months after officially organizing his church, Smith received a revelation instituting a practice of "common consent,"[13] ritualizing adding of doctrine to the Mormon canon through a process wherein LDS members vote to sustain, or support, the addition. This early nod to democratic American norms figured in Mormonism's early practice but obfuscates the hierarchical nature of modern Mormonism.

Sustaining a new doctrine, much like sustaining the church's leaders as they are inaugurated, is an oblique process that Mormons often refer to as the litmus test of whether a particular teaching or belief is legitimately doctrine or not—and thus whether complicity to it is binding and can, implicitly, be used as a social means of gauging other members' standing. In current practice, a new doctrine (or leader) is sustained at the church's largest meeting, General Conference, in the Salt Lake City Conference Center by a show of hands.[14] Bodily investment is a necessary means by which religious ritual increases individual and group commitment to any religious community;[15] as a new doctrine is presented by leaders who are a priori deemed revelators in communication with the divine, Mormons raise their hands, literally putting their bodies on the line to signal their assent to the liturgical order. This question of bodily investment is further implicated in the issue of caffeine consumption, as we will see.

Like all rituals, meant to be faith affirming and cohesion inducing, the process of sustaining new doctrine is largely symbolic; votes are not counted. As the process is not clarified in LDS scripture, it is unclear if a majority or unanimous vote is required for a new doctrine to be canonized, but that matters little, since negative votes are rare. While doctrine must be approved by a sustaining vote of the members, a bishop or other presiding authority can then move forward with whatever decision regardless of opposing voices. In April 2015, for example, when the General Conference congregation was asked to signal that they sustained their leaders, a small protest group stood and yelled "Opposed!" Despite gathering some media attention, the protest had no noticeable effect on proceedings.

Still, the process of proposing, sustaining, and recording new teachings in the Mormon scriptural canon is counted as evidence of a teaching's status as "doctrine," which lends it the status of divine mandate and implies group commitment to the terms of the doctrine. The myth of common consent, that the church's positions and leaders are unequivocally supported by the entire membership in a democratic voting process, contributes to feelings of unity and imagined community. Indeed, some members have told me that when new officers are proposed and voted on in their local congregations, dissenting voters are sometimes taken aside afterward by the bishop and asked why they opposed the vote. In this way, the process of sustaining new leaders publicly serves to identify contrary opinions among the congregation.

Because doctrine is seen as divinely revealed, acceptance of it is generally taken as a necessary requirement for belonging within the Mormon community; indeed, today's biggest threats to groupwide cohesion in Mormonism often stem from claims by marginal groups and individuals that challenge status quo interpretations of doctrine (e.g., claims by Mormon feminists that women should hold the all-male priesthood or claims by progressive LDS that same-sex marriage should be recognized or at least not opposed by the church). Among countless points of doctrinal distinction, adherence to the Word of Wisdom is one way that Mormons mark their bodies as properly Mormon.[16] In Mormonism, proper belief (or orthodoxy) is implicit unless stated otherwise; but it is through *doing* things the right way that Mormons signal their assent to the church's regulations, thus communicating their normative membership and submission to the group. But when the wording of Mormon doctrine is ambiguous (and it nearly always is) and when leaders offer no clarification, individual Mormons must determine how to follow it according to their own interpretation, which they often refer to emically as *agency* and which involves a negotiation of practical considerations, social expectations, and an affective, subjective feeling about what is right. This navigation underscores the tension between structure and agency in Mormon identity construction.

Bureaucratic Norms and Control

In addition to the divine appointment of latter-day prophets, Smith taught that Christ's ancient priesthood was restored, giving authority in various increments to all worthy men over the age of twelve. Priesthood authority refers to this divine authority, received through the laying on of hands, to conduct ritual ordinances and give blessings (special prophetic prayers) in God's name. A woman's access to the priesthood and its power is limited to what she can gain secondhand through marriage or another close association with a male priesthood holder. The concept of priesthood authority not only sets Mormonism apart from other Christian groups but also creates a structure within the LDS culture that gives both spoken and unspoken normative authority to those with a divinely sanctioned voice. In practical terms, this means church leaders have more sway than congregants, that men have more authority than women, and that ultimately the refusal to accept or submit to counsel from leaders is tantamount to rejecting God's chosen leadership and thus God himself. The stakes are high in a culture built on the concept of priesthood authority.

Partially because of this leadership hierarchy, the LDS church has evolved to become an institutional monolith, highly bureaucratic and authoritarian in structure, with a clearly demarcated chain of command among those in leadership positions. Headquartered in Salt Lake City, Utah—where early Mormon pioneers settled under the leadership of Brigham Young to avoid persecution and prosecution—the leadership of the church is structured hierarchically and known as the "General Authorities," comprising five interrelated governing bodies. At the apex of authority is the prophet, as of 2024 Russell M. Nelson, who together with his two counselors makes up the First Presidency; these, especially the prophet, are the church's spiritual and temporal figureheads and carry the most normative weight as mouthpieces of God on Earth. The normative authority of the prophet cannot be overstated; he is revered and nearly worshipped in a fashion similar to the Catholic pope.

Below the First Presidency in structural authority is the Quorum of the Twelve Apostles, who primarily travel and give religious talks (LDS parlance for the equivalent of sermons or homilies). Continuing down the chain of command is the seven-member Presidency of the Seventy, who primarily preside over the First and Second Quorums of the Seventy, both of which may have up to seventy members at a given time. Below all of these is the Presiding Bishopric, who oversee the Aaronic Priesthood and are responsible largely for administrative affairs.[17] All of the hundred-odd General Authorities are men (female auxiliary leaders were only recently added to the flowchart and have been dubbed General Officers), and the vast majority are American, white, and from upper-middle-class business backgrounds. Men are divinely "called" to all these positions generally after years of faithful local service and success in their secular careers.

In addition to the all-male General Authority structure, General Auxiliaries consisting of a president and two counselors oversee church programs. These include Primary, Relief Society, Sunday School, Young Men, and Young Women General Presidencies. Women's leadership at the structural level is relegated to presiding over other women (in the Relief Society and the Young Women General Presidencies) and over children (Primary). Auxiliary leaders have less normative sway than General Authorities but considerably more than local leaders or, especially, lay members.

Mormons' Scripted Roles

Mormons' individual roles within the structure are constrained by various additional considerations. Traditionally, the church has been firmly bounded and closed, meaning membership access is difficult, and internal cohesion and control are high.[18] Categories that emphasize the embodiment of faith through practice (orthopraxy) classify individuals' standings in the faith: a *member* assents to the church's teachings verbally and is subsequently baptized by someone with priesthood authority. While membership is the least necessary requirement to be counted as Mormon, membership is itself a multivalent category: an *active member* embodies his or her assent to the organization through attendance and service, fulfilling voluntary service called callings, tithing 10 percent of his or her income, and following prescriptions for morality and daily living. An *inactive member*, generally someone who has been baptized but no longer attends services, has fulfilled the basic obligations but has neglected practice—thus this category includes as diverse a group as believing Mormons who have fallen out of habit to individuals baptized as children but who left the church as adults and never autonomously accepted the doctrine. A *nonmember*, then, is one who has never been a part of the faith or who has resigned his or her membership or been excommunicated (although, in practice, I have never heard a Mormon refer to someone who was excommunicated as a nonmember with no other qualification). Occasionally, and only in internal discourse, an even stronger term demarcates outsiders: they may be referred to as Gentiles, the ultimate outsider to the Mormons' chosenness.[19]

These emic terms—*active*, *inactive*, and *nonmember*—serve to reinforce organizational boundaries through us and them distinctions and help increase and maintain group solidarity. Based on the church's emphasis on individual praxis, it seems easy to judge a Mormon as in or out of the firm boundaries provided by the institution and to categorize them according to the church's taxonomy. But the terms also create an illusion of homogeneity within the faith itself, conflating participation with assent to the tenets, doctrines, and even history of the church; and this illusion is complicated by the understanding that individuals with heterodox perspectives must keep them to themselves or face social and/or institutional sanction.

As an institutional tactic to maintain a high level of member control, pervasive rules for members function as commitment mechanisms and contribute to group cohesion and member retention. Members are effectively rank-ordered in terms of personal worthiness: the institutional church primarily emphasizes orthopraxy—right action or rule-keeping—to distinguish legitimate members from outsiders; but the church also prizes orthodoxy, or right thinking, as a central characteristic of model or worthy members. To be temple-worthy and thus able to partake in the highest rites of the church, members must engage in appropriate moral action (such as tithing 10 percent of one's income, keeping the health code known as the Word of Wisdom, conforming to the Law of Chastity, and after going through esoteric temple ceremonies, wearing particular undergarments). These are ways individuals embody Mormonism. Temple-worthiness is lauded as the ideal status for Mormon faithful: as Elder Russell M. Nelson of the Quorum of the Twelve Apostles put it, "The Lord would be pleased if every adult member would be worthy of—and carry—a current temple recommend [a credential authorizing admission to LDS temples]."[20]

But temple attendance also requires that Mormons verbally testify to the church's truthfulness (and, implicitly, its literality). Moreover, members are expected to give regular talks in the church and "bear their testimonies," emphasizing that they *know* the church is true.[21] Additionally, requirements and social expectations for active membership include attendance at weekly church meetings and other special meetings, volunteer service in various capacities, the responsibility to visit assigned ward members, and many other expectations, all of which are time-consuming and make church the primary social sphere for a faithful member. In this way, the church constructs a scale of belonging—necessary requirements for mere membership privilege action and embodiment, but to be worthy as an ideal member involves belief and implied internalization of the church's teachings. Tellingly, several members have told me in interviews, "As a Mormon, you can believe anything you want—as long as you don't tell anyone." This tension between orthopraxy and orthodoxy—and the mixed messages the church sends about which it prioritizes—is integral to the framework or structure against which modern Mormon identity is negotiated.

Situated within this web of structural constraints shaping LDS identity lies the distinct Mormon dietary code known as the Word of Wisdom. Juleen Jackson's public declaration that she eschews caffeinated beverages and *Rock Center*'s offhanded representation of this as a peculiar, and peculiarly Mormon, edict represents a contentious if common interpretation of this code, outlined in section 89 of one of Mormonism's sacred scriptural texts, the Doctrine and Covenants. To understand the function of the Word of Wisdom in Mormon praxis, it is necessary first to explore its origins.

The Word of Wisdom and Beyond: Rule-Keeping and Mormon Identity

History is a vital reference point for Mormon identity, and the history of the Word of Wisdom at once elucidates the ways Mormons embody it today and provides an illustration of the way norms are circulated and advanced within the community. Revelations received by the acting prophet and recorded as doctrine are historically contingent textual creations that, stamped with the title of "official church doctrine," become inexorable truth for Mormon faithful. Despite the aura of factuality they garner, Mormon doctrines' specificity as historical products matters when considering evolving Mormon identities. This history marks the ways that religious rules become part of an invented tradition and, taken together, create a religious ethos around which the community is structured.[22]

The Word of Wisdom was received and recorded by Joseph Smith in 1833 after his wife Emma complained about Smith and his colleagues' habit of chewing and spitting tobacco in her home during their meetings. Smith said he prayed about tobacco use and in response received the divine revelation that would later become Doctrine and Covenants section 89. In addition to tobacco, the passage specifically mentions avoidance of "wine," "strong drinks," and "hot drinks" and goes on to prescribe proper uses of various foodstuffs, including eating scant meat, relying on grain, and consuming only seasonal produce. But the wording of the passage is ambiguous, leaving room for personal interpretation: verse 9 simply says, "And again, hot drinks are not for the body or belly." Debates over what constitutes "hot drinks" and whether these are prohibited or simply cautioned against highlight LDS efforts to define clear boundaries for the community and help explain the accompanying emphasis on orthopraxy that these boundaries inculcated in the early church.

In 1842, Assistant President (and brother to Joseph) Hyrum Smith clarified in the church's magazine *Times and Seasons* that "hot drinks" referred specifically to coffee and tea.[23] Still, LDS faithful continued to view the Word of Wisdom as a health code, more sound advice to take or leave than a command; in fact, Joseph Smith's doctor recorded in his journal that Smith had tea with his breakfast in 1843.[24] It was not until the later presidency of Heber J. Grant, who served from 1918 to 1945, that strict observance of the Word of Wisdom became a moral code, reinforcing the church's political posturing during America's movement toward Prohibition.[25] It was also at this time that observance of the Word of Wisdom was rhetorically reduced to specifically refer to a prohibition against alcohol, tobacco, coffee, and tea. By 1934, observance of the Word of Wisdom was listed in the *Handbook of Instructions* as a requirement for admission to the temple and thus participation in the church's highest sacraments.[26] Since that time, according to religious historian Matthew Bowman, "the Word of Wisdom has become perhaps the most recognizable social marker for Mormons in America,"[27] both marking Mormons as different from those in non-LDS society and serving as an in-group marker of commitment and status.

Proscriptions like the Word of Wisdom are found in most religious traditions and were particularly common among groups established during the Second Great Awakening, when Mormonism was born. As Rosabeth Moss Kanter shows in her study of nineteenth-century utopian societies, swearing off particular practices like drinking coffee and tea prior to baptism is not unique to Mormonism. The ritual practice of requiring new members to sacrifice particularly dear luxuries and pleasures increases the success of a community by asserting control over individual members. Pervasive rules function as commitment mechanisms and contribute to group cohesion and member retention.[28] Kanter defines commitment as "the process through which individual interests become attached to the carrying out of socially organized patterns of behavior which are seen as fulfilling those interests, as expressing the nature and needs of the person."[29] In modern lived Mormonism, the Word of Wisdom functions to increase commitment to the faith and stands as a public and visible symbol of that commitment.

Yet the arbitrariness of avoiding alcohol, tobacco, coffee, and tea as primary markers of LDS commitment and differentiation is perhaps best highlighted by noting that other elements of the Word of Wisdom are not rigidly adhered to by faithful LDS. For instance, the Word of Wisdom advises to only eat seasonal produce and to eat meat sparingly and suggests that while members should avoid wine, the exception is wine taken in the sacrament, which should be "pure wine of the grape of the vine, of your own make."[30] Contemporary LDS sacrament consists of sliced white bread and water, never wine, and no emphasis is placed on proper consumption of other foodstuffs beyond admonitions to treat the body as a temple and thus eat healthfully (an admonition that does not bear the weight of divine command among most Mormons, known for their love of ice cream and superb home-baked goods). While alcohol, tobacco, coffee, and tea may be arbitrary, their proscription is a frequent and public reminder to faithful Mormons of their commitments to Christ and his church. As one LDS bishop explained, as a businessman who frequently entertains clients, he must explain and defend his religious convictions on a regular basis with high stakes for his own social standing and income. The Word of Wisdom forms a boundary between Mormons and non-Mormons, as a commitment to keep the Word of Wisdom is one of several requirements for baptism into the church in the first place.

The quotidian ways that Mormons practice the Word of Wisdom hint at a broader cultural emphasis on orthopraxy even beyond the "letter of the law." Although caffeine itself is not mentioned in the Word of Wisdom, its avoidance has become a signifier of orthodoxy in many Mormon communities, particularly in Utah, where the LDS population predominates. Since Hyrum Smith's elucidation that the textual phrase "hot drinks" is meant to refer to coffee and tea, some LDS leaders have publicly speculated that coffee and tea are to be avoided specifically because they contain caffeine, which is habit-forming and thus harmful to the Mormon value of agency;[31] noncaffeinated herbal teas are not verboten.

Mormon discourse around the proscription of caffeine focuses on its deleterious effects: it is framed as a habit-forming, harmful drug. A 2008 article in the church-owned magazine *Ensign* describes "caffeine addiction" and lists its potential side effects: insomnia, heart disease, depression, and even death. "Addiction," a devil word in Mormonism, suggests the sacrifice of agency to evil influence. The word is applied regularly in Mormon discourse not only to obvious culprits like alcohol and illicit drugs but also to caffeine, pornography, and masturbation, all signifiers of a lack of mastery over the body. The author of the *Ensign* article further notes that the Word of Wisdom "does not specifically prohibit caffeine" but also says, "If we follow the spirit of the Word of Wisdom, we will be very careful about what we consume, particularly any substance that can have a negative impact on our bodies.... This includes caffeine."[32] In firmly bounded communities, "pollution beliefs can uphold the moral code" and often function as a way of policing the community.[33] In Mormonism, caffeine, as a pollutant to the body, has been moralized and stigmatized.

Because of these implications, many modern Mormons, particularly those raised in the Intermountain West, grew up in families that decried caffeine consumption not only in coffee and tea but also in the form of soft drinks—exemplified by the Jackson family featured on *Rock Center*. But this avoidance of caffeine is a particularly contentious cultural construction that some Mormons differentiate from "official" doctrine in a rhetorical move that underscores the function of authority, norms, and rule-keeping within the LDS tradition. After *Rock Center*, when the issue was confronted and debated in 2012 by both the LDS institution and its members, fractures in the LDS community became publicly visible on the internet.

Mediated Fallout: Public Declarations, Private Control

After Juleen Jackson's high-profile public declaration that she does not consume caffeine and *Rock Center*'s implication that this is a distinctly Mormon proscription, the church issued a statement through its Public Affairs Department via its online Newsroom website.[34] The Newsroom launched in 2000 in anticipation of the 2002 Salt Lake City Winter Olympics with the tagline "The Official Resource for News Media, Opinion Leaders, and the Public."[35] Over time, this site became not only a source for news media and the curious public to access reliable information about the church but also a platform for the church to publicly correct misconceptions or misrepresentations of Mormonism (particularly its more controversial doctrines), giving the church a say in the public construction of Mormonism and attempting to police that construction following the tradition of correlation. Today, the Newsroom disseminates information via its website, social media accounts on Facebook and YouTube, and press releases.

Responding to *Rock Center*, the Public Affairs statement praised NBC for its "evenhanded" treatment of Mormonism, particularly its positive portrayal of church welfare programs, but took issue with the implied claim that the church teaches against the use of caffeine. The statement read, "Despite what was reported, the Church does not prohibit the use of caffeine. The Church's health guidelines, known in our scriptures as 'the Word of Wisdom' (Doctrine and Covenants 89), prohibits alcoholic drinks, smoking or chewing of tobacco and 'hot drinks'—taught by Church leaders to refer specifically to tea and coffee. The restriction does not go beyond this."[36]

After years of ambiguity on the issue of caffeine, the church had finally made its stance clear. Many Mormons took to Facebook, Twitter, and personal blogs to celebrate this unique example of church leadership clarifying an ambiguous point of contention within LDS culture, many echoing the lighthearted celebration evident in a *Salt Lake Tribune* headline that read, "OK, Mormons, Drink Up—Coke and Pepsi Are OK."[37]

But the next morning, the Newsroom's statement had changed; with no notation that the entry had been altered,[38] it now read, "Despite what was reported, the Church revelation spelling out health practices (Doctrine and Covenants 89) *does not mention the use of caffeine.* The Church's health guidelines prohibit alcoholic drinks, smoking or chewing of tobacco, and 'hot drinks'—taught by Church leaders to refer specifically to tea and coffee."[39]

The Newsroom's parsing of words differentiated carefully between "not prohibiting" caffeine versus "not mentioning" caffeine, and the phrase "The restriction does not go beyond this" was omitted, which left many Mormons scratching their heads as to whether church leadership—and by extension, God himself—actually did have an opinion on caffeine consumption. If caffeine is *not* frowned upon, why did the wording warrant alteration? The vagueness signaled to some members that the church, in fact, *does* prohibit the use of caffeine, or at the very least does not recommend it, while still leaving room for the interpretation by other members that caffeine consumption is acceptable.

Amid the ensuing discussions, some began to ponder the statement's implications. The *Salt Lake Tribune*'s religion writer, Peggy Fletcher Stack, noted that the confusion over whether caffeine is prohibited might stem from the fact that Brigham Young University (BYU), a church-owned institution, did not sell caffeinated beverages on its campus; its vending machines and beverage fountains had been exclusively stocked with caffeine-free sodas.[40] Known for being a strict and conservative campus, BYU is often seen as a Mormon microcosm, and its lifestyle edicts are often extrapolated as broader cultural ideals; even a 2009 food service industry newsletter, *Food Management*, conflated LDS culture and teachings in an article that highlighted BYU's dining services: "To draw customers, [dining services director Dean] Wright must tap into the needs of a fairly unique student population. BYU is an institution of the Church of Jesus Christ of Latter-Day Saints (LDS). Among other things, that means not just no alcohol, but no caffeine either."[41]

BYU's caffeine issue highlights generational and geographical peculiarities in a worldwide church still so enmeshed in and reflective of white, upper-middle-class Utah culture. At BYU, students bring their cultural baggage from all over the world and encounter the stark reality of a deeply conservative culture. One caffeine-abstinent BYU professor explained to me that the Word of Wisdom is as much a communicative strategy as it is a health code; just as Jewish dietary laws are intended to set them apart from other people groups, the Word of Wisdom is one of many Mormon practices that says, according to the professor, "I'm telling you who I am. This is my notice that tells you what I am and what I believe." At BYU, where everyone is assumed to be LDS, caffeine use could be interpreted as a lack of commitment to the group. He went on: "Here at BYU, if I were to walk around with a Coke in my hand, I'm making a statement that I'm not all the way in. Culturally, here, that's what that means. Regardless of whether I think caffeine is good for me or not. In New Jersey, if I'm holding that Coke in my hand, it doesn't make the same statement."

After the *Salt Lake Tribune* pointed out the irony that BYU does not sell caffeinated beverages despite the Newsroom's clarification that the church has no position on it, confusion abounded about the relationship between BYU's policies and LDS expectations. In response to media queries, BYU campus spokesperson Carri Jenkins explained that the university's abstention "was not a university or church decision, but made by dining services, based on what our customers want," and that there is "no demand" for caffeinated beverages on the campus.[42] Yet BYU's online newspaper, the *Digital Universe*, reported that BYU's dining services director, Dean Wright, stated that while dining services conducts online surveys to determine its offerings, they had never asked students about caffeinated drinks and had no plans to do so.[43]

BYU students took to social media to petition the school to change its position and to illustrate that there was indeed a demand for caffeine at their school. An online petition at Change.org titled "Brigham Young University: Please offer caffeinated beverages on campus and at venues" gathered 1,040 signatures in a matter of days. One BYU senior and returned missionary, Skyler Thiot, created a community page on Facebook titled "BYU for Caffeine" to illustrate enough demand to sway campus policies. Comments on the page, primarily by other BYU students and alumni, ranged from support for "dispelling a Mormon myth" to accusations of "stirring the pot." Within two weeks, despite garnering over 2,300 page "likes," Thiot removed the page because the issue had become "too contentious."[44]

A second anonymous "BYU for Caffeine" Facebook page popped up, promoting a policy protest on BYU's campus that would entail distributing free cans of caffeinated soda on September 14, less than a month after the *Rock Center* episode ignited the whole debacle. The issue was settled, at least for the time being, after only three minutes and fifty free cans of soda: BYU campus police arrived on the scene and asked the two lone student protestors to leave, citing their lack of a permit to assemble.[45] Despite the flurry of attention, the issue of caffeine on campus quickly died down with no further clarification from church or BYU leaders. In Utah at least, nonnormative interpretations of the Word of Wisdom had been silenced.

Three years later, as the caffeine issue seemed to dissipate, another intrepid caffeine fiend at BYU, Austin Mills, circulated a new Change.org petition: “Offer Caffeinated Beverages on Campus.”[46] The petition garnered just 504 signatures, less than half of the original petition.

Just weeks later during General Conference, Second Counselor in the First Presidency Dieter Uchtdorf joked that learning how to use a computer took lots of effort and “many liters of a diet soda that shall remain nameless.”[47]

In 2017, the university unceremoniously reversed its decision and began selling caffeinated beverages across campus. After over sixty years of refusing to sell it on campus, students could now purchase caffeinated sodas across campus and at sporting events. Much can be said about the timing of this shift, but it seems certain that student demand ultimately drove the decision, while the policy change was withheld until critical attention had shifted away from the university’s policies.

Today, some more traditionally conservative Mormons at BYU still abstain from caffeine on principle, but the issue is no longer central to marking insider or outsider status. As culture moves, so do Mormon mores of belonging.

Authority, Normativity, and Voice in LDS Identity Construction

Why do everyday Mormons, like the students protesting BYU’s caffeine ban and the Mormons who criticized them for it, disagree about proper practice? Is it possible that faithful, lifelong Mormons such as the Jacksons, avid eschewers of caffeine, could somehow misinterpret church doctrine? When did church Public Affairs become the mouthpiece of Mormon leaders and, by extension, God himself, clarifying important points of contention for both the media and the faithful? Why is it that with changing institutional expectations, even those that go without explanation, social norms naturally shift into alignment?

These questions highlight major pitfalls in locating the boundaries of modern LDS identities, all of which are compounded by the expansiveness of the internet as a mediating technology and the visibility of online participation that renders these identities susceptible to surveillance and policing. First, various strategies for interpreting the Word of Wisdom and the concomitant controversies around these interpretations highlight the ambiguous role of authority and normativity in Mormonism as a disciplinary structure. Next, the Word of Wisdom and Mormon rule-keeping as particular points of cultural contention underscore the tension within Mormonism between mainstreaming with the broader American culture and self-segregation via purposeful differentiation, issues of both organizational strategy within the marketplace of religion and individual navigation of cultural norms in identity formation. Finally, the challenges in parsing how Mormons embody various interpretations of the Word of Wisdom and what these interpretations tell us about Mormon identity illustrate the difficulty in simplistically categorizing Mormonism in toto and hint at the role of individual agency in Mormon identity construction.

Doctrine and Authority: Who Speaks for Mormons?

Who defines what it means to be Mormon and draws lines to determine who is in and who is out of the bounds of the legitimate community? Answering that question requires starting at the top: in this theologically and pragmatically top-down organization with clearly demarcated hierarchy, Mormon leaders are considered divinely installed, and their words are revered as messages from on high. As mentioned previously, these leaders are annually sustained by active members of the church—both during biannual General Conference proceedings as a community and in personal worthiness interviews that assess a member's standing to determine whether they may participate in the temple—as divinely appointed and inspired to lead righteously. But the status of Mormon authority is steeped in paradox, much like other aspects of Mormon belief and identity.[48] This paradox makes it difficult to delineate where structure and its constraints end and agential choice begins in LDS identity construction. When are leaders offering normalizing discourse? When are Mormons choosing? While General Authorities, especially the First Presidency, are said to be called to their positions by God himself, the church is quick to emphasize to the non-Mormon media that not everything a General Authority says is said with authority, illustrated in this 2007 statement from the online LDS Newsroom.

> Not every statement made by a Church leader, past or present, necessarily constitutes doctrine. A single statement made by a single leader on a single occasion often represents a personal, though well-considered, opinion, but is not meant to be officially binding for the whole Church. With divine inspiration, the First Presidency... and the Quorum of the Twelve Apostles... counsel together to establish doctrine that is consistently proclaimed in official Church publications. This doctrine resides in the four "standard works" of scripture (the Holy Bible, the Book of Mormon, the Doctrine and Covenants and the Pearl of Great Price), official declarations and proclamations, and the Articles of Faith.[49]

That is, a leader is speaking authoritatively when he says things that have already been given normative weight through the esoteric process of canonization. These caveats and obfuscations around what counts as doctrine versus what is opinion or outmoded teaching respond to critics' and the media's tendency to draw out controversial yet mostly peripheral teachings, often the pet teaching of long-dead Mormon leaders, and emphasize them as central to the faith, such as the past practice of polygamy or the belief that God resides near a star called Kolob.

For many faithful members who revere their leaders, the question of what counts as doctrine and what is mere opinion is of little practical concern. Members are taught from an early age that their church is uniquely led directly by God through its leaders. Many members express their ultimate faith in *anything* said by someone in leadership—right down to the local bishop, who serves on a volunteer, rotating basis with no ecclesiastical training. In many ways, the degree to which members accept *all* words of General Authorities as divinely inspired and binding is a generally accurate way to measure LDS orthodoxy and conformity to Mormon institutional norms. Faithful members generally treat General Authorities' public addresses and publications as weighty with authority and inspired by God; when pressed, they express a reliance on affective evidence to decide whether these messages are right or true. One missionary explained to me, "When the prophet speaks, I feel warm and happy. And I know what he is saying is true."

This common affective response stems from not only the actual words of a church authority but a deep, personal conviction that each authority is divinely installed. It was not uncommon in my interviews and observations for faithful Mormons to become visibly emotional or even weep as they bore their testimony of the divine inspiration of General Authorities and their complete confidence in their words, especially those of the prophet. The tendency for orthodox Mormons to accept leaders' messages on their face is often mocked and used by those on the outside and even by internal critics as a way of denigrating Mormons as sheep who blindly follow their shepherds. One rather obscure line from a 1945 issue of *Improvement Era*, the church's official periodical, provides an overly simplistic yet incisive explanation for this confidence in leadership: "When our leaders speak, the thinking has been done."[50]

Still, the utility of defining specific church teachings as doctrinal (or not) was reflected in a 2012 General Conference remark by Elder Neil L. Andersen, who acknowledged that some Mormons "question their faith when they find a statement made by a Church leader decades ago that seems incongruent with our doctrine." Andersen continued, "There is an important principle that governs the doctrine of the Church. The doctrine is taught by all 15 members of the First Presidency and Quorum of the Twelve. It is not hidden in an obscure paragraph of one talk. True principles are taught frequently and by many. Our doctrine is not difficult to find."[51]

The discursive strategy of distinguishing between culture and doctrine relies on the Mormon emphasis on continuing revelation; merely by not speaking frequently of a once-common teaching, Mormon leaders thus imply its lack of official status in the here and now.

Yet in lived experience, Mormon doctrine is indeed difficult to find. Allow me to share a brief anecdote to illustrate this difficulty: During a conference of mostly Mormon academics, during a question-and-answer session, I expressed consternation at pinpointing where the line falls between doctrine and culture. The audience laughed knowingly, and one prominent Mormon academic shouted across the room, "Welcome to our world!"

The ambiguity around what counts as doctrine (and is therefore true) and what is merely culture or policy is not relegated to curious outsiders and detractors looking for chinks in the church's armor; indeed, faithful, lifelong LDS cannot always pin down where doctrine ends and culture begins. For instance, "The Family: A Proclamation to the World," a statement issued in September 1995 by the First Presidency just months after the LDS church's failed attempt to influence a Hawaiian court to nullify same-sex marriage, summarizes the church's position on gender roles, marriage, and family.[52] Most of its 630 words reassert accepted doctrine; but it also appends the concept of gender as an essential and eternal characteristic (that men and women were gendered before, during, and after being born into earthly life), which, among other issues, raises important questions about the status of transgender or intersex people. Although it is framed and prominently displayed in the homes of many LDS faithful, frequently cited in ecclesiastical talks, and widely considered inspired, it has never been officially canonized, and it is unclear if its contents are doctrine or not. For members, ambiguity concerning the doctrinal status of certain teachings such as those in the family proclamation can lead to sectarian disputes and policing of other Mormons' legitimacy.

The bureaucratic discourses surrounding differentiating doctrine (which is binding) from mere culture, policy, or opinion (which is elastic) serve two important functions in Mormon identity construction, which can be characterized as outward-facing and inward-facing rhetorical devices. In the most basic sense, it is a defensive organizational communicative strategy designed to divert or dissolve criticism from outsiders (and internal pot-stirrers). As critics of the church point out, ambiguity around what the church considers to be doctrine is a convenient (and, they say, intentional) way for church leaders to claim plausible deniability and easily sidestep controversial doctrines or historical teachings.[53] In this view, the church can de-emphasize or gloss over past leaders' statements that have now fallen out of cultural acceptability without ever retracting them or apologizing, such as Brigham Young arguing for the death penalty for miscegenation,[54] simply because the objectionable teaching is not current.

Ambiguity around doctrine can be linked historically to the defensive communication strategy long employed by the Saints. Linguistic anthropologist Daymon Smith has noted that particularly around the history of polygamy, the Saints have adopted and adapted this strategy, a process of evasion or obfuscation involving telling one story to outsiders and reserving another for insiders.[55] The Mormon defensive strategy traces back to Joseph Smith himself, who—in various, often contested accounts—claimed to be morally outraged when he was accused of polygamy, when in fact he had been practicing it for years. Smith was, in the view of apologists, protecting the church from federal interest in the question of polygamy.[56] To others, he was establishing a narrative tradition for dealing with those on the "outside," particularly those with normative influence that might help—or hinder—the church's progress.

In one oft-cited modern instantiation of this defensive strategy, during a 1997 interview with *Time* magazine, then-president Gordon B. Hinckley responded to questions about the LDS teaching that God the Father was once a man by hesitating and then ambiguously explaining, "I don't know that we teach it. I don't know that we emphasize it… I understand the philosophical background behind it, but I don't know a lot about it, and I don't think others know a lot about it."[57] The teaching that God was once a man, while ambiguous, is central to the LDS doctrine of eternal progression, giving every faithful LDS man hope of becoming divine; but it is Mormon peculiarities like this one that create friction with the broader Christian mainstream, who reject it as heretical. Hinckley's response on this fraught issue shows a careful parsing of words, essentially refusing to give a straight answer because such an answer is too risky. Critics like Sue Emmett, the great-great-granddaughter of LDS patriarch and second president Brigham Young, call this rhetorical strategy "lying for the Lord" and claim that church leaders encourage members to lie or omit information to protect the church or avoid making negative impressions.[58]

For those faithful to the church, this strategy is not devious but instead makes pragmatic sense. One faithful Mormon told me that sometimes the church has to "simplify" its message to explain it to a non-Mormon public; because the witness of the Holy Ghost is required to understand more complicated (and controversial) elements of the Mormon faith, it is important to present "milk before meat," a biblical reference conjuring images of an infant who cannot digest solid foods and first requires sustenance from simple liquids. The implication is that transparency around the full history of issues like polygamy, the church's racial past, or other complicated subjects would alienate a noninitiated audience before they have the chance to gain a spiritual witness of the truthfulness of the church.

On a personal rather than institutional level, the LDS tendency to bifurcate between doctrine and culture serves another important function: it provides a cognitive and discursive strategy for members who are themselves struggling with tough issues. For members who disagree with particular teachings or policies, contested points can be written off as "not doctrine" even if the issues are still normative among most Mormons. Thus, individual Mormons can reasonably navigate and dismiss nearly any peripheral issue that they do not fully support (ranging from the church's stance on same-sex marriage to the question of whether polygamy will be practiced in the heavenly celestial kingdom). Speaking during a conference panel on LDS women and agency, emerita Columbia University professor and Mormon feminist Claudia Bushman explained, "Mormons choose which doctrines to feel strongly about.... We define doctrines that we don't approve of as policy."[59] Her words were followed by knowing laughter from the academic crowd, suggesting the ubiquity of this strategy for dealing with dissonance. Progressive Mormons like Bushman can maintain their LDS identity in the face of what they consider gender, racial, or sexual orientation discrimination, among countless other issues, by parsing such mistreatment as cultural baggage, separate from the nature and contents of the true church. Innumerable issues on which the church has taken a normative stand cannot be said to be official church policy or doctrine, despite real-world consequences of the church's normative sway. Instead, they can be discounted as culture when members find them unacceptable or when outsiders react to them as particularly strange or noxious.

Still, using this strategy to keep one's Mormon identity intact can still leave individuals on the periphery of Mormon belonging: despite the 2007 Newsroom statement (tellingly directed outward at the non-LDS media and public, not inward at Mormons themselves) to clarify what counts as doctrine, it is almost always ambiguous when leaders' words are meant to be taken as inspired and when they are simply sound advice or even opinion—that is, in Mormon parlance, when they are "speaking as a prophet" or "speaking as a man." After all, LDS leaders are considered divinely installed. This ambiguity makes it taboo for Mormons to criticize their leaders or suggest that anything they say is merely opinion (or, much worse, entirely wrong) until and unless higher leaders have offered a public correction of the offending words. Mormons who publicly reject teachings on even minor points mark themselves as not completely committed to the Mormon community and risk surveillance and even ostracism for doing so.

Authority and Church Media: A Growing Reliance on Public Affairs

The rhetorical differentiation between doctrine and culture serves as a unique communicative strategy that both is particularly Mormon and complicates the bifurcation of Mormon identity into tidy "structure versus agency" boxes. Increasingly, the church's reliance on online Public Affairs efforts to communicate with the membership by way of the broader public accentuates the strategy of functional ambiguity surrounding Mormonism. As seen in its official responses to the issue of caffeine consumption, rather than ecclesiastical leaders themselves directly communicating with the membership or the public, the LDS Newsroom has increasingly become the primary source for "official" church information. Updates, postings, and press releases from the LDS Newsroom are generally published with no byline, leaving the audience with no knowledge of the source or process through which the information came about—a rather unusual development in a church so committed to process, procedure, and proper authority. This circuitous way of communicating with both the inside and the outside is highly problematic in this top-down system, as the relationship among "official" information, rhetorical public relations spin, and doctrine (e.g., truth) remains unclear.

Even before the church began to focus much of its efforts online, sociologist of religion Armand Mauss referred to those working for the LDS church but not in official ecclesiastical positions as its "civil service bureaucracy" and noted that there was "a certain amount of ambiguity (some of it perhaps calculated and functional)... associated with operational directives out of the bureaucracy."[60] In the case of the LDS Newsroom, this functional ambiguity centers on what it means that the page is official. Are the Newsroom's outputs simply strategic marketing rhetoric, or do they provide information that is both relevant and binding for Mormons and how they conduct their lives?

Church leaders are not unaware of questions of authority regarding public affairs information; one LDS spokesman told me on the condition of anonymity that church officials specifically chose the title "Public Affairs Department" rather than "Public Relations" to avoid associations with unreliable and biased PR spin. Still, the Newsroom is, ostensibly, primarily directed at the media and non-Mormon public, not the church body, which raises questions of insider and outsider discourse. To what extent is the Newsroom meant to clarify ambiguous teachings for Mormons? Is it, rather, intended to control public discourse about the church by putting a particular spin (dreaded though the term may be) on points of contention with the broader American public?

Although it is represented as an official church website and is increasingly used as a voice for the church, the authority of press releases, articles, and blog posts from the Newsroom is unclear. The institutional church is highly bureaucratic, and proper processes and procedures are emphasized in all aspects of both administrative and sacred rhetoric and praxis; members recognize that the process of receiving and sustaining doctrine is necessary to make a given teaching official. Yet the Newsroom is billed as official, bypassing the process that grants this necessary approval. It is unclear whether church leaders have any input on what is written there, and this seems strategic: by including no bylines but still bearing the church's logo and name, Newsroom content communicates an aura of authority, however ambiguous, and thus functions to establish norms for the community. This ambiguity allows the church to respond to important threats to its perceived legitimacy in ways that inculcate it from criticism.

The problematic nature of the Newsroom as an official voice for the church is perhaps best illustrated by an episode centered on the heated issue of race and church history. On February 28, 2012, the *Washington Post* quoted a BYU religion professor on the origins of the notorious "priesthood ban" that, before the 1978 revelation that reversed it, barred Black men of African descent from the priesthood that all otherwise worthy Mormon men hold.[61] In the article, Professor Randy Bott noted what he called some "possible" theological explanations for the ban, grounded in ambiguous Mormon scripture and historical teachings by leaders of the church: in one iteration, dark skin is interpreted as the curse of Cain, the first murderer; in another, Black people are cast as having been less valiant than white people in their premortal existence and thus cursed with dark skin and barred from the priesthood of God.

The views Bott relayed in his interview with the *Post* are obviously culturally fraught and divisive and shined an unflattering light on a church struggling to join the mainstream. But his views directly mirror historical teachings promoted by church leaders and folk teachings passed on by many conservative Mormons even today. Since the *Post* article was published during a time of intense national scrutiny—Mitt Romney's presidential run—the online Newsroom responded immediately with its own statement.

> The positions attributed to BYU professor Randy Bott in a recent *Washington Post* article absolutely do not represent the teachings and doctrines of The Church of Jesus Christ of Latter-day Saints. BYU faculty members do not speak for the Church. It is unfortunate that the Church was not given a chance to respond to what others said.
>
> The Church's position is clear—we believe all people are God's children and are equal in His eyes and in the Church. We do not tolerate racism in any form.
>
> For a time in the Church there was a restriction on the priesthood for male

members of African descent. It is not known precisely why, how, or when this restriction began in the Church but what is clear is that it ended decades ago. Some have attempted to explain the reason for this restriction but these attempts should be viewed as speculation and opinion, not doctrine. The Church is not bound by speculation or opinions given with limited understanding.

We condemn racism, including any and all past racism by individuals both inside and outside the Church.[62]

Problematically, of course, Bott's statements *did* reflect "teachings and doctrines of the Church," albeit *past* ones—a distinction that makes all the difference in a church built on the doctrine of continuing revelation but can be lost on a public that does not share its epistemological orientation to truth. While church leaders have distanced themselves from these teachings in recent years (I'll revisit this episode in chapter 6), our previous discussion of the confounding canonization process makes clear that Public Affairs statements do not an official doctrine make.

Orthodoxy versus Orthopraxy: The Linchpin of Mormon Identity

While the Word of Wisdom is inarguably a plank in the structural framework around which faithful Mormons construct their identity (that is, its observance is mandated by the institution as a prerequisite for belonging), its enactment in everyday life is also circumscribed by cultural expectations and norms that—despite their much-touted nondoctrinal and thus nonofficial status—also become structural constraints that are in many ways just as powerful as doctrine itself. Similarly, the distinction between doctrine and culture is an emic one that overlooks the cultural nature of doctrine itself, locating it discursively beyond normative critique among faithful LDS; this is, as anthropologist of religion Clifford Geertz reminds us, how religious symbolic systems function, by maintaining the sense that they are natural and not naturalized.[63] Labeling some things as doctrine and others as culture also overlooks the authority of culture in establishing norms that are powerful, pervasive, and binding as preconditions for membership in any community. Thus, effectively, all doctrine is always already culture, and all culture has the potential to become doctrine in Mormon praxis.

The functional ambiguity in Mormon discourse creates difficulty in identifying what is and is not requisite for belonging to the LDS church. Because a source of information may be viewed as inspired but also may or may not be speaking officially and, regardless, may be debunked or disclaimed later, Mormons toe a line between institutional structure and personal agency that appears flexible to those on the outside while implicitly constraining those on the inside. This ambiguity is brought to the fore by the church's modern-day reliance on unattributed sources in digital media for disseminating information about the church and its teachings rather than direct instruction from leaders.

Just as individual Mormons must navigate the doctrine-culture distinction, rule-keeping and commitment in Mormonism rely on the practice of applying individual agency as an interpretive lens. Open-ended rules like the Word of Wisdom are instrumental in their vagueness, allowing for various interpretations. As BYU professor and LDS philosopher James Faulconer notes,

> Latter-day Saints often speak of the Word of Wisdom as a health law, and there is evidence for that way of understanding it. Nevertheless, there is no official explanation of its prohibitions and there is anything but a universal practice, especially regarding, for example, the consumption of caffeine. There is little consistency among LDS practices regarding caffeinated drinks and no more consistency regarding the explanations of those practices. Consider that many LDS abstain from all caffeinated drinks, presumably believing that it is the caffeine in coffee that makes it forbidden; and thus, other drinks with caffeine are also forbidden. However, few of them who abstain from caffeinated drinks in general will drink decaffeinated coffee, though consistency would dictate that decaffeinated coffee is not prohibited.[64]

While Faulconer's comments are specific to the Word of Wisdom, the sentiment extends to many rules in Mormonism that rely on what Mormons often refer to as personal agency, despite the lack of true choice available when cultural and doctrinal constraints abound. Still, this vagueness is intentional and utilitarian, allowing individual Mormons to engage in self-surveillance and concomitantly to judge the worthiness of others based on a mutable scale that varies generationally, geographically, and according to countless other individual factors.

As the 2012 controversy around Mormon caffeine use illustrates, doing things the correct way, or religious orthopraxy, matters among faithful Mormons. It matters so much that when the correct way is not spelled out by leaders, Mormons themselves take a position on the issue and rationally defend it using belief as the basis for practice. For both those who find caffeine off-limits and those who find it acceptable, arguments around the proper orientation to caffeine often privilege the LDS value of agency. Caffeine users will appeal to the letter of the law: the Word of Wisdom, as the church noted through its public affairs statement, does not mention the use of caffeine, and therefore Mormons are free to choose for themselves. This choice is the essence of Mormon belief, which values agency above all other human traits. Those who avoid caffeine appeal to what they consider the spirit rather than the letter of the law, claiming that caffeine is an addictive substance, and its avoidance is one way to secure their agency as unfettered by outside influences. These divergent orthodoxies, though contradictory, each work to establish individual praxis as doctrinally sound.

These rhetorical strategies illustrate ways in which Mormon identity does not neatly fall into etic categories of "orthodoxy" or "orthopraxy" (to be sure, a nuanced understanding of any religion is likely to complicate those binaries). To be faithful and temple-worthy, Mormons must both *do* the right things and *believe* the right things (or at least say so). Of course, surveilling internal belief is challenging for any religion and is often less pragmatically important as a mechanism of group cohesion. As one self-described Mormon apologist noted during an academic panel on Mormonism, Mormons can "believe anything they want as long as they don't teach it."[65] The social consequences of voiced heterodoxy are the institution's primary concern; indeed, grounds for excommunication include not heterodox beliefs themselves but the public dissemination of heterodox beliefs (recall, for example, the September Six, prominent Mormons disciplined or excommunicated in 1993 for public criticism of LDS leadership or doctrine).

For the apologist and other Mormons, because belief is not strictly policed by church leaders (beyond, perhaps, standard temple-worthiness interviews that ask whether one has "a testimony" of Christ and the restoration of his church and whether one sustains current leaders as "prophets, seers, and revelators"),[66] actions speak louder than words, so to speak. But broadcasting one's heterodox perspective is taboo, and many unorthodox LDS fear the social consequences of coming out as such, underscoring the implied premium placed on correct belief *as well as* correct practice in the form of observance of LDS narrative norms. As Skyler Thiot illustrated when he shut down his "BYU for Caffeine" Facebook page, social policing is the standard Mormon response when a member publicly breaks the norms of acceptable speech. The Mormon who wants to appear faithful, even if they harbor heterodox beliefs, must fall into line in practice to avoid social censure.

If Mormonism is not strictly a faith that privileges orthodoxy over orthopraxy or vice versa, Mormon blogger Alan Hurst offers a third way. He explains that Mormonism is about not just doing the right things or believing the right things but covenanting the right things. Mormonism begins with a baptismal covenant to keep Christ's commandments, which is renewed weekly in sacrament meeting and culminates with a temple covenant to consecrate the faithful Mormon's life and possessions to God and the church. For LDS faithful, writes Hurst, "both to make that covenant and to remain faithful to it, a mixture of physical acts and inward intentions is required."[67] Yet Hurst also explains that Saints often create a "hedge about the law" as a safety net to avoid breaking the law, which implies that not only are Mormons orthoprax, but often more so than is technically required by the institution.

The concept of idealized Mormonism as a covenant identity explains, in part, why some Mormons and not others may find caffeine acceptable. Mormonism as a culture paradoxically prizes both institutional rule-setting, thought to be divinely inspired, and personal revelation; it is a tension between "authority and radical freedom."[68] For some Mormons, the tension is easiest resolved by avoiding any practice that is unclearly defined, out of an abundance of caution, by *not acting* as a form of faithful *acting*. For others, exercising freedom in gray areas is a way of highlighting trust in the ultimate guidance of the institution and/or the affective guidance of divinity, which would no doubt create parameters for behavior if they were required for righteousness. Parsing "culture" and "doctrine" at different fault lines creates ambiguity around Mormon identity—what it means to be Mormon will vary depending on the values and opinions of each Mormon practitioner as well as their cultural location within various Mormon universes.

The Digital Fractures of Mormon Imagined Community

In Mormonism as in all cultures, the "dominant cultural order" is made up of codes so naturalized that they appear to not be constructed at all.[69] The institution, through its naturalization of processes around doctrine, authority, and revelation, creates these codes in its disciplinary structure, normalizing them and embedding them in daily life. The differences between Mormon belief and culture and mainstream American society render Mormonism incomprehensible and thus easily misconstrued and maligned, leading to the institution's defensive Public Affairs strategies and its outward-focused voice. This tension also manifests in the institution's careful balance between mainstreaming and differentiation so emblematic of religious communities but present, indeed, in any type of alternate community. Individuals, then, negotiate this line, factoring in values and discourses particular to their own specificities (of place, of generation, etc.); for faithful Mormons, the line must be toed with care, and divergences from mainstream norms must be examined and rhetorically justified to maintain a place in the community.

This rhetorical practice not only maintains Mormon identity; it creates it in the first place. Mormon identity itself is a thing signified—that is, referenced across various intelligible signs that confer meaning. French deconstructionist Jacques Derrida described the sign as "deferred presence," explaining that "every concept is inscribed in a chain or a system within which it refers to the other, to other concepts, by means of the systematic play of differences."[70] Religion, then, is defined or "constituted 'historically' as a weave of differences."[71] As with other aspects of identity, it is defined socially against what it is not; functionally, religious identities are boundary markers, categories for exclusion or inclusion. Within Mormonism, rule-keeping on issues like caffeine consumption—along with numerous other signs of varying importance—is an inscription within an inscription, and its situatedness denotes commitment, community, agency, and priority.

If correlation once provided a worldwide imagined Mormon community that was united in purpose and vision, the internet has punctured this myth of homogeneity and cohesion. Despite institutional attempts to craft a holistic image of Mormon identity in the minds of both its members and the broader public, Mormonism as a community is increasingly fractured. Nowhere is the fracture more evident than on the internet, which provides space for alternate voices. The mediated conversations about caffeine use and Mormon belief and praxis highlight growing trends among Mormons online to challenge the traditional status quo in ways that at once threaten imagined Mormon hegemony and potentially enable new, or at least previously private, forms of Mormon life. Just as the internet provided the forum for the church and its members to explore the seemingly benign issue of caffeine, Mormons on the web are exploring the limits of belonging on every issue from homosexuality to temple attendance to female ordination. Beliefs, practices, and the bounds of what it means to be Mormon seem to be up for grabs as Mormon communities reinvent themselves in public view.

3

Mitt Romney and Bifurcated Mormon Representation

From the Mormon perspective, [their] radical difference is the believer's sign of blessedness. But from the opposite perspective, such difference is threatening and dangerous; opposing it becomes a display of patriotism, not intolerance.

—Terryl L. Givens, *The Viper on the Hearth: Mormons, Myths, and the Construction of Heresy*

Religious criticism, confronted by indigenous American visions, is compelled to become a national criticism, aware that we are a dangerously religion-soaked, even religion-mad, society.

—Harold Bloom, *The American Religion*

On September 18, 2012, less than two months before American presidential votes were cast, a preelection bombshell hit the media circuit. In clandestine video footage of a closed-door session with elite campaign donors, Republican candidate Mitt Romney derided opponent Barack Obama's supporters, declaring that nearly half of Americans would vote for Obama because of some innate sense of entitlement and dependency. Romney argued that 47 percent of the population believes "they are entitled to health care, to food, to housing." He conceded that these voters would never support his own candidacy because they are "dependent on government," "believe they are victims," and would never "take personal responsibility and care for their lives."[1] Romney's strong and condemnatory language, unusual for the generally guarded and equivocating candidate, was swiftly (if predictably) circulated in the media to underscore his seeming elitism and lack of empathy for average Americans. In some circles, moments like this one were not just used to dissect Romney's politics; they were also used to question his faith.

When Mitt Romney announced his presidential candidacy in June 2011, media commentators immediately pinpointed his Mormonism as an anomaly and a liability: the media had already identified Romney's "Mormon problem" during his earlier quest for the nomination in 2007,[2] an epithet that extended into the 2012 race.[3] Soon, pundits began speculating on whether Romney would attempt to explain, justify, or use his difference to his advantage as a candidate in a party typically swung by Evangelicals—or whether he might "pretend it away" altogether. Although it ultimately did not impinge his ability to clinch the nomination, Romney's Mormonism was a constant talking point, and not just among the mainstream media: it also came under fire from closer quarters. Disputations concerning the relationship between Romney's politics and his religion marked divisions within Mormon ideological communities—divisions that were made visible and amplified by digital media and that visibly reimagined the borders of Mormon belonging.

Drawing on the previous chapter's exploration of group monitoring and idealized normativity, in this chapter I examine media representations of Mitt Romney's faith during his 2012 presidential run—but rather than considering only mainstream, non-Mormon media, I also focus on internet-based media largely produced for and by Mormons. Doing so enables an investigation of not only the still-contested role of Mormon identity in American society but the ways that mediated scrutiny informs intergroup dialogue and, in the case of the fraught issues of politics, contributes to an intensification of internecine conflict.

First, I situate discourse about Romney's faith by locating Mormonism within a broader national political context, showing the cultural push and pull that paradoxically establishes Mormonism as both quintessentially American and simultaneously foreign and suspect. The remainder of the chapter analyzes the major narratives about Romney's faith that emerged during his run from three major stakeholders invested in the public's perception of Mormonism: from the mainstream press, from Romney himself and his conservative supporters, and from progressive Mormons who did not support Romney's candidacy. Finally, I show how these latter two narrative trajectories underscore the divide between conservative and liberal Mormons and ultimately highlight the tensions between structure (e.g., roles and norms) and agency (autonomy and individualization) in modern Mormon identity.

Contextualizing Romney's "Mormon Moment"

Inevitably, Mormonism's paradoxical relationship to mainstream America colored political pundits', religious insiders', and detractors' attempts to interpret the significance of

Romney's faith in the context of U.S. politics. In some ways, Mormonism's solid place in American culture seems incontrovertible. It is increasingly commonplace—in academic writings, in news reports, and in conversation—to see the Mormon faith described as quintessentially American: an American invention, a reflection of American creative genius, the embodiment of American values and priorities.[4] Noted literary and religious critic Harold Bloom goes as far as to label Mormonism, as the innovation of an "authentic religious genius" and the embodiment of American history and ideals, as *the* American religion.[5] The LDS church is an entrepreneurial religion, so the argument goes; it was founded in the heat of nineteenth-century pioneer imagination and triumphed through hardship and persecution, unabashedly setting itself against popular and traditional norms for religious belief, culture, and practice. Its founding myth—the incarnation of the American dream—involves an uneducated plowboy innovating religion from the dust and through hard work and unfailing commitment creating an institutional empire that now exerts global influence politically, economically, and socially—not to mention its undeniable spiritual pull felt by millions the world over.

Not only is the faith solidly American, but Mormons themselves may be the most patriotic of any American religious group. Their scriptures place America at the center of ecclesiastical drama, calling it "the land of promise" and positing that Christ himself came to the Americas after his Resurrection and will return to gather his church in western Missouri;[6] that God uniquely cares about America, divinely directing Christopher Columbus's discovery and foreordaining the American Revolution and its outcome;[7] and that the Constitution of the United States is divinely inspired.[8] One enigmatic prediction attributed to Joseph Smith, known as the "White Horse prophecy," even foretells that the U.S. Constitution will one day be "on the brink of ruin" and "the very verge of destruction" and will be saved by the Latter-day Saints[9]—a prophecy later echoed among a handful of staunch Romney advocates and cited in some corners of the media to ridicule Romney's candidacy.

Despite the church's international growth, which means most members today live outside the United States, Mormon culture, doctrine, and practice continue to be deeply intertwined with American history and culture. And yet for all its Americanness, Mormonism stands at odds with the mainstream as one of the most contested groups in America: in addition to a history of persecution and distrust, Gallup polls in 2011 indicated that the percentage of Americans who said they would not vote for a Mormon candidate—about 22 percent—was more than double those who would not vote for a Hispanic or Jew and quadruple those who would not vote for a woman or Black person. Public reluctance to elect a Mormon, which was unchanged since Gallup first asked the question in 1967, was only surpassed by opposition to a homosexual or atheist nominee.[10] Evangelicals, who at the time composed about 30 percent of the

Republican voting base, exhibited the highest rates of prejudice and distrust toward Mormons.[11] While 21 percent of mainline Protestants and 22 percent of Catholics said Mormonism was "not a Christian religion," that number was 47 percent among white Evangelical Protestants.[12]

As detailed in earlier pages, the tension between Mormonism and the American mainstream can be traced to the faith's inception; Mormonism has always "threaten[ed] as an example of radical otherness that [does] not blatantly manifest otherness,"[13] a living instantiation of Ernst Jentsch's (and later Freud's) notion of the uncanny.[14] Because Mormons are both "Christian" and "not Christian," they are familiar to American Christians. They quote from the Bible, and though they use many of the same esoteric phrases, they often have a very different meaning in mind (think "baptism," "heaven," and "damnation"). Throughout their history, Mormons have been viewed with ambivalence and often fearful hesitancy. Their status in American society at any given time is an important cultural marker precisely because of Mormonism's inherent Americanness and the American tendency to reject it out of hand.

In 2012, Mormonism's fraught history as both a respected and established part of the social fabric and a distrusted impostor required not just Romney as candidate but *Romney as Mormon* to be both vetted by and interpreted for the public. His Mormonism was automatically a weakness to his candidacy, his first and most obvious "flaw" as a potential American leader, because it marked him with unclear social expectations. The American public would inevitably demand this difference be accounted for and justified; the Romney candidacy put the Church of Jesus Christ of Latter-day Saints itself in the limelight merely by virtue of his affiliation.

What would it mean for a candidate to be a lifelong, committed member of this little-known and less-trusted faith? What would be the implications of a Mormon presidency? Mormonism needed to be spelled out, delineated, and defined to satisfy a concerned and curious citizenry. It was a perfect storm: Nationwide, the media and public demanded a clear, palatable schema through which to interpret and assess Romney's differences, and the stakes could not have been higher. Individuals and groups with vested interests in controlling public perceptions of Mormonism found a rare opportunity to put forward diverse interpretations of Mormon identity for consideration in a national public referendum on what it means to be Mormon.

Religion in American Presidential Race Coverage

To be sure, during any high-profile campaign, journalists and media organizations approach candidates' personal lives and identities with very different strategies: Predictably, adversarial reports depict candidates cartoonishly, digging for salacious details and prodding potential weaknesses. Undeniably, controversy sells (or, more accurately in the digital age, feeds the algorithm). Meanwhile, other media outlets, in a bid for journalistic purity, will do their best to "stick to the issues" and, as a result, may avoid or downplay personal differences (e.g., race, religion, gender) to avoid being seen as prejudicial or discriminatory. Rarely, intrepid journalists will tackle the elephant in the room, attempting to describe and, even less often, *explain* candidates' relevant differences with the goal of a more informed voting public. These classic press informers are the exception to the media's often bifurcated approach to candidates' latent personal differences.

Religious difference is one aspect of a presidential candidate's profile that seems to evoke discomfort among the media and voters. On the one hand, a staunch tradition of the separation of church and state, canonized as an essential element of American democracy, makes commentary on a candidate's religion taboo. Although American jurisprudence on the topic is vague, the Constitution expressly forbids (but does not define) a "religious test" as a requirement for public office.[15] On the other, candidates' religious beliefs and practices are almost always gauged and discussed in the media, often in coded language. In what Jürgen Habermas calls today's postsecular society, religious discourse during a campaign is expected but must conform to established norms.[16]

In many ways, just as U.S. presidents have historically been male and (with one recent exception) white, their religious affiliations have also been mostly predictable: American presidents are nearly always Protestant. The country has had five Unitarian/Deist leaders (Adams, Jefferson, Quincy Adams, Fillmore, and Taft) and two Catholics (Kennedy and Biden). At the time of the Obama-Romney candidacies, 37 out of 42 U.S. presidents had been Protestant—a whopping 86 percent. Perhaps more importantly, since the 1980s, the Religious Right's Moral Majority movement has coordinated a tight national campaign to foster the perception that the United States is and always has been a Christian nation.[17] The outcome? In today's presidential politics, Americans simultaneously claim to eschew a religious test and then apply one.

During the campaign cycle, media coverage often includes information on the denominational preference and church attendance of Protestant candidates. Candidates themselves are not expected to be too forthcoming or transparent on the minute details of their faith. It is generally enough that they claim a Protestant heritage, attend church at least some of the time, and evoke God or faith vaguely but regularly on the campaign trail. Such faith-based but generic discourse is part of the liturgical language of campaign season rituals.

Evangelical candidates in particular are increasingly vetted by the media and by conservative voters for the degree of orthodoxy and literality in their belief, a litmus test of sorts of their commitment to what have become Republican norms since the rise of the Religious Right.[18] For Evangelical candidates, the test is whether they are Christian enough—an entirely different question than what Romney would face, as many Americans were already convinced that he was not Christian at all.

The Media Tackles Romney's Mormonism

In this religiopolitical context, Mitt Romney's Achilles' heel was apparent from the start. Wealthy, white, Harvard educated, business minded, and from a family of politicians: little about Romney as candidate was foreign to voters, save his lifelong involvement with the Church of Jesus Christ of Latter-day Saints. Romney was raised LDS, served in a two-year religious mission in France, and devoted his adult life to service in his local congregations: his Mormonism was not subtle and could not be disguised during the invasive frenzy of a campaign. Perhaps more than any other Christian denomination or group, a Mormon candidate faces unique obstacles: proving his Mormonism is not "weird," that it is not threatening to the Christian status quo, and that he is not a puppet of his church or its leaders.

Faced with the challenge of a presidential candidate with such an obvious and contentious difference, mediated narratives about Romney's Mormonism tended to take one of the three approaches I've already hinted at: adversarial discourse that intentionally picked apart Mormon history, doctrine, and practice to frame Romney as an outsider/other; ambivalence toward and sometimes reticence to delve into discussions of Romney's religion, primarily reflected in debates about the place of such critique in politics; and the rarest approach of all, attempts by true press informers to parse out Mormonism's possible areas of relevance to a potential Romney presidency.

Adversarial Discourse

In the 2012 campaign, major contenders for the Republican ticket represented various faith groups: conservative Baptist Ron Paul; Baptist Herman Cain; Catholics Newt Gingrich and Rick Santorum; Lutheran Michele Bachmann; conservative Evangelical Rick Perry; and Mormons Mitt Romney and Jon Huntsman Jr. American familiarity with Protestantism and Catholicism immediately placed the last two on the outside. Huntsman was identified early on as a nominal Mormon, less committed and much less orthodox than Romney (a cultural member, sometimes called a "Jack Mormon" in LDS circles). With Huntsman irrelevant as a challenge to the religious mainstream, Romney became the primary object of difference, a target for media attention that would dissect salacious details from Mormon history, belief, and practice.

Adversarial discourse on Romney's faith focused on distrust, fear, and the Otherness of Mormons in American society, bringing to the fore obscure Mormon beliefs and other particularities that place Mormonism at odds with mainstream society. Much of the negative or salacious coverage of Mormonism occurred during the early stages of the campaign before Romney had clinched the nomination in attempts by competing conservative candidates to establish Romney as dangerous and Other. In fact, the most circulated Mormonism-related episode during the entire election cycle centered on controversial comments Romney made in October 2011 during the heated battle for the Republican nomination.[19]

On October 7, a Southern Baptist megachurch pastor named Robert Jeffress introduced Republican Party candidate Rick Perry to the audience at the Values Voter Summit by contrasting Perry's Evangelical faith with that of his top challenger, Mitt Romney. Jeffress stated, "In a few months, when the smoke has cleared, those of us who are Evangelical Christians are going to have a choice to make. Do we want a candidate who is skilled in rhetoric, or one who is skilled in leadership? Do we want a candidate who is a conservative out of convenience, or one who is conservative out of deep conviction? Do we want a candidate who is a good moral person, or do we want a candidate who is a born-again follower of the Lord Jesus Christ?"[20]

Playing on long-held antipathy between the Moral Majority and the Mormon faith, Jeffress's dog whistle cued the common Evangelical belief that Mormons are *not* born-again followers of Jesus. But it was his comments following the summit, in a candid moment with reporters outside the venue, that went viral on the news and the internet as a potential precursor to the type of rhetoric around a Romney candidacy. Jeffress invoked the word *cult* to describe the Church of Jesus Christ of Latter-day Saints, explaining, "That is not some right-wing, fringe view, that Mormonism is a cult. The Southern Baptist Convention, which is the largest Protestant denomination in the world, has labeled Mormonism as a cult. So that is a mainstream view, that Mormonism is a cult."[21]

Jeffress's use of the cult label to describe the Mormon faith was widely circulated in the news media and on social media sites like Facebook and Twitter. Some reports decontextualized the "cult" remark, finding in it a calculated political strategy to alienate Evangelical voters.[22] Head of LDS Public Affairs Michael Otterson immediately issued a response not only countering Jeffress's suggestion that Mormons are not Christian but going a step further to insist that Jeffress's view was *not* mainstream: "I've known a lot of wonderful Baptists over the years and this outburst was not at all typical of those I've met."[23]

Given the history of Mormon representation and the relationship between Mormonism and the Christian mainstream, comments like Jeffress's reference to

Mormonism as a cult came as no surprise before Romney had secured the nomination. But Romney's reception as America's first Mormon presidential nominee from a major party in the August 2012 primaries signaled at least a tentative acceptance of this ostensible "cult member" by the Republican Party.

In October, news media described another major shift in Evangelical discourse about the LDS church that seemed to confirm this acceptance: after its eponymous founder met with Romney, reports circulated that the Billy Graham Evangelistic Association officially scrubbed Mormonism from its website's "cult list."[24] In fact, the website never had a definitive list per se. Rather, in a question-and-answer section of the website, Mormons were mentioned along with other groups in response to the question "What is a cult?": "A cult is any group which teaches doctrines or beliefs that deviate from the biblical message of the Christian faith.... Some of these groups are Jehovah's Witnesses, Mormons, the Unification Church, Unitarians, Spiritists, Scientologists, and others." The site described "features common to most cults," including the following: "They do not adhere solely to the sixty-six books of the Bible as the inspired Word of God.... They do not accept that our relationship to Jesus Christ is a reality 'by grace through faith' alone, but promote instead a salvation by works.... They do not give Jesus Christ... full recognition as the second Person of the Trinity."[25]

By Graham's definition (a sectarian one to be sure, unrelated to the already problematic and imprecise sociological use of the term), Mormonism is indeed a cult. But then so are all non-Protestant religions, including Islam, Judaism, and Catholicism, although this detail was never highlighted in media coverage. More to the point, the fact that questions over Mormonism's "cult" status—and concerns over its acceptance by Evangelicals—were afforded so much airtime during the early stages of the campaign speaks to Americans' nervous anxieties about Mormon secrecy. While other presidents who have been less than forthcoming about the intimate details of their faith or religious practice have not been called "secretive," the stigma was used to evaluate Romney's reticence based on a long-standing public concern, part and parcel of public perception of Mormonism since its seclusion in the Great Basin in the nineteenth century.[26] Though the seclusion has ended, the stigma has endured: in a 2007 Pew Forum survey, respondents were asked to say the first word that comes to mind when they hear "Mormon." The most frequent word reported was "cult."[27]

Media critiques of Romney's faith played on Americans' fears of secrecy and hidden agendas. In an op-ed for the *New York Times*, Bloom articulated these fears in a seemingly drastic departure from his earlier praise for Mormonism and its founder. Portentously writing of "omens that will darken a year hence," he described the modern-day LDS church as a secretive, money-hungry bureaucracy and a Romney presidency as one of allegiance to Salt Lake corporate oligarchs and a Mormon theocracy.[28] Bloom's 2006 praise of Joseph Smith's creative genius and nineteenth-century Mormonism certainly does not extend to its twenty-first-century iteration, which he distrusts as concerned with money and ever-growing power. Bloom articulated, somewhat fantastically, the basis of American reticence toward Mormonism.

Similarly, press attention to the "White Horse prophecy," with its accompanying suggestion of the LDS church overtaking the country, crystallized American fears and paranoia about the sinister intentions of a Mormon candidate. In what reads like an exposé of Romney's fanatical Mormon machinations to overtake the country, Salon writer Sally Denton describes Joseph Smith's own presidential ambitions and then claims, "Smith viewed capturing the presidency as part of the mission of the church." She further asserts that, despite Smith's own failure to do so, "the time is now for a Mormon leader to usher in the second coming of Christ and install the political Kingdom of God in Washington, D.C." After providing a sinister and dark depiction of Romney's faith, Denton claims that "Mormonism define[s] not only Mitt Romney's character, but what kind of president he would be and what impulses would drive him in both domestic and foreign policy," implying that Romney's character is also sinister and dark and that a Romney presidency would be marked by that darkness. She goes on to argue, "The seeds of Romney's unique brand of conservatism, often regarded with intense suspicion by most non-Mormon conservatives, were sown in the secretive, acquisitive, patriarchal, authoritarian religious empire."[29]

While other stereotypes and depictions of Mormonism as "weird" circulated in the media, their overriding focus was always on secrecy and esotericism. Mentions of Mormon undergarments, hidden from public view, marked fear of the unseen and thus unknown and unknowable. ("Under his pants he is wearing magic underwear. Magic underwear!" joked magician, comedian, and outspoken atheist Penn Jillette.[30]) Discussion of polygamy and other controversial elements of Mormon history underscored fears of a hidden and sinister past with real but unknown repercussions in the present ("They are pretty much over that extra wives thing," quipped an article in *Esquire*[31]).

Public fear of secrecy has deep roots in American political discourse, where openness and transparency are vital for the success of the democracy and for keeping political powers in check. As Harvard political theorist Archon Fung articulates, unfettered access to information is central to democratic processes, enabling citizens to "use information to exercise influence . . . and to navigate life choices in ways that are more likely to advance their own welfare and flourishing."[32] Thus, transparency is central to the notion of an informed voting public, who are rightly alarmed by institutions or individuals that refuse disclosure. Secrecy in politics is an added threat, as it prevents fully informed voting behavior in the public's best interests.

But accusations of secrecy hit a nerve among Mormons, long distrusted by Americans on precisely this account. The tendency of media voices to use this socially embedded stereotype of LDS secrecy against Romney was noted by Brigham Young University journalism professor and active Mormon Lane Williams, a frequent columnist for the church-owned *Deseret News*. For Williams, painting Mormonism as "secretive" leads to conclusions that there is something "sinister" about the faith (indeed, noted antitheist and polemicist Christopher Hitchens opined in *Slate* that Romney espouses a "weird and sinister belief system"[33]). Williams relies on a familiar Mormon strategy when he goes on to argue that Mormons are not secretive at all but rather choose "to not disclose cherished beliefs with those who wouldn't appreciate them, who wouldn't or couldn't hold them sacred." It is worth noting that while the rest of Williams's prolific blog series from this period seems to still be stored on the *Deseret News*'s website, this article is nowhere to be found. Perhaps a glitch... or perhaps counter evidence to Williams's assertion in the article, "No, we are not secretive. We love to share."[34] Still, the secrecy-versus-sacredness rhetorical flourish underscores a deep Mormon cognizance of the American social taboo against esotericism, and yet the same defensive communication strategy has long been employed by LDS authorities to dissuade members from disclosing controversial temple practices, personal spiritual experiences, and countless other elements of faith and practice.

The Role of Religious Critique in Politics

Despite these salacious and widely circulated exceptions, religion was mostly downplayed by most major news outlets throughout the 2012 campaign season. Pew found that just 1 percent of major campaign coverage focused on the candidates' religions or the role of religion in the election, about the same as in 2008; of that, only 18 percent focused on Mormonism specifically. Still, Romney was the subject of twice as much religious reporting as Obama, although only 8 percent of religion stories were prompted by statements or actions from the Romney campaign. More specifically, 43 percent of the coverage of Romney's faith focused on whether conservative Christians and other groups would support a Mormon candidacy. Only 30 percent focused on his personal beliefs or background, and that figure includes both deep profile features and mere mentions of his Mormon faith.[35]

Rather than merely dissecting or critiquing his difference, many press outlets used the Mormon moment to discuss whether refusing to vote for a Mormon amounted to a religious test as prohibited by the Constitution. Some argued that it is useful and sometimes necessary to "question a political candidate about the implications of his religion for public policy."[36] Professor and feminist Mormon Joanna Brooks noted on National Public Radio's *All Things Considered*, "It is fair to ask questions about the culture of leadership Mitt Romney was raised in and that he assumed as a young man in Mormonism, both in terms of the networks of power he's associated with and the way he was raised as a Mormon to think about what it means to be a leader."[37] Columbia religion professor Randall Balmer wrote for the *New Republic*, "What ought to interest us about Romney's faith are not the vagaries of Mormon theology, fascinating as they are, but how he understands that theology, how his faith informs the way he lives, his sense of responsibility toward others and how that might affect the way he governs."[38]

Often, a call for open discussion of Mormonism was embedded in a larger partisan critique, as when Hitchens described Mormonism as a deeply vicious and closed system and insisted that voters are "fully entitled to ask Mitt Romney about the forces that influenced his political formation… and his voluntary membership in one of the most egregious groups operating on American soil."[39] Journalist and one-time Mormon Stacey Solie, in the Daily Beast, challenged presidential debate moderator Jim Lehrer to ask Romney, "Why do Mormons continue to treat women of the faith as second-class citizens?" She wrote that a "perverse instance of religious tolerance" is the only way to explain the fact that Romney had not been asked to account for his faith's treatment of women.[40]

Likely because of this transparency argument being used as a front for what many saw as deeply offensive religious bigotry, others contended that discussing difference in Romney's beliefs or practice at all was an indication of discrimination. Writing for *Time* magazine, Amy Sullivan observed, "Americans wouldn't accept an ethnic or gender test for office. Why then do so many voters impose a de facto religious requirement on their candidates?"[41] Tim Rutten noted in the *Los Angeles Times* that "objections to the former Massachusetts governor's presidential hopes because of his Mormon religion mark a dangerous turn in American politics."[42] In the *Jerusalem Post*, Rabbi Shmuley Boteach asked, "Are Mormons any weirder than the rest of us?" He argued that criticizing Mormon beliefs as "weird" is always hypocritical and shortsighted, since all religious beliefs are fantastic; candidates, he suggested, "should be judged on their merits as people and politicians, whatever their faith and whatever their beliefs."[43] Together, these arguments put Romney's Mormonism beyond the scope of proper democratic debate.

Mormon Press Informers

Amid these two extreme approaches to LDS faith found in these examples of gotcha journalism and avoidance, few press informers were able to adequately interpret Romney's Mormonism and its implications for his potential White House service.

These rare attempts, such as an October 2011 *New York Times* exploration of Romney's time as a Massachusetts bishop,[44] delved into the centrality of Romney's faith to his life and perspective; but even this lengthy piece did little to distinguish Mormonism from its Christian counterparts except to parallel it in procedural norms and terminology, such as by explaining that a Mormon bishop is analogous to a pastor or that a ward is akin to a diocese. These informative pieces, lacking in salacious intrigue, failed to go viral on social media, marking a lack of social interest in the representation of Mormonism as normal and safe.

However, one unlikely press informer working at a popular internet entertainment mill joined the conversation just in time. A former *Newsweek* journalist who joined the online social news and entertainment company BuzzFeed in January 2012, McKay Coppins used his insider knowledge as a Mormon himself to address issues of Romney's faith head-on with both sensitivity and accuracy. He addressed Romney's lifelong tithe to the LDS church alongside the institution's oft-criticized and rarely disclosed use of tithing funds; Romney's reluctance to speak about his faith and the roots of that reticence in both historical persecution and the modern Mormon experience; and even the much-discussed Mormon undergarment, which he demystified by normalizing it as a sacred vestment rather than a magical amulet.[45] Coppins made the media's pervasive but generalized anti-Mormon sentiment personal: recounting his time on the campaign press bus, he described how other reporters giggled discussing the Romneys' underwear, not realizing Coppins was also Mormon. He noted that by the end of the campaign, "Romney's career had provided a national education" on Mormonism.[46]

But it was Coppins who provided a useful model for engaging in democratic dialogue about the potential impact of Romney's faith on his candidacy. It was not merely his status as a Mormon insider that left him qualified to interpret Mormonism for the public. He also became a model of journalistic objectivity (which is never truly objective but aims for self-reflection to reduce bias) and the importance of nuance and detail in reports on religious faith. Coppins's lone voice during the campaign spoke to the urgency of a more comprehensive religious education for would-be journalists and content creators in an era when candidacy for national office seems no longer restricted to white, predominantly Protestant men.

A poll conducted in December 2012 by the Pew Research Center's Religion and Public Life Project found that 82 percent of Americans claimed to have learned "little or nothing" about the Mormon religion during the campaign season, and most respondents were unable to answer basic questions about LDS teachings and history. Still, between Romney's campaign, the LDS church's "I'm a Mormon" campaign, and pop-cultural nods to the church like *The Book of Mormon* Broadway musical, American sentiment seemed to warm slightly toward the church: the same poll found a slight decrease in the percentage of Americans who considered Mormonism "very different" from their own beliefs (65 percent in November 2011, down to 61 percent in 2012) and a slight increase in the number who said Mormonism had "a lot in common" with their own beliefs (from 25 percent in 2011 to 31 percent in 2012).[47]

Mormon Candidate, Mormon Narratives

The narratives that circulated about Romney's faith in the press differed not only in substance but also in function from those circulated in closer quarters. Among Mormons, the Romney candidacy became a momentous opportunity to define Mormonism for public consumption. The ways Mormons discussed Romney's faith showcased the diversity in modern Mormon identity and ideology. Mirroring the political polarization embodied in the American two-party system, Romney's run brought out two particular camps—conservative and progressive Mormons—who aggressively presented two very different interpretations of Romney's Mormonism for the public. In these discussions, what appear to be simply differences of political opinion among citizens mark deeper ideological orientations to the whole of Mormon identity and practice, where many Mormons increasingly find themselves forced to align with a conservative status quo or to mark themselves as progressive, the Other in Mormon communities.

During Romney's run, mounting tensions between these two ideological groups came to a head on the internet, where their narratives were circulated and reproduced. Rather than reflecting a cohesive faith community, both groups used the Romney moment as an opportunity to advance their own visions of ideal Mormonism, visions that contrasted sharply and no doubt left mainstream observers more befuddled than ever before about what constitutes true Mormon identity. First, Romney himself and his conservative Mormon supporters depicted Romney's faith as nonthreatening and generic (when they depicted it at all), reflecting the institution's defensive communication strategy for dealing with those on the outside. At the same time, however, progressive Mormons took the opportunity to deride Romney as a false face of their faith, attempting to make their agenda a part of the national conscience. These narratives highlight the tension between structure (e.g., roles and norms) and agency (individualization and interpretation) in lived Mormon identities today and provide insight into the available strategies Mormons of varying orthodoxies use to cohere with or criticize their religious community.

Obscuring Difference: Mitt Romney and Conservative Mormons

Although Romney's Mormonism was marked as significant and a potential weakness by strategists, pundits, and the press during his first presidential run in 2007, Romney's discursive strategy throughout his 2012 campaign involved a practiced avoidance of the subject of religion; Romney was consistently tight-lipped on the particularities of his faith.

But pure avoidance had not always been his tack. In December 2007, at the start of his first unsuccessful bid, Romney attempted to head off concerns about his "Mormon problem" with his one and only "religion speech" at the George H. W. Bush Presidential Library in College Station, Texas. Analysts recognized the speech as the narrative progeny of John F. Kennedy, whose 1960 address famously quelled public concerns about his Roman Catholic faith and has been cited as a model rhetorical strategy for a minority religious candidate.[48] Kennedy assured his audience at the Greater Houston Ministerial Association that were he elected, neither the papacy nor any other ecclesiastical body would influence his public policy.

Like Kennedy in his day, Romney recognized the urgency of retaining the Evangelical vote, which was then swinging to his competitor, Arkansas governor and Southern Baptist minister Mike Huckabee. To that end, Romney used his address to target Evangelical concerns about potential LDS institutional influence on White House policy. Just as Kennedy had done, Romney promised that "no authorities of [his] church, or of any other church for that matter, [would] ever exert influence on presidential decisions. Their authority is theirs, within the province of church affairs, and it ends where the affairs of the nation begin." Throughout the speech, Romney avoided details about his Mormon faith and practice, suggesting that his reticence to delve into particularities was an expression of tolerance and civic compartmentalization. In remarks that presaged the "religious test" debate in the media during his 2012 run, Romney rebuked the public for questioning his Mormon identity: "There are some who would have a presidential candidate describe and explain his church's distinctive doctrines. To do so would enable the very religious test the founders prohibited in the Constitution. No candidate should become the spokesman for his faith. For if he becomes president he will need the prayers of the people of all faiths."[49]

Although Romney attempted to replicate the Kennedy moment, he was no Kennedy. Where Kennedy was received as warm and engaging, Romney was seen as robotic and controlled. And where Romney devoted his life to his faith, Kennedy was a nominal Catholic, believable when he insisted that his faith would not dictate his policies. Moreover, as religion reporter Dick Ostling has noted, "non-Catholics expected Kennedy to say his faith would make no difference, which is hardly what today's Republican Christian conservatives want to hear."[50] Most importantly, by Kennedy's time, prejudice against Catholicism had lessened in America, and Roman Catholicism was not seen as so esoteric; its rituals and teachings were open and transparent to non-Catholics despite their prejudices against Catholic dogma. Mormonism, on the other hand, is still largely perceived as secretive and cultlike—due in part to its esoteric temple rituals that are shielded from nonmembers but also because of intentional institutional obfuscation of teachings, practices, and history.

Perhaps partially due to his failed 2008 bid, Romney took the opposite tack in 2012: He did not address his faith or its role (or lack thereof) in political discourse. Instead, whereas Kennedy worked to assure the public of his independence from papal dictates, throughout Romney's second campaign, it was his church that stressed its own political neutrality. The LDS church issued press releases to this effect, along with letters to be read in every Mormon congregation urging members to vote but reaffirming the officially neutral position of the church itself.[51] Rather than swear allegiance to his country over his faith, Romney allowed the church to do the talking—a poor move, given the public's general hesitancy to trust the Mormon institution and generalized social fears of LDS institutional control.

The church's PR strategy of claiming neutrality was also complicated by the pervasive conservative political culture in almost all stateside LDS congregations, especially those along the geographic Wasatch Front. The church's ongoing support of conservative legislation across the state, including its official stance on hot-button political topics like gay marriage and abortion, made this orientation hard to ignore. In 2008, for example, the church's efforts to influence California's Proposition 8 were widely circulated. Local church officials urged their congregations to donate millions of dollars and vote in favor of the proposition to define marriage as between a man and a woman. Despite continued claims of neutrality, the church also sponsored keyword search advertisements on Google, ensuring that searches for "Mitt Romney" returned a sponsored ad linking to an official church website—albeit a link reaffirming the church's neutrality.[52] (They sponsored no such ad for the term *Barack Obama*.)

Throughout his 2012 race, Romney rarely addressed his Mormon problem. As Coppins noted, he "spent much of 2012 publicly evading the subject of his faith. In speeches, he conducted all manner of rhetorical gymnastics to avoid uttering the word 'Mormon.' In interviews, he quickly changed the subject every time the topic came up. And to his staff, his instruction was to dodge and deflect all questions regarding his religious beliefs. He regularly employed variations of the declaration, 'I'm not running for pastor-in-chief.'"[53]

Romney was so keen to eliminate his faith as a factor that he assembled a team of strategists who were tasked with ensuring campaign discourse avoided discussion of Mormonism altogether.[54] Their responses to media inquiries were reportedly unreceptive and even hostile: journalists including Coppins and *CNN Belief Blog*'s Jessica Ravitz reported resistance from Romney's campaign strategists to answer questions on his faith. According to Ravitz, campaign spokeswoman Andrea Saul responded to inquiries with the following email: "What makes no sense to me is how you continue to push forward in writing about Gov. Romney's faith journey when we've made it clear in every way possible that this is not a story we want to participate in."[55]

Perhaps recognizing that his reticence was feeding rather than assuaging suspicion among voters, toward the end of the race Romney softened slightly about religion. He began to allow reporters to attend church services with him in August 2012 but continued to use generalities when discussing his religion, conflating it with mainstream Christianity and talking broadly about "faith" rather than addressing Mormonism's particularities. His hesitancy was attributed in part to his fear that open discussion would result in his faith being "dragged through the mud."[56] Ironically perhaps, Romney's choice to downplay and normalize his faith obscured rather than addressed the differences that make Mormonism what it claims to be: the one true church, distinct from rather than analogous to other forms of Christianity, which Mormonism has framed since its founding as bastardizations of Christ's true church.

Romney's conservative Mormon supporters used similar strategies when engaging the broader public on the topic of Mormonism. Rarely did these commentators opine on the particularities of belief or practice. Instead, they presented Romney as a trusted politician not needing explanation or details. As they attempted to obscure his distinct Mormon attributes and downplay the role of faith in his life, Romney was painted as a patriot, a good American, but one missing personal details and individuality.

When conservative Mormon supporters did address Romney's faith, it was in an attempt to mainstream the religion by talking about it in ways Protestants would identify with. Conservative talk show host and Mormon Glenn Beck minimized differences between Mormonism and mainstream Christianity by calling polygamy "a perversion of what we believe in" and dismissing concerns over esoteric temple rituals by claiming, "There's nothing that you'll find in the Temple that you won't find in the Old or New Testament."[57] LDS church–owned *Deseret News* attempted to water down the significance of Mormonism and its potential to sway the vote: citing other reports, one article suggested that Americans may be warming to the idea of an LDS candidate.[58] Another noted that "the perceived biases that potentially derailed Mitt

Romney's 2008 presidential campaign are dissolving and, lo and behold, a member of the Church of Jesus Christ of Latter-day Saints could realistically be elected president of the United States in 2012."[59]

Supporters also focused on his patriotism and policies rather than his religious affiliation; this trend was noticeable beginning in Romney's first campaign. In a now-deleted blog written for the *Idaho State Journal* in 2008, one supporter contrasted Obama's one-time pastor Jeremiah Wright's remarks about America ("God damn America!") with the LDS prophet Gordon B. Hinckley's ("Bless this chosen land!"), attempting to deflect criticism and point to Obama as the true impostor.[60]

In 2012, supporters continued to downplay the role of faith in obtaining votes. At church-owned Brigham Young University, students were energized by Romney's candidacy, but as election night neared, according to BYU College Republican co-social media chairwoman Emily Kinard, "Just because Mitt's Mormon, I don't think it's necessarily turned votes. Lots of people are pretty aware and making their decision issue-based."[61] Other Mormons presented Romney as a positive, inspiring face of the faith but did so without detailing or describing Mormonism itself: hotel chain mogul J. W. Marriott gushed, "There has never been as much positive attention to the church, thanks to the wonderful campaign of Mitt Romney."[62]

Some conservative Mormon writers wished Romney would talk more about his faith. They suggested that he should frame it as central to his life and character but that he should not detail its doctrinal particularities. Lane Williams again spoke up, criticizing the religious content of Romney's convention acceptance speech. But rather than suggest Romney should differentiate himself, Williams lamented that Romney had not done more to "tell the story of the Latter-day Saints that puts them at the heart of the American story," for example, by describing the Mormon climb from despised and persecuted to nominated for the highest office in the land or by telling "America the story of the handcart pioneers or the Mormon Battalion."[63] Journalist and supporter Pat Bagley even went so far as to sacralize media criticism of Romney's Mormonism as part of a long history of press criticism, making it part of Mormons' sacred duty to passively accept it: "Our great grandparents bore up under the ridicule, so Mormons today might as well get used to the scrutiny and let the nonsense roll off their sturdy tabernacle-turtle backs."[64]

In the *Deseret News*, authors Linda and Richard Eyre opined, "For the most part, Mitt has avoided speaking about his faith, and there are good reasons for this. The problem is that his faith and The Church of Jesus Christ of Latter-day Saints are so much a part of who he is that it is almost impossible to know or understand him and Ann without knowing at least some things about the church." They went on to claim that "most of Mormonism is very much like most other Christian churches, including the central focus on Jesus.... We are also very similar to other churches, synagogues, mosques, and other major faiths and places of worship." They described some "unique" aspects of Mormonism they felt Romney ought to share, including its lay ministry and emphasis on family. Although they asserted that "understanding and appreciating the unique aspects of our faith can help us know each other better and trust each other more,"[65] the agenda they proposed for Romney precisely avoided all mention of controversial or less-understood areas of Mormon practice and belief.

These were, of course, the areas the public cared about the most. The avoidance of details about Romney's faith was pragmatic, to be sure; if they had addressed and explicated it for the public, the American mainstream would have largely rejected these orthodox believers' religious ideas out of hand. But as religion scholar Randall Balmer noted, "Not only does [Romney's] caginess reinforce his image as evasive, his reticence about his faith reflects Mormonism's lack of openness."[66]

In chapter 1, I described in some detail the long history of Saints evading scrutiny through obfuscation. As linguistic anthropologist Daymon Smith explains, persecution resulting from the nineteenth-century Mormon practice of polygamy led to the development and maintenance over time of a uniquely Mormon defensive communication strategy for dealing with those on the outside by obscuring differences that make a difference.[67] The approach taken by Romney and his conservative Mormon supporters, then, mirrored this historical tendency of the institutional LDS church, as well as their public relations efforts like the "I'm a Mormon" campaign and the online LDS Newsroom, to downplay and even ignore the role of difference. In that way, Romney and his supporters were acting particularly Mormon by attempting to illustrate Mormonism's assimilative capacity rather than addressing its true difference. And still, Romney and his supporters' tendency to deflect and hide ultimately conferred a measure of validity to American concerns about LDS secrecy and obfuscation.

Progressive Mormons: Othering Romney

Because conservative Mormons chose not to speak about Mormonism, they gave an opening to voices from minority and often fringe strains of the LDS community: heterodox members. On the blogosphere and social media especially, progressive Mormons used Romney's visibility as a public resource to both put forward their vision for proper Mormon identity and justify their own agendas for Mormonism. Romney became a convenient and publicly available mechanism through which to offer up a countercultural vision for Mormonism and in some circles became a way to bypass taboos and surreptitiously critique Mormon culture and even the institutional church itself.

Recall the incident with which this chapter opened: Romney's video-recorded "47 percent" gaffe in September 2012. The footage was released and immediately went viral, and elite progressive Mormons responded publicly and vocally. The very next day, on September 19, scientist, philanthropist, and Mormon historian Gregory Prince declared in the Huffington Post, "Mitt Romney Is *Not* the Face of Mormonism." Prince expressed fear that Romney's prominence would lead Americans to misjudge Mormonism and correlate it with Romney's conservative views, which Prince felt "sullied" the faith. He went on to explain that "the very basis of Mormon community" is service to the poor and needy; Mormons, he argued, are obligated by their faith to support and give to those in need.[68] Implicit in his argument was Romney's failure to live up to this central Mormon tenet; indeed, Prince suggested that Romney's Mormonism was itself a bastardized and substandard version of an inherently caring, giving faith. Prince's eloquent and emotional denunciation concealed his status as a minority voice in his own faith; as an outspoken liberal, Prince is hugely outnumbered in his highly conservative faith, and his personal distaste for Romney's perceived elitism was as much politically as religiously founded.

Soon Democratic Mormon senator Harry Reid was quoted agreeing with Prince's condemnation of Romney's brand of Mormonism, asserting that members of the church "understand that [Romney] is not the face of Mormonism."[69] Noted historian and Mormon Kathleen Flake similarly argued that Romney's harsh words reflected less his religion than his political posturing: "That's Republicanism. That's not Mormonism."[70] Mormon religion writer Peggy Fletcher Stack criticized Romney for his shortsighted 47 percent gaffe, pointing out that many LDS couples end up relying on welfare because they are encouraged by the institution and by Mormon culture to have large families early in life.[71] These prominent public figures attempted to create a visible public narrative of Mormonism as a socially conscious and even liberal institution.

Bloggers also swiftly took Romney to task, sometimes with less equivocation than these prominent public figures. One feminist LDS blogger said she was "deeply uncomfortable about sharing a faith community with him, and frankly anyone like him," and opined that his Mormon constituents had "painted broad brush-strokes on our religious identity without getting permission from the rest of us." She went on to literally call Romney and his supporters to repentance: "I have a few words to say to the vocal minority who have so brazenly claimed a religious identity for Mormonism that they had no right to manufacture in the first place—its [*sic*] time for you to repent!" She argued that *true* Mormonism, finding its roots in the grand narratives of the Book of Mormon, opposed all that Romney and his supporters represented.[72]

Heterodox blogger Jana Riess concurred, noting in a since-deleted post, "The Book of Mormon is unequivocal in its insistence that a society succeeds or fails on the basis of how it treats the poor—and that our very salvation is related to how well we heed that call." While thus expressly calling into question Romney's salvation, Riess went on to acknowledge that indeed, Romney does represent *a* face of Mormonism, albeit "one that has always celebrated wealth and success," as Mormonism's "communitarian impulses to help the poor and share the load have often been counterbalanced by an acquisitiveness that has perennially equated financial prosperity with spiritual blessing."[73]

Writing for the *CNN Belief Blog*, Brooks vowed that she would not vote for Romney regardless of their shared religion.[74] What's more, she turned public concerns on their head by asking not whether Mitt Romney is too Mormon to be a good president but whether he is not Mormon enough. In her words, "What if it's not that Romney is *too Mormon*, but that faith has played virtually no role in shaping his approach to foreign policy issues?"[75] Brooks verbalized the view of many progressive Mormons that Mormonism is at its core a truly progressive, not conservative, faith and that a truly faithful Mormon's politics and faith should mutually reflect that.

Beyond criticizing Romney's politics or lived religion, these types of opinion pieces carried less-than-subtle critiques of the institutional church itself. By publicly proclaiming their version (or vision) of Mormonism, they claimed it for all of Mormonism, including the very conservative institution. The ideals they advanced strategically ignore the structural, doctrinal, and historical aspects of the LDS institution that have been criticized ad nauseam in progressive Mormon forums—critiques that depict the church as a bureaucratic oligarchy that builds vast temples and shopping malls rather than concerning itself with the needs of the poor. These pronouncements, rather than critiquing or attempting an objective description of reality, are more akin to ritual performatives: by claiming their ideal version of Mormonism, these Mormons hoped to create it.[76]

Simultaneously, progressive Mormons offered this vision of Mormonism in a language only other Mormons were likely to understand: By claiming that Romney's lack of social consciousness was evidence of his wrongheaded interpretation of Mormonism, they called into question both his righteousness and, by implication, the righteousness of scores of Mormons (including most Mormon leaders) who adhered to the same political perspectives. They also offered a surreptitious critique that the institutional church—which reifies the same conservative, capitalist impulses—was also falling short of these imagined progressive standards. Since criticizing the LDS church was and continues to be taboo and tantamount to criticizing God's divine order,

Romney provided a convenient work-around that allowed progressive Mormons to air their heterodoxies in ways that remained discursively faithful to the church—and thus above reproach.

Constructing a Mormon Candidate

As national attention focused on the LDS faith during Mitt Romney's candidacy, these three major stakeholder groups seized upon the opportunity to interpret Mormonism variously for public consumption. The press, with its own tensions between the duty to inform and the need to entertain, wavered between avoidance and salacious digging, hinting at Mormonism's precarious standing in the national conversation between mainstream and decidedly weird. The dearth of true press informers points to a need in American journalism to seriously consider the ethics and methods of reporting at the intersection of religion and politics.

Romney himself and his conservative Mormon supporters obscured his Mormonism, depicting him as a patriotic, blue-blooded American for whom Mormonism was simultaneously a central and a peripheral aspect, a paradox the public never quite untangled. The seemingly contradictory perspective that Mormonism can be a central, determining part of one's identity while *also* being insignificant and yet *still* inappropriate for dissection by an impartial, democratic public parallels the modern LDS church's public relations quandary: how to successfully downplay significant differences while gaining acceptance in the broader American mainstream. No doubt this is why the public remained ambivalent about Mormonism; *Mormonism* is ambivalent about Mormonism.

For their part, progressive Mormons supportive of Barack Obama's incumbency used the political moment to depict Romney as a poor example of lived Mormonism (indeed, as a bad Mormon), simultaneously advancing their own vision of proper Mormon identity and critiquing the larger conservative impulses of the institution. Because Romney and his conservative supporters took the church's cue and evaded frank talk about faith and difference, instead focusing on Mormonism's assimilative capacity, heterodox Mormons had almost unchecked freedom to dictate the public conversation about the meaning of Romney's faith. His conservative, bureaucratic faith mirrored his conservative, bureaucratic politics and served as an easy point of critique for liberal and heterodox Mormons. By critiquing Romney, they circumnavigated taboos around critiquing the institutional church itself. The open platform of the internet allowed minority voices to publicly mark him as a black sheep. By suggesting that his Mormonism was a poor representation of the broader church, these progressive Mormons both misrepresented what is largely a politically conservative membership and simultaneously reimagined a Mormon Church wherein voiced difference is acceptable and diversity of political opinion welcome.

Beyond increased visibility and public acceptance, the presidential candidacy of a Mormon certainly reverberated among Mormon communities. The clearest impact of Romney's run was a visible reimagining of the borders of belonging, solidifying the political diversity of the faithful. Mormons themselves used Romney as a talking point to question proper LDS identity norms. Indeed, the paradox of a faith that struggles between the impulses of liberalism and conservatism was on full display.

In terms of public perception, the viable candidacy of a Mormon provided legitimacy to Mormonism as an American faith on an unprecedented scale. Although the press behaved schizophrenically regarding Romney's difference, Mormonism's moment in the limelight certainly made the Church of Jesus Christ of Latter-day Saints a topic of household conversation. Moreover, despite Romney's ultimate failure to secure the White House, his nomination signals at the very least that Mormonism's one-time nemesis, Evangelicals themselves, may have finally accepted the LDS into their political, if not religious, fold.

Despite the fraught status of Mormonism in the American landscape, ultimately, Mitt Romney's religious identity was not clearly exploited as a primary weakness throughout the campaign.[77] While it was a curiosity for some reporters and many onlookers, its usefulness as a marker of weakness was limited to the primaries. After he secured the Republican ticket, his faith's erstwhile opponents among conservative Christians were largely silent on his faith. Instead, the most vocal postnomination opponents to Romney's brand of Mormonism were members of his own faith. While the media made Romney's faith into a minor joke to be exploited or a difference to be ignored, the internet-enabled visibility of in-group narratives around his presidential candidacy provided an interesting glimpse into processes of internecine conflict that work to build notions of proper Mormon belonging in the modern moment.

Mitt Romney's run unavoidably put the Mormon Church in the public spotlight, forcing stakeholders to take a public position on the meaning of modern Mormon identity. The lesson of his run may well be the multiplicity of meanings given to that identity. In modern America, Mormon identity is precisely this complex and multivocal amalgamation of competing narratives, each bespoken from a position of competing interests and ideologies. In a battle for narrative supremacy, who ultimately gets the final say in what makes a good Mormon is largely a product of who has the most visible platform.

If narratives about Romney highlight the public face of Mormonism, a simultaneous internal conflict, one that went largely unnoticed by the preoccupied and largely disinterested non-Mormon public, marks its innermost face. I turn to this conflict in the following chapter.

4

Wars and Rumors of Wars

Apologetic and Dissent Communities

In the Lord's Church there is no such thing as a "loyal opposition." One is either for the kingdom of God and stands in defense of God's prophets and apostles, or one stands opposed.

—Elder M. Russell Ballard, "Beware of False Prophets and False Teachers"

Liminal entities are neither here nor there; they are betwixt and between the positions assigned and arrayed by law, custom, convention, and ceremonial. As such, their ambiguous and indeterminate attributes are expressed by a rich variety of symbols in the many societies that ritualize social and cultural transitions.

—Victor Turner, *The Ritual Process*

A secret article. Somewhere in the ether, it circulated among staunch Mormon defenders and soon would be published for all to see. This was personal, and it contained proof, the hard-sought and meticulously cited evidence that might finally be the blow to take down that wolf in sheep's clothing so long amassing his forces against the church while pretending to be a friend of truth and a shoulder for the wounded. Finally, everyone would learn the truth.

Or was it nothing more than slanderous lies? A "hit piece," a personal, ad hominem attack in the guise of a one-hundred-page article written in the language of social science, designed to take the focus off the church's history of obfuscation and put it directly on the personal shortcomings of one wounded warrior?

As we have seen, Mitt Romney's unavoidably public run focused mainstream attention on the LDS church, resulting in competing representations of Mormonism strategically articulated to control public perceptions. Those representations, of course, were outwardly focused, designed to manipulate a skeptical voting public's perception of a controversial church. But while that public battle raged, private battles went largely unnoted outside of Mormon circles. Behind the curtains, conflicts among Mormons themselves revealed other facets and faces of modern Mormonism, arcane and only comprehensible to insiders. Like public contestations over the image of Mormonism, these private conflicts also drew lines in the sand, solidifying who is ultimately in charge of designating and policing proper Mormon identity.

One particularly intense internecine conflict resonated in online Mormon communities in 2012, highlighting the Mormon cultural practice of intragroup surveillance. For readers unfamiliar with Mormon goings-on from 2012, let me warn you that this whole scenario is convoluted and so esoteric as to be almost tedious. In fact, the details are so specific and personal that it may seem like nothing but a voyeuristic glimpse into the strange interpersonal conflicts between two men with penchants for online debate. But in hindsight, it is clear that the story I'm about to relay shifted a balance of power at one of church-owned Brigham Young University's academic research centers and no doubt reverberated in the type and contents of work produced by that center in the years that followed. At the same time, the conflict and ensuing discourse drew attention from the church more broadly, resulting in yet another pendulum swing toward enforced institutional control over public perceptions of Mormonism.

The dramatis personae in this highly circulated and contentious episode included members of two opposing communities on the periphery of Mormon identity: apologists and dissenters. These groups are not composed of typical Mormons, who largely practice their faith quietly or, when sharing it, do so with deference and tact. Apologists and dissenters, especially during this time when so much public attention and internal energy was focused on debates about proper Mormon identity, are vocal minorities in Mormonism. They are exceptions, not the rule.

The conflict itself was largely instigated by certain associates of an old-guard apologetics group known as the Foundation for Ancient Research and Mormon Studies (known as FARMS), established in 1979 as an independent collaboration of LDS apologists. In addition to what they positioned as scholarly defenses of the church's historical claims, these writers and academics were known for their work separating the wheat from the tares, unabashedly calling out what they saw as disingenuous threats to authentic faith. In 1997, FARMS was invited to join BYU as a research foundation. In 2006, it was formally integrated into BYU's Neal A. Maxwell Institute for Religious Scholarship. While FARMS officially disbanded in 2010, some apologists who were previously affiliated with the group continued their apologetic work through the Maxwell Institute.

The largest and most well-known LDS apologetic organization, FAIR, also played a major role in the proceedings.[1] Founded in 1997 with a specific mission to counter online anti-Mormon sentiment, FAIR is a registered nonprofit run entirely on volunteer labor. Its website features a blog, an answers wiki addressing difficult topics, embedded videos, podcasts, and an online bookstore; aside from its annual conference, it exists as a virtual entity. FAIR and FARMS often overlapped in purpose, approach, and membership and would often promote each other's publications and writings to magnify their efforts. Although FAIR has always been considerably less abrasive in style, today it continues in the tradition established by FARMS and with the support and participation of many former FARMS writers and contributors.

While most work from FARMS and FAIR involves compiling faith-promoting resources and essays, both groups have sometimes used their platforms to call out particular sources of what they see as misinformation regarding Mormonism. In 2012, the target of the apologists' fervor was a well-known if contentious podcaster named John Dehlin. A vocally heterodox and sometimes doubting Mormon at the time, Dehlin founded the *Mormon Stories* podcast in 2005 to explore the church's history and truth claims from various perspectives.[2] His hour-long interviews feature people with all types of relationships with Mormonism, from prominent Mormons to academic researchers and heterodox, former, and "anti-Mormons." He is known for his unorthodox explorations and outspoken critiques of Mormon teachings and practice, tackling subjects ranging from controversial Mormon mission practices to Joseph Smith's polygamy to archaeological evidence for and against the Book of Mormon's truth claims. As of mid-2024, Dehlin and his colleagues have produced 1,930 hour-long podcast episodes. But in 2012, as I conducted my ethnographic research on the drama at the center of this story, there were only around 320 *Mormon Stories* episodes. Dehlin was then quickly rising in prominence (and notoriety) as both a figurehead for dissenting and ex-Mormon communities and a lightning rod for controversy.

If Mormon identities encompass a range of possibilities tethered to a structural ideal, communities of apologists and dissenters map the borders of acceptability. At one extreme, apologists such as those associated with FARMS are known as orthodox, conservative, and devout; Dehlin and his allies are comparatively considered heterodox, liberal, and secular. Both groups tend to be educated, dogmatic, and sometimes abrasive, positioning themselves as the apotheosis of real Mormon identity and vilifying the other as a bastardization of that identity. The antipathy between Dehlin's community and apologists ran deep; each viewed the other as representative of the most cogent threat to Mormonism. Still, the resulting conflicts were primarily disembodied: in a perpetual war of words, the most engaged supporters of each group spent countless hours in online debates and arguments, often reverting to seemingly juvenile personal attacks and site-to-site stalking.

These dynamics peaked in 2012, when Canadian medical doctor-cum-Mormon apologist Gregory L. Smith completed a detailed article dissecting the implications of Dehlin's internet activity in a point-by-point takedown. As a FARMS-affiliated author, Smith intended to publish the piece in *FARMS Review*, a peer-reviewed journal then sponsored by FARMS and BYU. Doing so would escalate and legitimate this ongoing conflict by confirming it in the academic record. But although he did eventually publish the article, it found its home elsewhere, after the dissolution of the entire FARMS enterprise, the ejection of the board of directors of the Maxwell Institute, and a complete reconfiguration of BYU's approach to religious studies—a restructuring that came as an institutional attempt to dissociate from marginal, extreme orthodox voices such as Smith's and that foreshadowed later events in 2014–15 that would similarly distance the church from extreme heterodox voices like Dehlin's.

Smith described his article as an analysis of *Mormon Stories* and of Dehlin's assumed role of exit counselor for those disgruntled Mormons who ultimately leave their faith. Smith circulated it among his colleagues, some of whom approached me to discuss its contents on the condition of anonymity. Some of these firsthand reviewers described the article as objective, scholarly, and well supported, while others saw it as personal, decidedly unscholarly, and unprofessional.

In March 2012, one such reviewer and Maxwell Institute employee, after reading an early draft of Smith's article, surreptitiously contacted Dehlin to alert him to its impending publication. Using his own social media channels, Dehlin then spread word of the article, and the leak led to prolific message board discussions and speculation about the mysterious article's contents.[3] Although at the time Dehlin and his supporters had not read it and could only guess at its contents, they began to refer to it as "the hit piece." Dehlin's community predicted it would be an aggressive attack on Dehlin's character, a speculation based on Smith's well-established combative rhetorical style and on information from anonymous tipsters.[4] Some said it would attempt to link Dehlin to the untimely death of his mission companion twenty years before; others said it would paint Dehlin as a dangerous apostate and present a case for his excommunication.

These guesses were not unfounded. Smith had long been openly critical of Dehlin's online activism. For instance, in 2011, Smith wrote that the *Mormon Stories* podcast was "hostile to the truth of the Book of Mormon" and implied that Dehlin was a biased "cultural Mormon" who was ignorant of the Book of Mormon.[5] This type of critique of those he considered marginal Mormons was nothing new; just the year before, Smith had written a similar piece blasting the website Mormons for Marriage and its organizer and painting her as a faithless hypocrite.[6]

As an ethnographer, my own role in this unfolding story was an interesting and complicated one. I first met Dehlin in late March 2012 when we, together with FAIR president Scott Gordon, discussed Mormons and the internet on a conference panel at Utah Valley University. The tension between Gordon and Dehlin was palpable and a strong contrast to the warmth and affability I usually sensed in my academic interactions with Mormons. After the panel, I watched as Dehlin was confronted by Louis Midgley, a FARMS apologist and retired BYU sociology professor. I did not hear what was said, but I saw Midgley shake his finger in Dehlin's face and yell angrily. Later that day, I had lunch with Dehlin, and he took a phone call he said was from a General Authority. Later, I was told the call concerned the article.

In August, I was invited to be the first non-Mormon to speak at FAIR's annual conference. After my talk, I was approached individually by several men who claimed insider knowledge of the article. I received unsolicited personal emails and phone calls from various sources who wanted to tell their side of the story (anonymously, of course). It was clear that both sides saw me as a potentially unbiased outsider who could help them publicly construct their narrative to their advantage. Piecing together an objective account of these happenings became less important than understanding how the two communities constructed history for their own ideological purposes. (This was lucky for me, given the challenge of pinning down an accurate history!)

Finally, in November 2012, after the drama surrounding Smith's article had largely dissipated yet before it was published, Smith himself sent me a copy of his article to review. I'm still not quite sure why. I did not know the man, but I suppose he must have heard through the smallish Mormon studies community that I was looking into this story. I also imagine that my status as a non-Mormon academic might have played a role, since many informants throughout the course of my research approached me with information they felt I would be interested to know. Whatever the reason, it certainly proved interesting.

Titled "Dubious 'Mormon' Stories: A Twenty-First Century Construction of Exit Narratives," the 116-page article was framed as an academic review, treating Dehlin and *Mormon Stories* as texts to deconstruct and debunk. Using the rhetoric of both a social scientist and a religious purist, Smith began with a caution concerning the digital era's potential to dilute Mormon sensibilities, as the internet offers a platform for groups that he called "New Order Mormons" (a moniker corresponding to an internet community of that name) or "leavetakers from traditional or literal-interpretation Mormonism."[7] What followed was a heavily cited, intricate timeline of Dehlin's activities and teachings, primarily online, brought together as a rhetorical deconstruction of "cultural Mormonism" using *Mormon Stories* and Dehlin as representative of what Smith described as a dangerous trend. Painstakingly cataloging Dehlin's (mostly) public online activities, Smith argued that Dehlin was a wolf in sheep's clothing, playing the role of an exit counselor in the tradition of the Evangelical ex-cult movement while claiming to be simply letting folks tell their stories. While the article was ostensibly about *Mormon Stories* as a community and as a social project, Smith used Dehlin as a stand-in for dissenting perspectives more generally. Developing his argument by intertwining social scientific literature and Mormon scriptures, Smith examined Dehlin's online rhetorical strategies and, both implicitly and explicitly, criticized him as an insincere and dangerous Saint. For Smith, Dehlin was a foe to the faith who used his expert status as an insider to defiantly guide others away from the church, all while feigning sincerity as an advocate for Mormons to remain active and faithful.

But the article would never be published with FARMS. Within weeks of rumors of its existence leaking online, more news spread that the article's publication had been suddenly halted. Speaking anonymously out of fear for their jobs, two employees of the Maxwell Institute explained to me that the article was suppressed personally by BYU president and emeritus General Authority Cecil O. Samuelson with additional influence from another unnamed General Authority whom Dehlin had contacted to plead for an intervention.

The fallout from the controversial article did not stop at its censorship. Just months later in June 2012, the editorial board of the erstwhile *FARMS Review*, including its founder and editor Daniel Peterson (a well-known figurehead among LDS apologists and conservative intellectuals), were unceremoniously dismissed and the twenty-three-year-old journal's publication halted. Maxwell Institute executive director Gerald Bradford issued his only public statement on the episode via the institute's website, indicating that the journal would be relaunched under a new title and restructured as an outlet for Mormon studies research and that the replacement of the editorial team was intended "to better position the new *Mormon Studies Review* within its academic discipline."[8] The Maxwell Institute as an entity, and BYU by extension, seemed to be moving away from abrasive apologetics and positioning itself as an objective scholarly organization, a historic move for an institution centered so precariously between academic and faith-based magisterium. The apologetic efforts to remain associated with BYU would be solely "pastoral and faith-promoting" rather than "polemic," one employee told me.

Peterson's scathing letter of resignation from his position as director of advancement was leaked on various Mormon message boards; it was unclear if the source of the leak was the same source that leaked news of Smith's article, another party at the Maxwell Institute, or perhaps Peterson himself. In the letter, Peterson referred to the event as "my public crucifixion."[9] Two months later at the August 2012 FAIR conference, during a question-and-answer session, he expressed disappointment with the involvement of General Authorities in the debacle, saying it had felt like he, rather than Dehlin, "was the one being disciplined."[10] Rather than simply redrawing lines for appropriate and inappropriate university behaviors, the firing of Peterson and the rest of the editorial board suggested censure of aggressive apologetics as a rhetorical style befitting Mormons. Indeed, the firing of Peterson was a form of institutional discipline.

Throughout the debacle, Smith remained unconvinced whether church leaders were involved at all and wondered whether the story of General Authority involvement in the article's suppression was fabricated to justify a purely political decision by BYU. Eventually, Smith published a one-hundred-page revision of the article on February 23, 2013, in *Interpreter: A Journal of Mormon Thought*, an open-access apologetic journal founded by Peterson and others after his ouster from the Maxwell Institute.[11]

For his part, Dehlin continued his vocal online heterodoxy through social media, particularly his personal and *Mormon Stories* Facebook pages, publicly expressing doubt in the truthfulness of many central Mormon tenets and historical narratives and calling for greater institutional transparency around these troubling issues. For instance, in a since-deleted post on the *Mormon Stories* website, Dehlin stated,

> I am deeply troubled by [church leaders'] historical and current treatment of women, racial and sexual minorities, and scientists/intellectuals.... I am also troubled by their historical and current approaches to faith/doubt, sexuality, the pursuit of vast commercial interests along with financial non-disclosure, the coercion/shaming of members through the withholding of temple and priesthood privileges, and the current culture of leader worship within the LDS church. I believe that the discouraging of criticism of LDS church leaders is possibly the single most pernicious and damaging aspect of LDS church culture—and that sunlight and candor are ultimately the best disinfectants.

Dehlin soon came under investigation by church leadership, the third time over the course of his involvement with *Mormon Stories*, and in mid-2014 was contacted by his local authorities for a disciplinary hearing with the possibility of excommunication. In a formal letter, Bryan C. King, Dehlin's stake president, explained that the hearing was called on account of Dehlin's expression of views that were "not in harmony with the revealed doctrines of the Gospel of Jesus Christ." He explained that Dehlin's dissemination of these views was central to King's decision to bring forward an investigation: "Through your podcasts and Internet posts, you have broadly disseminated these views. Additionally, you have provided a forum for others to criticize the Church and to disseminate their views that are contrary to the revealed word of God."[12] The timing of Dehlin's investigation coincided with the high-profile and controversial excommunication of feminist activist and Ordain Women founder Kate Kelly (discussed in the following chapter), which together with Dehlin's case drew national media attention.

After months of postponements, Dehlin was excommunicated by local leaders in February 2015 on charges of apostasy. Discourse concerning the reason for Dehlin's excommunication did important boundary work: Dehlin framed the disciplinary action as a direct result of his LGBT and women's ordination advocacy, while church leadership described it as resulting from his public and repeated questioning of church leaders and teachings. More broadly, although this extreme ousting from his faith community is not on par with Peterson's firing from an academic position, both highly mediated instances underscored strict boundaries on Mormon speech, reminding marginal members of their always-precarious place in this bureaucratic faith.

Disputes concerning the Smith article, the firing of Peterson and dismissal of his board, and the disciplining of Dehlin underscore what is at stake in these ongoing, online wars for control over representations of proper Mormon identity. Conflicts between members of apologetic and dissenting groups are par for the course on the dialogic and interactive Web 2.0. Internecine conflicts involving religious interpretive communities are nothing new; in-group fighting in Mormonism is as old as the religion itself and not noteworthy in and of itself. Still, the rhetorical strategies used by these groups during volatile exchanges shed light on the ethos of the group: the ways that apologetic and dissent groups fight, and subsequently the ways they are reigned in and disciplined by the larger institution, underscore essential elements of Mormon identity and mark moments of renegotiation of group boundaries.

In the remainder of this chapter, I explore how these arcane communities operate within the structural constraints of their faith and the implications of their roles for the ethos of the broader institution. I begin with a detailed history of the relationship between these two vernacular communities, contextualizing their ongoing conflict. Then I generate a two-part analysis of this conflict and its closure: first, I establish the normative expectations for proper interpersonal exchange, built on shared values of placing community over self and deferring to authority. But ongoing, volatile conflicts between apologetic and dissent groups violate these norms, marking moments of agential renegotiation of group boundaries. I argue that the disruption of fundamental Mormon traits in these groups' performance of a sort of "Mormon machismo" places them outside the limits of acceptable discourse, jeopardizing their roles in the broader Mormon community. In the second part of my analysis, I show how the public censuring of members of these groups by the LDS church illustrates the importance of the ritual of boundary maintenance for ongoing Mormon cohesion. I argue that the outcome of this dramatic episode, rather than asserting or supporting marginality as a viable Mormon identity construct, instead serves to reassert the authority of the institution and of the hegemonic status quo.

Apologetics and Dissent in Modern Mormonism

Before exploring the role of apologetic and dissent groups in modern Mormonism, we must first establish working definitions for our terminology. First, *apologetics* refers to a rhetorical practice and a social exercise rather than a static identity, and so the term *apologist* generally refers to an individual taking on a particular social role at a particular time and in a particular place. In practice, apologists are defenders of the institutional party line. They are social activists, seeking out what they see as misinformation (any information that contradicts the institution's official position on any matter or even opinions or perspectives that fail to present the institution in a flattering light) and employing a combination of rhetorical strategies to defend the institution. This definition is not limited to Mormonism, and in this sense, it is true that any Latter-day Saint may act as an apologist by actively engaging in these defensive debates, starting with the assumption that the church's teachings are literally, historically true and the LDS church is the legitimate church established by Jesus, reestablished through Joseph Smith, and maintained through the process of continuing revelation through subsequent prophets.

But the term *apologist* as a demarcation of identity within the Mormon community has a more specific connotation, referring to a conservative, faithful member who dedicates considerable time and effort to actively seek out opportunities to engage in apologetics (generally in internet forums), as a hobby or self-appointed responsibility, and who self-identifies as an apologist. These Mormons form social networks on- and offline around shared apologetic enterprises: amassing their intellectual and textual efforts using rational argument, scripture, and hermeneutics to confront challenges to the church on websites, blogs, and social networking sites (primarily Facebook). They circulate their textual work with other apologists and socialize around these efforts in disembodied online space. Among some dissenting and heterodox Mormons, the term *apologist* is itself a devil term denoting a blind allegiance to authority, the privileging of religious narratives over empirical evidence, and an abrasive interpersonal style.[13]

Mormon apologists are—and this is key—almost exclusively highly educated, white, older American men. In Mormon circles, no well-known women are referred to consistently as apologists; although apologetic websites may occasionally feature women authors and apologetic conferences may feature women speakers, in my ethnographic work only men self-describe and have been consistently referred to as apologists. They are often highly regarded professionals and professors (most often at BYU but also elsewhere), the most prominent of whom have backgrounds in fields such as ancient languages, political science, and history. Some of them are academics whose apologetic work is tied to their research; others are not academics but lawyers or medical doctors who take up apologetics exclusively as a hobby or volunteer effort.

Mormon dissent communities, particularly online, are much more diverse and prolific. I use the term *dissent community* as a wide net, including a range of groups from sympathetic reformers to those who are hostile to the church, its leadership, and even its people. It should be noted that some groups I classify as dissenting might take issue with my use of that term, which carries connotations of unfaithfulness in Mormon culture and bifurcates Mormon identity in problematic ways. Yet I find it a useful term because it refers to an active, not passive, withholding of assent or approval; these groups are unified by their active doubt, by open criticism of some major or minor aspect of Mormon culture, history, or practice. The term *dissent* underscores that, unlike groups that fully assent to (or, in Mormon parlance, sustain) the institution, these groups do not necessarily start from the perspective that the church is true or that its policies or doctrines are right, a perspective that in and of itself is anathema in a church reliant on full and unconditional doctrinal and practical acceptance. In that way, these communities dissent from the party line in ways that make them outsiders to idealized Mormonism.

Dissent groups are slightly more demographically diverse than apologetic communities but are still dominated by educated white American men. They tend to be a slightly younger demographic, in the thirty to fifty age range. Their demographic similarity to apologetic communities is an important feature I will return to. In this chapter, I, like Greg Smith, use John Dehlin's *Mormon Stories* communities as representative of dissent groups more generally. The *Mormon Stories* communities are of particular interest because of their size, reach, and visibility (when I conducted most of my research a decade ago, the main *Mormon Stories* Podcast Community group page on Facebook had over 6,700 members; today, it has over 20,500); because of their interaction with and codependence on Mormon apologetics; and because they represent approaches to heterodoxy and dissent that employ distinct rhetorical styles and strategies. But the *Mormon Stories* groups are best understood as a community center or hub around and beside which other groups have formed; their membership, ideologies, and discursive strategies overlap with and depart from other distinct dissent groups.[14] Even among dissent groups not directly affiliated with *Mormon Stories*, Dehlin is widely considered a figurehead and spokesperson for the disaffected and dissenting.

Community may be the most problematic term in use here, and rightly so: in our increasingly fractured digital age, it is problematic to make claims about community, once a place-based identifier. When I refer to these groups as communities, I am highlighting specific features: the members of the groups interact frequently; share central values, goals, and motivations; and most importantly, by self-selecting into the affinitive community, self-identify as members of the group and signal the adoption of a particular identity construct. I do not mean to suggest that members of these groups socialize on an individual level or even know one another by name (in fact, many operate online under pseudonyms to protect their offline identity), although it is safe to say that group leaders and figureheads (like Peterson or Dehlin) are familiar to all. *Community* also should not be taken as a suggestion of establishment or permanence, or even of obligation to the group; especially in dissent communities, turnover is high and new members are added daily as others leave.[15]

While apologetic and dissent communities serve a variety of functions that could be analyzed separately for their impacts on Mormon identity, I am specifically interested in the ways these communities interact and what that interaction itself might reveal about Mormon identity construction and mechanisms for boundary formation. I rely on interviews with members of both communities (most of whom requested anonymity because of the precariousness of their own marginality) as well as discourse analyses of postings on social networking forums to analyze these communities' discursive strategies as self-reflexive ways of making sense of their standing and status as Mormons on the margins.

The LDS Tradition of Lay Apologetics

As a discursive strategy, apologetics makes use of mass communication technologies and public forums to speak back to public criticism. Apologists cull linguistic, historical, doctrinal, and other types of evidence to form systematic and cohesive arguments with the goal of defending church history, doctrine, and practice. As a communicative impulse, apologetics bridges that often-impossible gap between nonempirical issues of faith and belief on the one hand and reason and proof so valued by the post-Enlightenment purview on the other. Apologetics as a form of Christian rhetoric is as old as the religion itself; Catholics and Protestants trace the tradition from Christ's ministry to the New Testament letters of Paul through the Middle Ages and to the present day.[16]

Apologetics in the Mormon tradition is a necessary yet precarious undertaking. Since the founding of the always-controversial LDS church, Mormon writers have defended their beliefs to a skeptical and often hostile public in newspaper articles, book publications, and pamphlets. Generally, these early apologists were church leaders who held some normative sway, yet despite their authority, their apologetic work was often contested because of its autonomy. One illustrative example involves Orson Pratt, an inaugural member of the Quorum of the Twelve Apostles. From 1853 to 1854, Pratt very briefly published *The Seer*, a periodical commissioned by Brigham Young as a platform for explicating and defending the Mormon doctrine of polygamy, or "celestial marriage," to a skeptical and hostile national public. Yet despite his status as a church authority, and despite the official status of his publication, in 1865 the First Presidency issued a statement in the church-owned *Deseret News* publicly disciplining Pratt and denouncing his writings, including *The Seer*. This public rebuke called Pratt's doctrinal declarations "hypotheses and theories" and further explained the danger of speaking on behalf of the church.

> It ought to have been known, years ago, by every person in the Church—for ample teachings have been given on the point—that no member of the Church has the right to publish any doctrines, as the doctrines of The Church of Jesus Christ of Latter-day Saints, without first submitting them for examination and approval to the First Presidency and the Twelve. There is but one man upon the earth, at one time, who holds the keys to receive commandments and revelations for the Church, and who has the authority to write doctrines by way of commandment unto the Church. And any man who so far forgets the order instituted by the Lord as to write and publish what may be termed new doctrines, without consulting with the First Presidency of the Church respecting them, places himself in a false position, and exposes himself to the power of darkness by violating his Priesthood.[17]

The policing of apologetic discourse is central to its history in the LDS context. As we saw in chapter 2, unlike many other Christian churches, the LDS church sponsors no official theology, and official doctrine is in many ways undeveloped and often difficult for even lifelong members to pin down. Correlation and its legacy ensure that official church-sponsored messaging is consistent in content across speakers and throughout church media, and members are discouraged (officially and implicitly) from putting stock in unofficial sources of any kind. In keeping with the very top-down nature of the church hierarchy, even apologists who attempt to defend the church are not free to speak on its behalf. This policing of who can speak for Mormonism is reflected in the church's administrative policy handbook: "Members may not create websites, blogs, or social media profiles on behalf of the Church or to officially represent the Church and its views. However, they may create websites, blogs, or social media profiles to assist with their callings. When doing so, members must include a disclaimer such as 'This is not an official website of The Church of Jesus Christ of Latter-day Saints.' . . . As members express their own thoughts and feelings, they should not give the impression that they represent or are sponsored by the Church."[18]

Despite institutional ambivalence, in the first part of the twentieth century, many other church leaders, including apologists like Elders B. H. Roberts and John Widtsoe, engaged in defensive work. Interestingly, although Roberts lived and died a faithful Mormon, he wrote investigative studies on inconsistencies and anachronisms in the Book of Mormon, even suggesting that Joseph Smith may have plagiarized it.[19] These studies went unpublished until more than fifty years after his 1933 death and are now fodder for dissent groups who use his insider status to validate concerns over the Book of Mormon's authenticity.

Although leaders have long engaged in intellectualist apologetics, many modern apologists see prolific BYU linguist Hugh Nibley as a sort of founding father of Mormon lay apologetics. Nibley was one of the first lay members to engage in mass-media-driven apologetic work, publishing his extensive works through church-owned Deseret Book throughout the 1980s and '90s. An acutely intelligent academic (Nibley trained at UC Berkeley in the 1930s and was fluent in some sixteen languages) and a faithful member of the church,[20] Nibley established a tradition of what has come to be called "faithful scholarship," an approach that upends the scientific method by presupposing the veracity of all of Mormonism's truth claims on a range of topics from cosmology, to history, to linguistics, analyzing data in light of these foregone conclusions. Since Nibley, LDS apologetic work has been institutionally separated from the church itself, avoiding the risks of "official" sanction on whatever tactics and information the groups themselves employ.

Aside from individual apologists working to defend the church's claims, visible and active Mormon apologetic organizations are relatively new phenomena. The largest and longest lived, FARMS began in the late 1970s as an informal collaboration of Mormon thinkers interested primarily in historical scholarship. FARMS was officially annexed by church-owned Brigham Young University in 1998 under the direction of then church president Gordon B. Hinckley, who intended it to "provide strong support and defense of the Church on a professional basis";[21] in 2006 it merged with BYU's newly organized Neal A. Maxwell Institute for Religious Scholarship, which originally focused mostly on faith-affirming initiatives. FARMS-affiliated apologists continued Nibley's tradition of faithful scholarship until the effective dissolution of their organization in 2013.

As with many aspects of LDS culture, the internet revolutionized Mormon apologetics, allowing independent groups of researchers and thinkers to come together with a common goal of defending the church. Today's largest LDS apologetic organization, FAIR, largely owes its genesis as an organization to the internet. According to president Scott Gordon, in 1997 during the heyday of America Online message boards, one particular religion-themed board became a heated battleground for Mormons defending their faith. Fueled by the Mormon proselytizing impetus, faithful members and critics of the church (at that time largely Evangelical Christians, who no doubt saw their engagement on these boards as a form of proselytizing or witnessing as well) engaged in often heated discussions and debates around Mormon beliefs and practices. Frustrated at having to constantly retype the same rebuttals to misperceptions and challenges posed again and again by various detractors, Gordon and several others created the FAIR website as a centralized database of information and responses to these common critiques.[22]

Gordon said his motivation for starting the website centered on his desire to present correct and unbiased information about the church for individuals on the cusp of major faith decisions, particularly those considering leaving the church. He explained, "It's disconcerting to me when people make major decisions in their life based on information that I feel is either inaccurate or at least deserves a little more explanation before making a decision based on it. So... I just want people to have their eyes wide open. If they still make a decision one way or the other, that's OK with me. I mean I may be disappointed but... I'm OK with that because I feel like they've thought about it, they've thought it out, they've made their decision, and they've moved on."[23]

His intention, he explained, was to show doubters and seekers that they could make faith work despite difficulties. Today his nonprofit volunteer-only organization is headquartered online at the sleek website www.fairlatterdaysaints.org. It features articles by regular contributors on various hot-button topics like polygamy, the translation of the Book of Mormon, and Mormonism and science; a child organization called Come, Follow Me formatted for the public; a feature that puts readers in direct correspondence with FAIR writers (formerly called "Ask the Apologist," this feature has since been retitled "Ask FAIR, Get a Direct Answer," which seems to suggest a move away from the "apologist" label); an expanding podcast; and a wiki updated by apologists with information and rebuttals to various challenges of the day.

The internet has made Mormon lay apologetics both more difficult and more necessary, according to FAIR's public relations representative Steve Densley, a corporate lawyer who at one time devoted ten to thirty hours a week volunteering for the organization. In an interview, Densley explained that prior to the internet, anti-Mormon claims from both Evangelicals and former Mormons, often the most outspoken adversaries to the church, were generally easy to refute. In his recollection, critics then were largely ignorant or dismissive of complicated problems in church history and anachronisms or other textual issues in the Book of Mormon. Instead, challenges then focused on sectarian quibbles, generally nonfalsifiable claims like whether God has a body or esoteric aspects of Mormon practice raised to paint the church as a dangerous cult.[24]

In those preinternet days, some in-depth criticisms did exist, such as the book *No Man Knows My History: The Life of Joseph Smith*, a notorious 1945 exposé by historian and former Mormon Fawn Brodie,[25] or the mimeographed writings of Jerald and Sandra Tanner, former Mormons turned Evangelicals who founded the Salt Lake City–based Utah Lighthouse Ministry in the 1960s, publishing exposé-style writings on church history and beliefs.[26] The "former member turned critic," or what sociologists refer to as the apostate role of whistleblower, is a familiar trope in religious experience, particularly in controversial or marginalized religious groups.[27] Mormonism provides a simplistic heuristic for orthodox members to easily dismiss the critical writings of former members: they are "anti-Mormon."

Allow me to take a moment to underscore Mormon culture's easy dismissal of whistleblower activists. After I presented a talk on the narratives of former Mormons at FAIR's annual conference (as the first non-Mormon to present in its then thirteen-year history), a Mormon woman approached me and said, "This is all very interesting, but the real question is, Why do so many people leave the church, but they can't leave it alone?" That was not the first time I had been asked that question. Repeated often among conservative members, the question originates in authoritative discourse, masking the derision that many orthodox LDS express for those who have left the church but still invest time in discussing and deconstructing its teachings and history. Perhaps not coincidentally, it was Elder Neal A. Maxwell, namesake of the BYU institution that first housed FARMS, who coined the phrase as an epithet for former Mormons still actively engaged in conversations about the church. In 1980, Maxwell said, "Newcomers, you may even see a few leave the Church who cannot then leave the

Church alone. Let these few departees take their brief bows in the secular spotlight; someday they will bow deeply before the throne of the Almighty."[28]

Maxwell repeated the phrase even more forcefully and derisively a few years later in General Conference, expanding on the caricature to create what would become a standard heuristic among orthodox LDS to categorize and dismiss former Mormons and their critiques.

> Some real tares even masquerade as wheat, including the few eager individuals who lecture the rest of us about Church doctrines in which they no longer believe. They criticize the use of Church resources to which they no longer contribute. They condescendingly seek to counsel the Brethren whom they no longer sustain. Confrontive, except of themselves, of course, they leave the Church, but they cannot leave the Church alone.... Considering their ceaseless preoccupation, one wonders, Is there no diversionary activity available to them, especially in such a large building—like a bowling alley? Perhaps in their mockings and beneath the stir are repressed doubts of their doubts.... Therefore, brothers and sisters, quiet goodness must persevere, even when, as prophesied, a few actually rage in their anger against that which is good (see 2 Ne. 28:20). Likewise, the arrogance of critics must be met by the meekness and articulateness of believers.[29]

As recently as the April 2004 General Conference, Maxwell noted that in his lifetime, he had seen "a few leave the Church who could then never leave it alone. They used often their intellectual reservations to cover their behavioral lapses."[30] The idea that some disgruntled members leave the church but won't leave it alone became a cultural truism among many mainstream LDS, as did the idea that vocal criticism of the church was a mask for secret sinful proclivities. Whistleblowers were written off as apostates who left because they preferred to live a sinful life but, because of their shame and deeply embedded knowledge of the church's truth, could not leave the church alone.

In my own observations, the notion that leave-takers can't seem to leave the church alone does important cultural work in reaffirming hegemony. If Mormonism is the only truth, then those who have experienced its truthfulness and still choose to leave must forever harbor some vestige of its truthfulness in their hearts and minds. They leave, as Maxwell explained, because they cling to some sinfulness they cannot extinguish. Still, even after leaving, they feel drawn to the church, and this compulsion manifests in a blatant desire to fight against it. This notion is, of course, offensive and even laughable to leave-takers, who say that decisions to leave the church are complex and heartfelt and that their inability to "leave the Church alone" has to do with the depth of their Mormon acculturation, their embedded social and familial connections to Mormonism, their desire to understand their own spiritual histories, and often the concern they feel for those still in the fold.

Before the proliferation of internet use among American Mormons, partisan and vitriolic criticisms often founded in matters of fact, like those found in the writings of Jerald and Sandra Tanner, were generally dismissed as "anti-Mormon literature." These arguments were disregarded by apologists and adherents. Average Mormons were often unaware of these complicated issues and, being faithful, would be unlikely to engage with such material if they did come across it.

Before the internet, this simplistic approach to whistleblower exposés paralleled a simplistic approach to most lay apologetics. Serious issues like anachronisms in the Book of Mormon were rarely raised, and when they were, apologists often lacked access to advances in the fields of archaeology, science, and history, which made it challenging to craft sophisticated responses. Densley explained that many complicated issues had to be accepted on faith alone in those days, and apologists often had to admit, "I don't know. But I've prayed about the Book of Mormon and I'm confident that the Book of Mormon is the word of God.... We'll figure that out later."[31]

The World Wide Web changed the game, bringing together people who are or have been Mormon and thus have deep knowledge and concern for church history with unprecedented access to information about complicated and esoteric historical issues—Joseph Smith's polyandry, the Kinderhook plates, the Book of Abraham, and DNA evidence. These issues have been repeatedly cited in my interviews with former Mormons as contributing factors in their decisions to leave the church. These days, too, Evangelical Christians are no longer the church's biggest detractors. As Densley told me, "The stuff that has been more time-consuming, or the stuff that's captured the attention of the apologists more [today], are the attacks that are coming from Mormon dissidents."[32]

Today, disgruntled former Mormons organize websites like MormonThink (www.mormonthink.com), the internet-era version of Jerald and Sandra Tanner's work. MormonThink takes what it calls an empirical approach, featuring in-depth and heavily cited articles on dozens of sticky issues, dissecting the church's position alongside critical takes. FAIR is not alone in recognizing the dangers posed by critical former Mormons online: General Authority Neil L. Andersen recently noted in a church-wide address, "There have always been a few who want to discredit the Church and to destroy faith. Today they use the internet."[33] Because detractors gain a widespread audience online, apologists must go online to respond.

Because issues raised by former or dissident Saints threaten the church, Mormon apologists engage in a kind of surveillance of dissident groups. When asked how they gauge what issues to address on their own website, Scott Gordon explained that among other things, FAIR volunteers "monitor" various Mormon-related message boards (particularly those Gordon calls "hostile" and "anti-Mormon") and then address issues that are frequently cited in those venues.

This surveillance does not go unnoticed. Members of dissident groups are cognizant that there are often "moles" in their midst, which they attribute to a Mormon culture of tattling rooted in a history of peer surveillance: since at least the mid-1980s, the church has sanctioned the clandestine Strengthening Church Members Committee (SCMC), tasked with monitoring other Mormons (primarily but not exclusively their mediated writings related to the church) through reliance on tips or complaints from other members and then passing information to local leaders for potential disciplinary action.[34] By design, the SCMC has operated so surreptitiously that some members consider it little more than a folktale or by-product of anti-Mormon rumormongering. Although the existence of the SCMC has been confirmed by the church, the scale of its operations has never been clarified or even hinted at, but that may be beside the point; by its existence alone, it works as a sort of panopticon for members, especially in online groups where any lurkers might be operatives for the SCMC. On the other side of the coin, some orthodox members see surveillance and tattling as acceptable and even encouraged behavior, effectively electing themselves to the SCMC by reporting suspicious or unorthodox behaviors and words to church leaders. Members who are concerned about potential disciplinary action know to self-censor their speech to avoid the network of tattling that might lead to bishop notification of online dissent.

Despite the deep connections between surveillance and institutional mandate, the relationship between the LDS church and apologist groups is not clear-cut. Both Densley and Gordon see their work with FAIR as time given to their church and to God, but church leaders have remained ambivalent about the work of these and other lay apologists. As an independent organization, FAIR provides the requisite disclaimer at the bottom of its website: "Any opinions expressed, implied, or included in or with the goods and services offered by FAIR are solely those of FAIR and not those of The Church of Jesus Christ of Latter-day Saints."[35]

But FAIR's relationship to the church is more complicated. The disclaimer obfuscates what one FAIR writer told me is the actual function of the organization, to "say what the church can't say." He told me that he often chooses topics based on what he thinks needs to be said but might be "bad PR" coming from the church—controversial or complicated issues on which a definitive answer from Salt Lake would risk exposing naïve members to information for which they are mentally or spiritually unprepared. This writer said FAIR has received requests from General Authorities to cover specific topics on which the church would rather not go on record.

Gradually, the church began to take a more proactive, head-on approach, addressing some controversial issues on its official website through quasi-historical essays (necessitated, in large part, by the work of dissenters publishing for groups like *Mormon Stories* and MormonThink, who largely brought the issues to light in the first place). These institutional efforts (described in further detail in chapter 6) could soon make some apologetic efforts obsolete. Certainly, they represent some effort by the institution to divest apologetic groups of their influence by correlating even defensive arguments and information.

For now, though, apologists offer detailed defensive responses to many critical issues without the risk that comes with an official stamp of approval from the institution. While church leaders themselves have not endorsed FAIR, in July 2012 the church's Public Affairs spokesman, Michael Otterson, mentioned the organization's website as a reliable resource during a YouTube presentation describing how members should confront "anti-Mormon material."[36] (Otterson misstated the website address as "fair.org" instead of, at the time, "fairlds.org," which ironically directed faithful Mormons to an anticensorship media watchdog website completely unrelated to Mormonism.)

As chapter 2 indicates, the role of LDS public relations is a complicated one with intentionally ambiguous normative authority, so while Otterson's support of FAIR cannot be taken as proof of church endorsement, it at once signals approval and a certain strategic plausible deniability. Yet while it allows them a bit of rhetorical leeway, FAIR's unofficial status also leads to its marginality among many Mormons, particularly older members who are offline and unconnected to the shifting norms ushered in by the polyphony of the internet. As a residual effect of correlation, it is sometimes seen as taboo for lay Mormons to attempt to clarify doctrine and policy beyond official church statements; it is viewed as impertinent and borderline sinful to speak up for the church out of an overabundant caution to "follow the manual" (that is, the *General Handbook*), which warns members to only use approved materials when teaching about Mormonism. These conservative members understand the legacy of correlation to mean that unless the church officially issues a statement on an issue, members should not opine. In interviews, some members have said they consider apologetics work to be "against church policy" because Mormons should turn the other cheek and not argue with naysayers: "If someone wants to believe a lie about the church, let them," one former bishop told me. These Mormons feel that "no one was ever converted through argument" and that the Holy Ghost must set the stage before anyone will feel the truth of the church; time spent in persuasion is better spent simply spreading the gospel. These Saints often seem oblivious to the sophistication, proliferation, and effectiveness of anti-Mormon claims online.

But for Densley, apologetic defense of the church finds its precedence in Christ himself: "How should we respond when people are attacking the church? You know, it is appropriate sometimes to step back and say, 'We still love you.' Other times it is appropriate to turn the tables of the temple over and pull out the whip."[37]

Mormon Stories at the Borders of Mormon Identity

If the internet provided the impetus for new forms of lay apologetic work, it also provided the platform for what might be considered the opposite: social communities formed around the common denominator of dissent. Where apologetic groups work to defend the church's party line, dissent groups deconstruct it.

In 2005, with his testimony shaken after learning about controversial parts of church history, John Dehlin felt unsatisfied with the support available for church members experiencing crises of faith. Even online, he said in an interview, there were only two options: blatantly anti-Mormon sites that were, in his words, "negative," "critical," and "cynical," and apologetic sites, which he felt were often "mean-spirited" and disingenuous, trying to "distract people with complexities about the difficult issues."[38] Hoping to create a space for objectivity and support for struggling Mormons, Dehlin launched *Mormon Stories*.

Through his own personal journey in and out of belief and practice and in and out of church discipline for his vocal heterodoxy, Dehlin acknowledged that the church may not work for everyone and that each person should weigh the evidence and decide for themselves whether they want to remain affiliated. This stance has led to accusations that Dehlin is nothing more than a "cultural Mormon," a term often used derisively to refer to people who are not true believers, not quite in and not quite out of Mormonism's bounds.

Dehlin has long established himself as a sort of spokesperson for disaffected Mormons, using his own research as a psychology doctoral student to represent Mormon teachings as dangerous and damaging. For instance, Dehlin took public stances against LDS proscriptions on homosexual sex, masturbation, and other Mormon orthodoxies, arguing that these teachings are psychologically and socially damaging and abusive. He has also argued that the LDS church has not been honest about its own history with members, leading to deep resentment and disillusionment when individuals discover the truth. His online reach is prolific: in addition to *Mormon Stories*, Dehlin helped establish seven sister sites,[39] all of which were initiated under his nonprofit organization known as the Open Stories Foundation. He also hosts several Facebook pages with thousands of members; on these, over eighty regional and affinity-based support groups have been created that, while unaffiliated with the Open Stories Foundation, have been linked through the *Mormon Stories* podcast site.[40] While most of his outspokenness has been relegated to the internet, Dehlin actively organized and traveled to regional *Mormon Stories* conferences and retreats, publicized and marched in gay pride parades to show solidarity with the LGBT community, and solicited and gave media interviews. In short, Dehlin has been one of the most visible and most polarizing figures in online dissent communities.

Many bloggers and participants in online forums share his perspectives, of course, but it is a combination of Dehlin's open skepticism and his charisma that at once make his online communities successful and pose a real threat to orthodoxy, making him a figurehead and target for criticism and surveillance. By creating communities for heterodox Mormons under the premise of providing support and psychological healing, Dehlin amassed a following in the thousands of former and current Mormons who say he has saved them. They flock to him at conferences and gatherings, effusively thanking him for his work with *Mormon Stories* and for providing an online space for them to be honest and authentic about their doubt. His status is part celebrity, part spiritual guru: when I met Dehlin at a conference on Mormonism and the internet at Utah Valley University, we had lunch together with a man on his way out of Mormonism. When Dehlin stepped away to take a phone call, this man turned to me and said, "I keep pinching myself. I can't believe I'm having lunch with John Dehlin!"[41]

While he is popular among many dissenters, most conservative Mormons who know of him consider him dangerous and heretical. His audacity in both laying claim to an LDS identity and openly criticizing the church—two things generally thought to be mutually exclusive by faithful Saints—has made him a figure of enormous reproach. The Greg Smith article was not the first time John Dehlin had been singled out for criticism by orthodox ranks and certainly would not be the last. As LDS writer Rosalynde Welch noted, "Dehlin is a charismatic figure and a lightning rod for the cultural tensions the church is experiencing in this political moment, and he has attracted both adulation and criticism."[42]

Of his motives for creating the *Mormon Stories* podcast, in an interview Dehlin said that while his publicly stated objective was to create open and honest dialogue, his private motivation was to keep people in the church. He explained, "I was sad any time someone left the church. I felt like *I* was able to make the church work, and I was naïvely optimistic that all I had to do was get these issues out on the table and let the critics do their thing. But then if I could get the believers to say, 'Yeah, I know all this stuff but I still believe,' that would be really compelling. If people were struggling, then those people would choose to stay in the church."[43]

The parallels between Dehlin's motives for starting *Mormon Stories* and Gordon's motives behind FAIR's founding are striking: both told me there was no objective information on the internet for people in crises, both said they were motivated by a desire to help people stay active in the church, and both believed that openness around difficult issues was the best way to keep people in the church.

Dehlin's narrative is not uncontested; his real motives for creating and maintaining *Mormon Stories* have been debated since the start. Many apologists and conservative members dislike his unorthodox approach and feel he is duplicitous, a wolf in sheep's clothing. When Dehlin remained active in the church and on his podcast, these members felt that despite his claims to the contrary, Dehlin secretly wanted to convince people to leave the church, not to stay, and that he was using his membership in the church and his purported goals of objectivity as masks to fool gullible Mormons in faith crises. One Facebook commentator asserted that Dehlin was leading a "campaign against Mormonism under the guise of unbiased research." It was this debate over intentionality that sparked the controversial article by Gregory Smith, wherein Smith attempted to expose what he saw as Dehlin's real motivations.

Whatever similarities or differences may exist between their origins and motives, FAIR and *Mormon Stories* continue to operate at odds. The incivility between the two is a microcosm of the hostility between apologetic and dissent groups more broadly. Every apologetic critique of a dissident for "leaving the church but not leaving it alone" is accompanied by a parallel accusation by dissidents that apologists are simply "lying for the Lord," knowingly obfuscating truth to protect the image of the church. Members of both communities often refer to the other camp in ways that suggest that the real battle of Mormon representation is between apologetics and dissent communities—between Mormons on the fringes.

In previous research, I noted narrative strategies among orthodox members who approach faith conservatively and literally and heterodox practitioners who approach religious identity progressively and nonliterally. These narratives challenge normative assumptions about what it means to be Mormon, belying the notion that Mormon identity is monolithic.[44] If possibilities for LDS identity form a continuum from conservative to liberal, or orthodox to heterodox, these two internet communities—orthodox apologists on the one hand and dissenting heterodox groups on the other—appear to map out the margins and define the borders of affiliation.

While there have always been communities on the margins of Mormon identity, the internet provides unprecedented platforms for the expression, expansion, and policing of these communities' narratives. Indeed, the very nature of life online—participatory, disseminatory, and heterogeneous—makes the proliferation of these communities at once possible and necessary: apologetic groups largely respond to "anti-Mormon" information widely circulated via the internet, and dissenting LDS often find anonymous and disembodied community online necessary to avoid perceived real-world threats to their heterodox beliefs or practices. Each of these online communities rejects the other as misguided if not disingenuous, illegitimate, and even dangerous representatives of the broader Mormon faith community and yet rely on the other as a foil for their own version of legitimate LDS identity.

Where Apologetics and Dissent Meet: Negotiating the Narrative Enemy

Not only does the ongoing conflict between the groups provide their respective raison d'êtres, but its volatility also makes them the targets of broader institutional monitoring and occasional discipline. Significant because of their scope, visibility, and normative sway, apologetic and dissent groups' conflicts violate central institutional Mormon norms that prioritize the institution's interests over and above the interests of the individual member. It is the violation of these norms that then places these groups beyond the limits of acceptable Mormon identity, jeopardizing their roles in the broader Mormon community. Because these major violations occur in influential groups and are circulated widely via social media, the church must respond in clear, punitive ways to reaffirm the boundaries of acceptable Mormon praxis.

In Mormonism as in all cultural systems, complex values and priorities contribute to normative expectations for proper public deportment and interpersonal exchange. Among these, the church's patriarchal values are central, crafting clear hierarchies within the structure that demand specific if often unspoken obeisance. It is important to note that rather than an etic, feminist classification of Mormonism as patriarchal, my use of that word honors its emic meaning. The patriarchal order is a Mormon phrase, not my own, describing God's eternal structure for both temporal family life and ecclesiastical hierarchy, as well as the eternal structures of the cosmos.

Mormonism is a quintessential American hierarchical corporation: its basic unit is the family, which is presided over by a husband and father; geographically close families compose a ward, presided over by a bishop; geographically close wards compose a stake, presided over by a stake president; and geographically close stakes compose areas, presided over by an area president. The entire organization of areas is the church, presided over by General Authorities. In every case, the presiding authorities are men who are the heads of those beneath them on the organizational flow chart but who must also submit to the men above them. The patriarchal order of Mormonism structures all relations organizationally and politically but also flavors relations in affective ways.

Let me illustrate briefly with a counterpoint: in Elizabeth Brusco's analysis of Evangelical churches in Colombia, gender-imbalanced conversion rates and the resulting predominance of women in religious leadership roles give Colombian Evangelicalism "a 'tone' or 'flavor' that is distinctly consistent with Colombian femininity: what we might call a 'feminine ethos,' [where] ethos sets a definite tone of appropriate behavior and a standardized system of emotional attitudes."[45] Similarly, the Mormon patriarchal order situates men above women as leaders in the church and in the home, giving Mormonism an American *masculine ethos*, a strong androcentrism, that is hard to miss.[46] Structurally, emphasis on priesthood authority yields a lack of leadership roles and visibility for women. Moreover, the highly bureaucratic corporation's top-down leadership composition not only is literally gendered (as only men can hold high-stakes leadership roles) but also reflects the gender bias in postmodern hierarchical organizations more broadly, which are a site of male dominance.[47] When women do hold leadership positions, their decisions and meetings must be presided over by male priesthood holders; even girls' camps must have men present to preside over and protect the women and girls in attendance.[48] Even in weekly meetings, men literally occupy the most visible positions; although women can and do frequently give talks or lessons, men preside over every meeting physically and spiritually, sitting on the stand in positions of authority.

Theologically, Mormons are unique among Christians for their belief in heavenly parents rather than just Heavenly Father, but absolutely no emphasis is put on Heavenly Mother's role. Merely mentioning her is taboo, but there is a clear if implicit understanding that in heaven as it is on Earth, the Father presides. The Book of Mormon itself can be read as a story about the relationships between fathers and sons—indeed, the record is said to have been passed down from father to son for safekeeping.[49] Ritualized rites of passage for men, like the emphasis on boys' activities like Scouting and the expectation that all men serve a mission, institutionalize masculinity and are "the price of admission to the Mormon' Good Old Boys' club."[50]

The patriarchal context is central to Mormonism's expectations regarding ethical and religious obligations in interpersonal exchange, which privilege a white male body and masculine authority. By default, the authoritative Mormon voice is a male voice.

Speaking, especially in public forums, is a male task; discussion is first and foremost a male activity. Understanding apologetic and dissent groups' interactions begins with a recognition that these are primarily male spaces in a culture where maleness is a privileged and idealized subject position. It is no small irony, in this hypermasculine context, that the violations that mark dissent and apologetic groups as outside the bounds of acceptable Mormonism are inextricably tied up in overzealous, stereotypically masculine rhetoric. These groups take their masculinity too far and, in doing so, usurp the bureaucratic chain of command.

When apologetic and dissent groups violate two interconnected normative expectations that are central to idealized male comportment, they cross unspoken and invisible lines that separate acceptable and unacceptable behaviors, pitting themselves against the religious institution and marking themselves as public offenders. When the institution reigns in this behavior, it reinforces the hegemonic status quo as definitive and authoritative. These two expectations include a community-over-self orientation and deferral to authority, which together have a powerful silencing effect on dissent.

A community orientation has long been a feature of orthodox Mormonism, from its early experiments with communalism to its modern emphasis on service, volunteerism, and self-sacrifice. To remain in good standing, members are routinely expected to sacrifice time in volunteer labor and money in a 10 percent tithe to the church. The church itself is a network envisioned as a worldwide community of Saints united through these sacrifices (any Mormon will tell you that one of the benefits of being LDS is always knowing that if you move to a new city, you will have a congregation ready and waiting to help you unpack). But along with this emphasis on cohesion comes a fear of disagreement and argumentation. Mormons shy away from contention (see chapter 5) and avoid rocking the boat or upsetting the status quo. This penchant for avoidance of contention leads to a phenomenon referred to by insiders, with tongue in cheek, as "Mormon nice"—the tendency to always be sweet, to force pleasantries despite ill feelings, to maintain a smiling demeanor at any cost.

Cohesion as a Mormon moral priority is closely linked to deferral to authority as a moral injunction. Avoidance of contention in the Mormon context means explicit and unconditional submission to authority figures as the exclusive proprietors of truth. As I have detailed, Mormon identity is hierarchically structured along lines of masculine priesthood authority, deferral to which is mandatory and symbolic of submission to God. Refusal to submit to one's authorities suggests a contentious spirit. Together, the cohesion impetus and deferral to ecclesiastical authority create and sustain a deeply embedded cultural fear of speaking. Structurally, lay members are not entitled to voice opinions that conflict with the church's teachings and certainly not to present these opinions as fact. When apologetic and dissent groups violate these norms—publicly and with mass followings—their violations cannot go unnoted by the institution. These groups must be reined in, and sometimes they must be punished.

Apologetic and dissent groups are on shaky ground online where they openly defy or renegotiate the institutional norms of cohesion and deferral to authority. During intense disembodied rhetorical battles, these groups violate norms of cohesion by promoting contention and norms of "Mormon nice" by engaging in and promoting ad hominem, aggressive attacks. Rhetorical violence is so standard among these groups that in 2014, one apologist organized what he called an annual "Friends and Foes Rendezvous" as "an opportunity to lay down your proverbial weapons and meet your Internet opponents face-to-face."[51]

Worse for Mormon orthodoxy, these groups defy authority by claiming personal authority. Of course, orthodox apologists tend to be more careful about this than dissidents, but line-crossing regularly occurs in both groups; Greg Smith's article was roundly criticized not only for its harsh tone but for its presumptuousness in taking Dehlin's worthiness to task, a judgment that should have been reserved for his bishop and stake president. This defiance is also a negotiation; each group attempts to lay claim to authority to validate their own political positions.

After Smith's article on Dehlin was suppressed by BYU's Maxwell Institute, two versions of events circulated online. In the version circulated by dissident Mormons and those critical of the apologists, the "shake-up" directly resulted from the attempted publication of the controversial article and church leaders' disdain for the ad hominem rhetoric style of FARMS's publications. In the narrative offered by Peterson and Smith, internal politics had soured at the Maxwell Institute, and its director, Bradford, went against the vision of the institute's namesake, Maxwell (himself a General Authority), by quashing the article. The question of church leadership involvement reflects these Mormons' reliance, regardless of their stances on issues of church infallibility, on authority to legitimize their position. That is, both camps invoke LDS General Authorities' viewpoints to give legitimacy to their own perspectives on appropriate LDS behavior and identity.

Despite these attempts to cull credibility from the invocations of General Authorities, some leaders and members of apologetic and dissent groups override institutional authority by directly contradicting the church or attempting to speak on its behalf. This paradox—relying on institutional authority and simultaneously ignoring it—is part of a deeper one at the heart of these groups. In their quest for authority, these communities ooze what I call "Mormon machismo"—an attempt to surpass and ignore the so-called feminine qualities of Mormonism as an affective faith that values spiritualism and sensitivity (that Mormon "burning in the bosom," the ubiquitous "Mormon nice") and instead privilege the supposedly masculine qualities associated with scientific discourse: logic, argument, and debate. In practice, empiricism in these groups occasionally gives way to another form of affect in which their rhetoric enacts violence and evokes war and plunder. In the 2012 case of FARMS and *Mormon Stories*, "personal attacks" and "hit pieces" pitted one side against the other in an ongoing territorial struggle for control over the narrative of Mormon identity.

The Ritual Role of Institutional Discipline

Because of the complex relationship between apologetic groups and the institution and because of the top-down structure of the church, which circumscribes tolerable dissent, tension arises between the agential construction of masculine identities (and their freedoms of speech as Mormon actors) and the institutional policing of these identities. Institutional discipline, whether official or implicit (though these distinctions are not insignificant within the community), creates a state of liminal indeterminacy wherein an individual's relation to the community is precarious and their status neither in nor out.[52]

An effective disciplinary process can have one of two outcomes: it can reincorporate an individual into the group by forcing public assimilation into the group's norms (via an abandonment of threatening practices), or it can cut ties with an individual altogether, banishing the perpetrator from the group to clearly designate acceptable behavior to those who remain. In this way, liminal figures are central to rituals meant to identify the group and its values: the resolution of the liminality of Mormons like Dehlin and Peterson legitimizes the status quo by showing where the borders are for affiliation.

In authoritarian religious systems, peripheral groups threaten the hegemonic status quo by offering alternative narratives around which members may organize their lives. In Mormonism, peripheral groups generally operate without institutional intervention, though surveillance of these groups is expected and assumed. Rarely, institutional discipline directed at members of peripheral groups is necessary, resulting from their disregard of central Mormon norms around authority and interpersonal comportment. The censure of both apologists and dissenters is a kind of institutionally imposed liminality, a social sanction designed to reify the limits of the group. Practically, the LDS church heads off schisms by censuring extremist voices, thereby catering to the more moderate middle ground. Ritually, the institution reinforces boundaries. The dissolution of FARMS, the ouster of Peterson from his priestly academic role, and the two-year-long discipline and ultimate excommunication of Dehlin all point to an authoritarian system in which limitations on acceptable speech are tightly policed.

In the case of apologetic censure, it might seem counterproductive for the institution to punish its most ardent supporters. Indeed, some supporters of Smith and Peterson maintained that the 2012 conflict was just "politics" at BYU and not reflective of a larger censuring of their speech. But Mormonism's tightly structured bureaucratic model, in which BYU is embedded, gives academic discipline at BYU larger ramifications in the Mormon community, even imbuing it with spiritual overtones. In another high-profile case of censuring (and censoring) out of BYU, discussed in chapter 2, religion professor Randy Bott retired from his position and left for a senior mission after his statements to the *Washington Post* on the priesthood ban on men of African descent were publicly reproved by the LDS church. Bott's statements regarding the "possible theological underpinnings" of the ban were not wrong, per se.[53] Bott accurately reflected what had long been taught to be true, that dark skin either reflects the cowardly behavior of Black souls in the preexistence or descends from the biblical Cain and Ham as a curse on their lineage and that God withheld priesthood from black-skinned men because prior to 1978, they were not prepared to handle the responsibilities associated with it (a sort of benevolent racism). And yet, those long-standing teachings (which were never demarcated as "doctrine" but were still pervasive in many LDS circles) led to Bott's infamy because he dared to speak them publicly during a time of national attention.

Of course, any speculation on the relationship between Bott's censure and his retirement is merely that. But where there are parallels between his situation and that of FARMS and Peterson, they support a reading of the Mormon institution as invested in policing even its most ardent and loyal supporters to ensure that even they do not detour from the approved discursive course. Peterson's punishment was not ecclesiastical, but because it came as it did in the context it did, it served the same function.

Punishing dissenting voices is a necessary way for the institution to police its boundaries and suppress dangerous talk. Dissenters, by definition, push back against institutional narratives; this pushback threatens institutional control over members' social, emotional, and financial commitments. In his letter of excommunication, Dehlin's stake president explained that the disciplinary council's decision resulted from Dehlin's "categorical statements opposing the doctrine of the Church, and their wide dissemination via [his] Internet presence, which has led others away from the Church."[54] Of course, it is not only insiders the institution must protect from this dangerous talk; it is equally important to mark this type of discourse as intolerable for the outside world to hear.

For Daniel Peterson and John Dehlin, public censuring acted as visible discipline for their overt Mormon machismo, reigning in dangerous displays that challenged institutional authority. The scale and type of discipline varied, with the culturally heterodox excommunicated and the conservatives publicly humiliated and brought to heel. But in both cases, the institution asserted its ever-watchful eye and ultimate disciplinary power over all participants in its cultural system.

5

Patriarchy, Feminisms, and Digital Discourse

All human beings—male and female—are created in the image of God. Each is a beloved spirit son or daughter of heavenly parents, and, as such, each has a divine nature and destiny. Gender is an essential characteristic of individual premortal, mortal, and eternal identity and purpose.

—The Church of Jesus Christ of Latter-day Saints, "The Family: A Proclamation to the World"

The taboo—it is stronger than prejudice—against women's entry into public discourse as speakers or writers, was in grave danger of being definitively broken in the mid-nineteenth century as more and more educated, literate women entered the area as imaginative writers, social critics, and reformers. The oppression of women within the dominant class was in no way as materially brutal as the oppression of women in the working class, but it had its own rationale and articulation.

—Cora Kaplan, Introduction to *Aurora Leigh*

In late 2012, in what prominent Mormon feminist Joanna Brooks called "the largest mass action of Mormon feminists in our history," a collective of LDS women around the world, united through social media, took a stand for gender equality in Mormon wards.[1] The event garnered international media attention, led to church disciplinary meetings for some participants, fractured the LDS feminist movement, and even incurred death threats against participants and organizers. Despite the outcomes, to outsiders the event itself was not readily identifiable as a radical or volatile feminist demonstration. Rather, it was the simple act of wearing pants to church, an act that did not violate any written policy or teaching of the church.

Structural constraints around idealized gender roles in Mormonism, particularly those articulated as doctrine in semantic "doctrine versus culture" debates, mark some things as clearly off-limits for faithful Mormons. Until recently, identifying as a feminist has been one of those things. But as I discussed in chapter 2, less-defined issues frequently become testing grounds for orthopraxy, above and beyond doctrinal requirements. In 2012, amid all the political and cultural attention on the LDS community, a series of highly visible events involving Mormon feminists highlighted tensions in the broader LDS community while also hinting at evolving institutional discourses about women and gender equality.

The evolution of the media event "Wear Pants to Church Day," as well as its mediated backlash, provides an illustrative glimpse into the structural constraints and cultural norms surrounding Mormon womanhood. It also highlights the ways marginalized members of already marginalized groups make sense of and locate their own identity within the confines of the group. That the event was made possible by social media marks an important development in the modern construction of social movement groups as well as the ways that modern feminisms are articulated and enacted. Mormon feminists navigate life on the fringes by appropriating Mormon narratives in digital space, creating community not despite but because of their shared Mormon roots.

"Wear Pants to Church Day" and Mediated Fallout

On December 5, 2012, Mormon feminist blogger Stephanie Lauritzen composed a lengthy post lamenting her growing disillusionment with Mormon feminism, which she felt was fighting "the same fight, generation after generation. Petitions signed and sent, marches organized, pamphlets distributed," all with no measurable effect on the LDS institution or its culture.[2] Despite her conviction that women are not treated equally within the church structure, she felt the LDS feminist movement had stagnated, and she expressed a desire to mobilize and provoke real change.

After her post was shared and discussed among members of the Feminist Mormon Housewives Society (fMhs) Facebook community group[3] (established by admins of the popular blog *Feminist Mormon Housewives*[4]), Lauritzen and her readers created a new Facebook community group, All Enlisted, as "a direct-action group for Mormon women to advocate for equality within our faith."[5] Rather than merely bemoaning inequality or discussing hopes for the future, the group would engage the institution strategically to instigate change from the inside. Modeling their efforts after the civil rights movement and female suffragettes, All Enlisted was a private forum for brainstorming and executing tangible actions on behalf of its members' conviction that women in the LDS church should be, but are not, treated and regarded equally. Their name was taken from an LDS hymn.

We are all enlisted till the conflict is o'er;
Happy are we! Happy are we!
Soldiers in the army, there's a bright crown in store;
We shall win and wear it by and by.[6]

The group's moniker foreshadowed criticisms from more orthodox Mormon ranks of militancy often associated with any hint of feminist ideology, while mirroring the warlike rhetorical moves of the apologist and dissent communities discussed in the previous chapter.

After a few days of brainstorming and contributing to an extensive list of possible activities for "peaceful resistance," All Enlisted members agreed on their first collective act. As a way of testing the waters, they planned an event that most assumed would be mild, faithful, and well received in their churches: "Wear Pants to Church Day" encouraged Mormon women around the globe to band together on one designated date to replace their standard Sunday dresses or skirts with dressy slacks as they attended weekly services at their local wards.

Wearing pants as a symbolic action is deeply rooted in struggles for women's equality throughout history; this self-conscious decision to appropriate clothing reserved for men in a particular cultural space parallels the actions of nineteenth-century female suffragettes, who also donned men's apparel as a symbol of equality (the term *bloomer* derives from its namesake, American suffragette Amelia Bloomer, who argued that women's apparel was restrictive and impractical).[7] The connection to suffragette pants-wearing, however, was not widely cited by Mormon feminists until after the pants-wearing event, likely an intentional strategy meant to avoid associating their sartorial act with radical feminism. Instead, early discussions of the event suggested it was intended to challenge unnecessary and sexist norms in Mormon culture that have no foundation in doctrine or policy.

The group moved quickly, organizing and promoting the event for Sunday, December 16, just eleven days after Lauritzen's initial blog post calling for action. Event organizers said they expected the event to receive little critical attention: after all, LDS women are not officially discouraged from wearing pants to church meetings. They are also not explicitly required or even encouraged to wear dresses or skirts. The church has set no policy on what to wear to church except to encourage members to wear "their best" as a sign of respect. A 1971 statement approved by the First Presidency and issued church-wide through the LDS magazine *New Era* states, "The Church has not attempted to indicate just how long women's or girls' dresses should be nor whether they should wear pant suits or other types of clothing.... We have not... felt it wise or necessary to give instructions on this subject relative to attendance at our church meetings, although we do feel that on such occasions they should have in mind that they are in the house of the Lord and should conduct themselves accordingly."[8]

Some All Enlisted members balked at the plan, concerned that merely wearing pants to church was too small to be a meaningful act of resistance and represented more of the nonaction that Lauritzen originally criticized. To make more of an impact, then, the group turned to the media: Event organizers sent out press releases, and the *Salt Lake Tribune*'s religion writer, Peggy Fletcher Stack, quickly issued a brief article on the event.[9] The story was eventually picked up by the news and popular press and was featured on National Public Radio and in the *New York Times*, the online feminist newsmagazine Jezebel, and the UK's *Daily Mail*.[10]

"Wear Pants to Church Day" struck a sensitive cultural nerve. In the week leading up to the event, its public Facebook event page garnered 2,026 commitments to attend (and 667 "maybes"). Because it was posted publicly and shared widely among feminists and nonfeminists alike, it also received heavy backlash. Many comments by those declining the invitation to participate echoed the sentiment of Jaimie Cummings, a commenter who wrote on the event page, "I don't think sacrament meeting [i.e., the weekly LDS church service] is an appropriate place to 'protest.' For me it's about renewing my covenants and worshipping God, not about 'proving a point.' As a woman, if I have ever felt unequal to men in the church, it is only because I have felt more special, more treasured than men, never less." Over the following two days, her comment received 12,043 likes and 1,233 replies, arousing heated debate about the dangers of protests and the proper roles of women and men. While All Enlisted members worked to gain the upper hand in these intense exchanges, the sheer amount of support for the orthodox status quo proved overwhelming, even on their own event page.

Not every person who posted on the event page was as tactful as Cummings. Many detractors called the event "stupid," "ridiculous," or a "non-issue"; one man called All Enlisted supporters "pants-wearing femanazis." Another commenter, Bret Bowman, expressed a sentiment at once misogynistic and homophobic.

> LMAO! Geez! haha... what the hell is WRONG with women in our society these days? If you're going to wear pants, they might as well get penis implants too, to make them even MORE masculine. I'm exhausted with feeling the obligation to be "half gay" in order to feel attracted to the "new and improved" arrogant "manly" women in American society. I'll tell ya, the damn liberal women's movement has all be [*sic*] destroyed God's amazingly beautiful art of "femininity". I'd love to 'weigh in', but a bunch of liberal HE-girls are not going to like my opinion of their angry, masculine ways! Haha.

While many comments like this seemed generically misogynistic, others relied on particular Mormon tropes to decry the impropriety of Pants Day. A commenter named David Waite, for instance, condemned the organizers in no uncertain terms:

> Go ahead and follow Satan's path carefully down to your own destruction. Apparently the prophet isn't the one who recieves [*sic*] Revelation for the Church anymore? Seriously you women who started this movement should be ashamed of yourselves. YOU are leading away MANY of God's children down the wrong path and some day you will have to answer for that. If you believe in the Church than [*sic*] by default you believe this is wrong. Period. End of story. I will keep you in my prayers that your lost souls will one day realize their mistakes and repent and come back to the True Church.

While the suggestion that the event had demonic connotations may seem extreme, it was by no means isolated or exceptional as a response to the event and its organizers. In addition to copious social media backlash, some conservative Mormons used their personal blogs as a place to address the issue and weigh in on what Mormon women ought to wear to church. The associate editor of the widely read, largely conservative online Meridian Magazine, Erin Ann McBride, opined that the "instigators" of Pants Day had "disappointed" her because sacrament meeting "is not the time or place for rebellion or taking a stand.... This call to action is an act of contention."[11]

The buzzword *contention* is often invoked by conservative Mormons as a powerful way to quash opinions that differ from the Mormon mainstream. (Recall from chapter 2 how Skyler Thiot's fear that his efforts to bring caffeine to Brigham Young University had become contentious led to his choice to remove his Facebook petition, and in chapter 3, "contention" was invoked as a reason why some orthodox Mormons are uncomfortable with the practice of apologetics.) McBride went on to quote at length from a Book of Mormon passage in which Christ tells his newly formed church, "And there shall be no disputations among you, as there have hitherto been; neither shall there be disputations among you concerning the points of my doctrine, as there have hitherto been. For verily, verily I say unto you, he that hath the spirit of contention is not of me, but is of the devil, who is the father of contention, and he stirreth up the hearts of men to contend with anger, one with another."[12] With one word, McBride communicated to her orthodox audience that wearing pants to church is a corruption inspired by the devil himself.

Vicious online trolling and threats of violence are par for the course when women dare speak in cyberspace, and Mormon spaces are no exception. Travis James

Richardson, whose profile described him as a philosophy student at church-owned Brigham Young University, posted publicly on the event page that "every person who is a minority activist, should be shot... in the face... point blank... GET OVER YOURSELVES...." (ellipses in original). Additionally, just days after the event page went public, an organizer reportedly received a direct message on Facebook threatening her life; All Enlisted organizers reported the threats to Facebook, to local police, and to Brigham Young University's Honor Code office. Those issues, coupled with many conservative Mormons' decision to report the Pants Day page as a Facebook violation (some reportedly claiming that the page itself was hate speech and represented religious intolerance), led to Facebook deleting the page completely on December 13, just three days before the planned event. Despite the controversies and threats, All Enlisted organizers forged ahead, organizing a separate community page also called "Wear Pants to Church Day."

For some, the cultural backlash from the event was not restricted to the comfort of cyberspace. In an interview, one of All Enlisted's members described being called in for a special meeting with her bishop to discuss whether she should be permitted to retain her temple recommend (that is, whether her involvement in the group compromised her worthiness as a Mormon woman to participate in temple rituals). She explained that her bishop questioned whether someone willing to publicly protest could possibly support the leadership of the church.

Amid this heated online rhetoric and the fear of offline reprisal, as the day approached, rumors—that pants-clad women would be asked to leave sacrament meeting or that orthodox Mormons would form a human wall outside the building to prevent their entry—began to circulate in several feminist Mormon Facebook groups, stirring the nerves of many would-be participants. Because of this uncertainty, some initial supporters of the event backed out, citing concern about social sanctions and backlash. Others felt the event had become too political and divisive, and because they identified as political moderates, they did not want to be mistaken by their ward members as "radical" feminists merely for showing up to church in pants. The term *radical feminist*, it should be noted, is routinely circulated in conservative circles (both Mormon and non-Mormon) to demonize any feminist ideas or actions, no matter how moderate.

Some women explained that even though they originally supported the event, they ultimately felt uncomfortable participating. These women saw the issues associated with Pants Day as increasingly fragmented, and they were not sure what statement they would be making by wearing pants. Indeed, the event had been described by some organizers as a stand against unfounded cultural practices that had become unduly normalized and granted doctrinal weight; by others as a way of supporting women who routinely wear pants to church (largely converts and investigators, thus already marked as outsiders) to help them feel less marginalized; by others as a show of solidarity with women who left the church on feminist grounds; and by still others as a way of drawing attention to greater issues of women's inequality in the LDS church, with pants-wearing standing in for the priesthood authority that women are denied. Some women insisted that wearing pants was not akin to protest but merely a demonstration meant to highlight inequality in the church; others explained it was neither a demonstration nor a protest—those words being too culturally loaded and signaling unfaithful, radical feminism—but instead a way of "mourning with those who mourn" (a carefully chosen and often-repeated scriptural reference, mentioned time and time again on social media and in interviews) or standing in solidarity with other sisters; and still others routinely and definitively called it a protest against doctrinally unfounded cultural norms that should have no place in church.

Polarizing participants even more was the frequent conflation of Pants Day with the idea that these women might want to "wear the pants," or take over leadership roles in the church through ordination to the all-male priesthood. In an interview broadcast on Utah's FOX 13 News, a reporter noted matter-of-factly that event organizer Lauritzen "hopes women will one day serve in the priesthood," a reference to the fact that while all worthy men over age twelve may be ordained, the priesthood is closed to women.[13] In fact, Lauritzen did not mention priesthood in any of her numerous interviews (most likely a deliberate strategy on her part). But because she had advocated for women's ordination on her blog in the past,[14] soon the idea that she was subversively using the issue of pants to grasp for priesthood became part of the oppositional narrative surrounding the event. Women's ordination remains a lightning rod for controversy among orthodox members and one of the more divisive issues among Mormon feminists, and because the televised report quoted the organizer of the event conflating that issue and Pants Day's symbolism (whether or not that was Lauritzen's intention), many women backed out for fear of marking themselves publicly as radical feminists opposed to God's order—the patriarchal order—in the church.

December 16 proved underwhelming. Although many women participated across the United States and in a handful of other countries, the event was small by all accounts. Although there are no clear data on the number of participants, only several hundred reported that they had participated; high estimates placed the number around a thousand. Based on my own interviews and information from private online groups, I estimate the number to be between two and four hundred participants worldwide, with the vast majority centered in the Intermountain West, where most U.S. Mormons reside.

Most Pants Day participants reported that they were the only woman in pants at their ward, while a few mentioned that they saw one or two other women in pants but could not be certain if it was for Pants Day. Many critics as well as feminists who did not participate and some male supporters reported that no women in their ward wore pants; anecdotally, I attended the Midvale third ward in Utah that day, in the heart of Mormondom, where zero of around eighty women wore pants (this includes two investigators and myself, an investigator of another sort).

Moreover, since Pants Day consisted of simply wearing pants to church with no other fanfare or discussion of the reasons why, it was by and large a silent action. Despite the media attention given the event, most Mormons seemed unaware the event was taking place. And even though rumors had circulated prior to the event that all women in pants at certain wards would be called in for disciplinary meetings or that women in pants would not be admitted to the church building, actual reported negative consequences were few. While some participants mentioned negative comments or perceived piercing glares from people at their wards, almost all reported no response at all.

None of this mattered, though, as Pants Day quickly became inscribed in the group's collective ethos. Despite the relatively small scale of the actual event, its outcome was circulated widely in the media.[15] In addition to bringing momentary national attention to the role of women in the LDS church, which put pressure on the institution to examine its own inequities, Pants Day served as a touchstone in the narrative of Mormon feminist identity in the months to follow. On the one hand, the day was frequently invoked as an example of the possibilities of a unified social movement. Mormon feminists in online spaces playfully encouraged one another with vague invocations like "You can do this! Because pants!" and sometimes used the term *the pants* to refer to someone or something that was both positive and boundary-pushing (e.g., when one woman dared to turn down a calling because she was too busy with other aspects of her life, a Facebook friend commented to her, "You're the pants!"). In addition to serving as an in-joke, the rhetoric around the event helped solidify Mormon feminist identity as unified and marginalized. Many Mormon feminists "came out" (their phrase) as such by wearing pants or posting about the event to their personal Facebook pages. Even when the sign went unrecognized by those in their wards, by wearing pants they marked themselves as different and chose to publicly align with the narrative of the Mormon feminist community. Wearing pants and sharing the experience online united Mormon feminists across space in ways that preinternet feminist activism simply could not do.

Inflammatory responses by conservative Mormons, almost exclusively found online, also became an important part of the feminist narrative. The shared experience of engaging in heated online rhetoric, and even the anticipation of negative social feedback, reinforced their outsider status and brought Mormon feminists together to talk back to conservative perspectives. Of course, vitriolic comments like those described in the preceding pages are incredibly common on nearly any topic in online spaces. People like these commentators are often written off as "internet trolls," individuals who take a strange pleasure in stirring up fights online. But despite their trollish nature, those comments and others like them became rallying points for the community, playing a vital role in the construction of Mormon feminist identity. Mormon feminists themselves employed these overtly misogynistic responses as foils for their own identity, recirculating these comments all over the internet in blogs, on Facebook posts, and even in media reports as representative of the type of challenge that Mormon feminism faces and as proof of the urgent role that Mormon feminism must play in LDS culture.[16] One Pants Day participant explained in an interview that the online misogyny and vitriol from conservative Mormons were emblematic of "what we're up against," indicating that these types of responses are not atypical or exceptional but mark the norm in feminist Mormon experience and reaffirming the us-versus-them mentality between Mormon feminists and traditional Mormons.

These social responses to "Wear Pants to Church Day" highlight tensions surrounding discourses of womanhood within the Mormon tradition. Similar "Wear Pants to Church Day" events were held with little to no media attention or social outcry annually for a few more years but eventually became less relevant as Mormon feminists focused their attention on other issues. And yet Pants Day is still recognized as a notable milestone in the LDS feminist movement. That Pants Day became a significant cultural moment for many Mormons illustrates that it is more than just "doctrine" that constrains women in the LDS tradition: like the expectations around caffeine consumption described in chapter 2 and the rules for proper male comportment identified in chapter 3, culture forms normative constraints on female identity. Expectations that women should wear dresses to church and the social outcry when these norms are violated illustrate the interplay of doctrine and culture that form intersecting and limiting narratives around what appropriate Mormon womanhood looks like in lived practice.

Examining the institutional rhetoric around gender and gendered roles, in the remainder of this chapter I draw on interviews and discourse analyses of online social networks and news media to explore the processes by which Mormon femininities are imagined and discursively produced against normative assumptions about Mormon womanhood. I argue that the church creates a culturally ideal feminine narrative around specific normative traits of LDS identity over and beyond doctrinal distinctions between men and women, which individual women then adopt or adapt. I begin with an exploration of the structural constraints on Mormon womanhood, including a look at historical discourse around gender and the institutional model for idealized womanhood. I then explore ways that women themselves experience gender and gendered roles as Mormons by considering the antithesis of Mormonism's idealized femininity found in the modern LDS feminist movement, which has seen unprecedented growth thanks to the internet. I then explore the rhetorical strategies used by Mormon feminists to locate themselves within the two marginalized and paradoxical identity constructs to which they belong (both "Mormon" and "feminist"). I conclude with a discussion of another once-fringe feminist movement, Ordain Women, to illustrate the interplay of choice and constraint in lived Mormon womanhood and how these are complicated by life online.

Let me be clear: this is not a feminist critique of Mormonism or a history or critique of Mormon feminism. Instead, I want to explore the ways that identity emerges as a social narrative project in a marginal community—in this case, a doubly marginal community, as Mormon identity is itself outside the American mainstream, and Mormon feminism finds itself marginalized by both the church and the broader secular community. The marginalization of Mormon feminism is, in fact, the crux of its identity narrative.

Contextualizing Mormon Womanhood: Structural Constraints on Gendered Identity

As an all-encompassing identity construct, Mormonism constrains identity to differentiate what Mormonism is from what it is not. One area in which these constraints are both highly pronounced and highly contested is the social construction and lived expression of gender. Like other aspects of normalized LDS identity, these structural constrictions have complementary nodes: those that are "official" in the sense that they are built into Mormon doctrine and religious teaching, handed down by religious authorities, and those that are "cultural" as normative expectations that develop within orthodox Mormon communities with little to no emphasis or explanation from leaders. Both the official and cultural constrictions are pervasive in the lives of active LDS women.

Before discussing trends in Mormon discourse around womanhood, we must first situate these narratives within the history and theology of the LDS church more broadly. Despite the conservative and rather rigid gender binaries in the modern church, the history of Mormonism reveals the role of social milieu in its evolving practices regarding lived gender roles. After the westward migration of the Mormon people to Utah Territory and the institution of the doctrine of celestial marriage, or polygamy, in the 1850s, Latter-day Saint women prior to the turn of the century were necessarily more liberated by modern standards than women throughout most of the United States. With husbands incapable of providing for such large families on their own and some serving time in prison on federal bigamy charges, many Mormon women sought employment outside the home when mainstream American society frowned on the practice.[17] In 1868, LDS president Brigham Young even sent several women to medical schools on the East Coast to learn useful skills and return to Utah to establish medical and midwifery practices, not out of a desire to promote gender equality, but out of a practical concern that obstetrical care should be both a Mormon and female province.[18] Moreover, partially to garner needed votes for statehood and to secure additional support for polygamy, in 1870 Utah became the second territory to grant women the vote—a full fifty years before the nation would adopt the Nineteenth Amendment.[19] Mormonism's gender roles have historically been nothing if not pragmatic, providing support for the institution's broader social goals.

After the cessation of polygamy, the church at the turn of the century began efforts to join mainstream American Protestant culture. However, it was not until the 1950s and '60s that the church took a sharp institutional turn toward promoting traditional family units and strict gender roles, with men exclusively serving as career-oriented heads of household and women as nurturing stay-at-home mothers.[20] These roles became increasingly strict as the feminist movement gained traction in the United States, coming to a head in the early 1980s. Indeed, under the leadership of Elaine A. Cannon, the general president of the church's Young Women organization (for girls aged twelve to eighteen) from 1978 to 1984, institutional rhetoric intentionally attempted to counter the cultural messages of the feminist movement. As Cannon explained, the feminist "movement was brilliantly presented [and was affecting] all the aspects of girls' lives—movies, clothes, press, etc. No longer was there a single voice saying that a woman behaves this way, thinks this way, does this, and so on."[21] The church responded to these social pressures by emphasizing traditional values and gender roles, tying these especially to women's spirituality and religious duty.

More and more since the traditional turn within the church, Mormonism's culturally constructed gender dynamics have gained increasing support from its evolving doctrine (as is often the case in conservative religions where social issues are interpreted through a strict reading of scriptures and traditions). While doctrine on gender roles was sparse in the church's early years, the church now officially states that women and men are gendered by divine order, an "eternal principle" that accounts for what are seen to be innate differences between the sexes. In the LDS origin story, all humans existed premortally as spiritual beings born of Heavenly Father—who is worshipped and discussed regularly—and his consort, a mysterious Heavenly Mother figure who is not described in any detail in any official Mormon teachings (in fact, whether there is only one Heavenly Mother or whether Heavenly Father is polygamous is an occasional source of quiet speculation). As spirit children in the preexistence, all souls are already male or female; gender is considered "an essential characteristic of individual premortal, mortal, and eternal identity and purpose."[22] It should be noted that gender and sex are conflated in LDS teachings and practice, and there is no official or cultural context among believing Mormons that allows for gender ambiguity or transgender identities. Updates to the official *General Handbook* and newly released church materials define gender as "biological sex at birth" and warn that transitioning, whether socially or surgically, is cause for church discipline.[23]

Structurally and theologically, because of gender's eternal nature, one's gender overdetermines one's roles in this life and in the life to come: men represent God through the priesthood and are the "presiding authority in the family,"[24] while women's roles are as nurturers, as they are considered to be naturally "compassionate, self-sacrificing, [and] loving."[25] Women are taught from an early age to "plan and prepare for marriage and the bearing and rearing of children," as it is their "divine right and the avenue to the greatest and most supreme happiness." This "patriarchal order," discussed in the previous chapter, follows its heavenly model: it is "the Lord's system of government," which "will continue throughout time and eternity" as "the Lord has told us that the patriarchal order will be the order of things in the highest degree of the celestial kingdom."[26] Men and women who are sealed, or married, in the LDS temple ritual create a dynastic bond that extends into eternity, as they are likewise sealed to their ancestors and to their progeny; thus marriage and child-rearing are imbued with immeasurable spiritual importance, quite literally influencing one's eternal fate.[27]

Patriarchal hierarchy is built into Mormon doctrine and practice. Worthy men and boys over age twelve are ordained first into the Aaronic Priesthood then at eighteen into the higher order Melchizedek Priesthood,[28] giving them both temporal and eternal authority to act in the name of God; thus only men can directly access the spiritual blessings and power that come with priesthood authority (one active, faithful woman who had served a mission, married in the temple, and dedicated her life to the church and to service lamented to me in an interview that her thirteen-year-old son held more authority in the eyes of her church than she ever will). Though they cannot hold it, church leaders repeatedly point out that women may access the priesthood and its accompanying blessings through their husbands and other worthy priesthood leaders. For their part, girls and women are taught to view motherhood as the highest possible womanly achievement, their equivalent of priesthood authority in its echo of the divine: "Eve and her daughters can become cocreators with God by preparing bodies for his spirit children to occupy on earth and later in eternity."[29] Some LDS leaders have even argued that during the preexistence, women chose the nurturing role of motherhood over the leadership role of the priesthood, the role of the "family heart" over the role of "family head."[30] The tendency to equate motherhood and priesthood follows the church's broader gender complementarity rhetoric: while men have the priesthood, women have motherhood; these callings are different but equally vital to God's plan. After all, only women can bring souls into the world through childbirth, and only men can help them get back to Heavenly Father through rituals and ordinances that must be conducted by holders of the priesthood.

Temporally, too, these cosmological underpinnings have consequences in the day-to-day operations of the LDS church. The patriarchal order in the home reflects the prominence of men in leadership positions. As discussed in chapter 1, the church's General Authorities are all men. Beyond spiritual and ecclesiastical decisions, the General Authorities direct the global financial operations of this incredibly wealthy organization; any input from women is at the discretion of the men in power.[31] As Brooks explains, "The global operations of the Church of Jesus Christ of Latter-day Saints are governed and directed by an all-male organizational chain of command. Mormon women may participate in some decision-making at the congregational level. But at all levels most forms of institutional power—from the power to shape the church's global policies and finances to the power to bless the sick, administer sacraments, baptize, and excommunicate—belong only to men."[32]

The historical and theological underpinnings of women's roles in the church create ambiguity around the place of women in the church today, an issue that is fraught with political and spiritual tensions. Speaking on condition of anonymity, one high-profile Mormon woman and church employee explained in 2012, "The church is really schizophrenic about women right now." For those on the outside looking in, the church's Public Affairs Department paints a view of unencumbered women free to choose their own personal educational, marriage and family, and/or career decisions, as epitomized in the prolific "I'm a Mormon" campaign. And it is certainly true that there are many successful businesswomen, politicians, and academics who are also Mormon, as well as those who have chosen other paths besides marriage and children. At the same time, internal discourse continues to privilege the stay-at-home mother as the ideal Mormon type and the most respectable life path.

The church's social media team aptly illustrated this tension in November 2012, when the now-defunct MormonMessages YouTube channel briefly posted a short video titled "You Are Not Alone." The video features a voice-over vignette and fairy-tale motifs as a deep-voiced narrator tells the story of a faithful Mormon woman whose greatest desire is to be a wife and mother. Unfortunately, she never meets her "Prince Charming," as the narrator explains, and eventually becomes an elementary school teacher instead. As the story develops, the woman becomes bitter about her lot in life; she yells at her young students and eventually sinks into a deep depression. At the end of the video, the woman has an epiphany: while she wasted years mourning her lost dream of marriage and family, she had all along been blessed with classrooms full of children to love and nurture. The video went briefly viral on social media, garnering dozens of comments and complaints from progressive Mormons and others condemning its misogyny and stereotypical representation of singleness and womanhood. It disappeared from YouTube just a few hours after it was published.

Despite the digital backlash against the video and its swift removal, the story line of "You Are Not Alone" neatly boiled down decades of LDS teachings about women's roles, highlighting the ways church discourse privileges motherhood as the highest womanly calling even when representing career-focused women. Its quick disappearance from social media signaled a slowly growing institutional awareness that gender oversimplifications don't play well in broader American culture—and the institution's willingness to bend to social pressure regarding its messaging.

Mormon Feminisms: Adopting, Negotiating, and Resisting Structural Constraints

In the modern LDS church, womanhood is idealized and constructed as a sacred calling yet devoid of authority and voice. The construction of idealized womanhood creates scripted roles for orthodox women to fill, roles that rely on specific cultural narratives and doctrine underpinning gender.

Idealized Mormon womanhood differs, of course, from lived experience, wherein Mormon women variously adopt, negotiate, and/or resist the constraints to their identities imposed by both the institution and the culture of their faith. In this section, I explore institutional and popular discourse surrounding a community of LDS women on the fringes of accepted belonging. These self-described feminists see the church as structurally and sometimes doctrinally oppressive and call for a reconsideration of the roles of men and women in the church, sometimes including advocating for women's ordination.

The use of the label "feminist" as a self-identifier mediates both orthodox and feminist Mormon women's experiences of gender.[33] The appropriation or rejection of the label is one way these communities draw lines in the sand, cordoning off identity as if it fits neatly into binaries of feminist or not feminist. Like other conservative groups, orthodox Mormon women often use the term *feminist* as a devil word, finding what they take as its connotations directly counter to their own self-perceptions. These women adopt the church's gender narratives as their own—narratives that promote separate but equal spheres for men and women. Many orthodox members consider LDS teachings to actually elevate women above men in some ways, giving women fewer spiritual responsibilities because they are viewed as spiritually superior and not in need of the accountability the priesthood demands. Faithful Mormon women often view and depict feminist Mormons as misguided, confused, or intentionally "stirring the pot" to cause contention because of their own unbelief, unrighteousness, or selfish attention-seeking. In the orthodox view, being a Mormon and a feminist marks one as clearly misunderstanding or refusing to properly internalize the church's teachings about gender.

Self-described feminist perspectives and critical attitudes toward the patriarchal structure of the church are not new in Mormonism. As institutional rhetoric around gender roles became more traditionalized, some small factions of LDS feminists began to vocally take issue with the implications of that shift. While there have always been advocates for gender equality in LDS communities, the issues came to a head in the 1970s, when some Mormons, most notably Sonia Johnson, supported the Equal Rights Amendment despite the church's vocal opposition. Johnson, it bears mentioning, was swiftly excommunicated for her involvement and stands as a foremother for the modern-day LDS feminist movement.[34] It was also during the 1970s that several East Coast Mormon women founded *Exponent II*, a progressive print quarterly meant to open dialogue about women's issues in the church. Still in publication as both a print magazine and an active website, Exponent II arguably instituted a tradition of using mass media to further the cause of Mormon feminism.[35]

The Internet and Feminist Activism

Although organized LDS feminism has been ongoing since at least the 1970s (a period some LDS feminists refer to as their first wave to underscore that despite the church's early adoption of women's suffrage, in most other ways Mormon women have been behind the curve in terms of equality in the faith), most of the concerns raised by these early feminists—such as the idealized relegation of women to the domestic sphere, the lack of female leadership positions in the church, and the issue of women's ordination—remain unchanged by the institution. So while today's LDS feminism is in (at least) its third generation, it remains in its first wave of concerns addressing basic institutional inequities.[36] The stagnancy of LDS feminism makes the role of today's online social networks even more striking, as the articulation and development of Mormon feminism in these spaces are unprecedented both in scope and in outcome. Because of increasing online access and participation, the perception of safety and anonymity by users, and the visibility of online activity, the internet provides a space for community building, identity policing, and increased exposure to culturally relevant feminist issues. In 2012, in a single year of online activism, Mormon feminists arguably earned several (albeit small-scale) institutional shifts that earlier articulations of feminism had only hoped for.

Beginning with small email listservs in the 1990s for mostly academic, progressive Mormons (who, like *Exponent II*'s readers, were largely centered on the East Coast rather than the more conservative, and more Mormon, Intermountain West), LDS feminists have consistently made use of internet space to find like-minded members and forge connections and communities. These communities were generally closed, private spaces until 2004, when Lisa Butterworth began Feminist Mormon Housewives (fMh) as a forum to discuss issues affecting Mormon women from a progressive perspective. The now largely defunct site was at its height from around 2010–14, boasting thirty thousand unique visitors a month in 2013.[37] During that time, fMh permabloggers and guest writers represented various orthodoxy levels (from completely inactive and nonbelieving to fully active, temple-worthy believers). These bloggers wrote under pseudonyms, but many of them became so prolific and active in the bloggernacle (a Mormon portmanteau combining blogosphere and tabernacle) that their offline identities were widely known.

Over time, fMh became a community hub and agenda-setter for pressing issues affecting Mormon feminists. Perhaps most significantly, it became a support group of sorts for (mostly) women who found themselves precariously situated between the expectations of their conservative religion and the ideologies and priorities of progressive feminism. In interviews and across internet platforms, many Mormon feminists cited fMh as the place where they first "cut their teeth" as feminists, learning the parlance of and issues specific to Mormon feminism after discovering the blog. They also credited fMh as the reason they were able to continue to identify as Mormons: without the group and the community support it provided, these feminists said they could not have remained in the faith at all, isolated and alone as they felt in their physical church buildings. Notably, I've noticed that many of the women I interviewed a decade ago about their involvement in fMh are no longer active there. Many of them are no longer involved in the church at all.

Several other blogs and forums developed around Mormon feminism, such as *Young Mormon Feminists* in 2012, and still others with progressive lenses began to address gender issues as an ancillary focus. Many of these groups created parallel closed Facebook pages (often overlapping in membership from one to the next) where thousands of individuals could network, strategize, and offer support through various faith struggles and transitions. In 2011, fMh organizers founded the Facebook group Feminist Mormon Housewives Society (fMhs), which changed the nature of online feminist activism. This group is closed but not secret, which in Facebook parlance means that users must request to be added to the group by a page administrator, and only members of the group can see postings to the group.

However, because it is not secret, anyone on Facebook can access the page's membership list. Conservative family, friends, and ward members might locate a clandestine feminist simply by noting their participation in the fMhs group. More problematically, as the group grew and became unwieldy, participants often expressed anxiety that "moles" might be in their midst. A handful of early reports of disciplinary actions against members of fMhs from participants whose ward members had reported them to bishops, coupled with Mormon surveillance culture, created some level of tension and nervousness among members. The fMhs group allowed participants to at once feel a sense of privacy and security while leaving them open and vulnerable to the real threat of surveillance.

Still, fMhs created unprecedented possibilities for networking not available on anonymous platforms like blog comment streams. On fMhs, Mormon feminists could see one another's real names, faces, and geographic locales and even identify mutual friends. Regional, national, and global networking was only a post away. Despite the threat of surveillance, in interviews feminist Mormons reported that they felt safe, or at least safer, to be real or authentic in these spaces. Although nothing is truly private on the internet, the closed nature of these forums provides a semblance of anonymity and privacy, allowing participants to feel secure sharing intimate aspects of not only their faith or doubt but also their personal lives and histories. Many participants in these groups express relief at having found an outlet for their frustration, venting to the group about issues that they feel unsafe sharing in their wards or on their open social networking accounts, which are visible to their offline family and friends. Because so many people participate in these groups, this open sharing is often rewarded with the empathy only available from others with shared experiences. These forms of online community often fill a void that cannot be duplicated offline; many LDS feminists say they have no other feminist friends offline and rely on support through the internet to maintain their status as Mormons.

While online communities provide support and networking, they also maintain and develop the identity constructs around which they are built. Just as faithful LDS women describe increased fulfillment in their own roles and strengthened testimonies of their rightness through their association with like-minded others, feminist Mormon women nurture and develop feminist perspectives by participation online. Many participants in online feminist spaces begin with one or two relatively small concerns—for instance, a frustration with institutional budgetary disparities for Mormon youth groups based exclusively on gender or a desire to participate in the baby blessing ceremonies currently relegated only to priesthood holders—and eventually come to recognize structural or doctrinal inequalities in other unrelated spheres. Like in all social circles in which we engage regularly, whether online or off, active participants in these online spaces adopt and replicate the narratives of the group.

Over the course of my study, many LDS feminists ultimately fell out of activity in the church, and some lost their testimony that the church is true in a spiritual sense. Like members of John Dehlin's *Mormon Stories* communities (discussed in the previous chapter), in interviews and in posts on social media, these women often attributed their loss of activity or faith directly to their online exploration of feminist issues in the church. This cycle from isolated initial issues with the church to full-blown disillusionment is not a feature of every online heterodox or feminist Mormon's experience, but it occurs with enough frequency and predictability that even some church leaders recognize the threat of the digital world to idealized Mormon womanhood.

Still, despite the power of the internet to forge new communities and strengthen communal sensibilities, its vastness makes Mormon feminism unwieldy as a unified community. While Mormon feminism is united by its overarching recognition of gender inequality within the LDS church, like many young social movement groups, it is disjointed at several basic levels. The Pants Day event and its on- and offline repercussions highlighted the fractures in Mormon feminism that threaten its cohesiveness as a social movement: it has no defined goals, no agreed-upon strategies, and no clear leaders to consistently articulate such points. Even its one point of unification, the recognition of gender inequality in the church, is ambiguous: What would Mormon gender equality look like? Is the doctrine of the church unequal or just the culture? Must women have the priesthood to be equal? Opinions vary wildly on these and other questions, and because the internet provides a platform for the full spectrum of feminist voices, Mormon feminism as a movement displays its fractured nature regularly.

Beyond these basic definitional issues, Mormon feminists have varied opinions concerning what the group's objectives, strategies, and tactics should be. There is little agreement around acceptable semantics for framing Mormon feminist activism for its nonfeminist target audiences: Should Mormon feminists actively campaign for change, lobby, raise awareness, protest, petition, demonstrate, or even ask their leaders to reconsider the church's stance on particular issues? In one case, a feminist Mormon told me she declined to sign a petition that "call[ed] upon the First Presidency… to thoughtfully consider and earnestly pray about the full integration of women into the decision-making structure of the Church and the question of women's ordination"[38] not because she was uncomfortable with the idea of ordination (she is not) but because she felt it was inappropriate to "call upon" God's chosen leaders to do anything at all, even merely to pray about and consider a new position. Her Mormon sensibilities found it presumptuous to suppose that an everyday member could make any demand on a divinely appointed leader in the first place.

In addition to its own framing dilemmas, Mormon feminism faces the challenge of confronting a preexisting organizational frame for its own movement. The conservative church has not been shy over the years in expressing its position that feminism is a misguided if not outright dangerous perspective. Elder Boyd K. Packer of the Quorum of the Twelve Apostles famously said in 1993 that the three greatest threats to members of the church came "from the gay-lesbian movement, the feminist movement… and the ever-present challenge from the so-called scholars or intellectuals."[39] To be sure, any movement that seeks to lobby for change is seen as suspect in a church that models its hierarchy after divine revelations.

Feminist Discourse: Rhetorically Locating within Marginal Communities

Facing institutionalized and cultural resistance, feminists rely on Mormon narrative strategies and coded speech to rhetorically locate themselves within the LDS community and publicly declare "We belong." These strategies mark an effort to legitimate their identities, reduce suspicion, and ultimately effect change from within. By appropriating idealized Mormon womanhood, LDS feminists speak the language of the institution and mark themselves as authentically Mormon despite discrepancies in belief, activity level, or sympathy with the organization. Their narrative strategies mark concessions to the larger ritual community's structural and cultural norms for belonging. By crafting these narratives, Mormon feminists illustrate a uniquely Mormon commitment to the community over and above individual rights.

As mentioned in chapter 4, this community-over-self orientation has long been a feature of orthodox Mormonism, from its early experiments with communalism to its modern emphasis on service, volunteerism, and self-sacrifice. The rearticulation of this priority in Mormon feminist circles underscores the value of community as a basic Mormon value. Most (but decidedly not all) Mormon feminists accept the church's paradigm for change: gradual and revealed rather than revolutionary. While some Mormon feminists hope for immediate and groundbreaking changes such as priesthood for women, most opt for strategies that privilege gradual cultural shifts over larger theological battles, exemplified by the choice to merely wear pants to church as their first large-scale group action. Despite views that make many of them marginal members by the church's standards, LDS feminists emphasize community and commitment to distinguish themselves from the liberal mainstream (that is, non-LDS) feminist movement, important because of LDS institutional and cultural suspicion of all things feminist.

Mormon feminists must strategically signal their commitment to the institution and thus their in-group status using coded speech. Their commitment to community over individual rights is discursively marked through two major strategies: a reliance on and appropriation of Mormon historical narratives and testimony sharing as a defensive communication strategy.

Appropriating History

One major motif undergirding modern Mormonism is its reliance on historical legitimacy. The use of historical accounts to garner legitimacy is an important strategy for marking oneself as part of the group (explaining in part the Mormon fixation on genealogy, which has eternal dynastic implications in LDS cosmology). Mormon identity fetishizes historical narratives, particularly concerning lineage and precedence; one important Mormon ritual involves a patriarchal blessing given to every member who discloses, among other things, the member's ancestral line in the ancient twelve tribes of Israel.[40]

Since a patriarchal blessing is largely private (though it is recorded and kept on permanent record in church databases), in practice it is many Mormons' genealogical roots to pioneer ancestors that serve to confer social authority and legitimacy. Institutionally, the church links itself to Christ's church; individually, members link themselves to Joseph Smith's. Mormons often identify their ancestry within the faith as a way of establishing their bona fides as members, with members claiming pioneer ancestry or ancestral ties to the early church having more legitimacy in many ways than others, especially first-generation converts.[41] Similarly, institutional and bureaucratic processes in the early church are often taken as blueprints for such processes today.[42]

Like their conservative counterparts, modern Mormon feminists find their identities intricately rooted in their histories. As both a means of constructing identity and a political rhetorical strategy, LDS feminists historicize the nineteenth-century roles of women in the church to illustrate women's intended equality in Mormonism (and even, among some feminists, their claim on priesthood authority). As blogger Caroline Kline has stated, "Women who want expanded roles for women's leadership have only to go back to our own Mormon past to see women who were really running their own programs, controlling their own funds, and highly visible in their callings."[43]

Mormon feminists have long relied on this type of appropriation of traditional LDS sacred narratives: much of the early work of Mormon historian and feminist Linda King Newell, for example, explored the ritual roles of women in the early church.[44] Such research imperiled some members of the September Six, notoriously excommunicated in part for feminist interpretations of LDS doctrine and history.[45] Today, these narratives are circulated in blogs, podcasts, and forum discussions, evidence of feminists' engagement with and privileging of Mormon history. In 2013, Brooks argued that Joseph Smith intended women to have priesthood power all along: "He ordained his wife Emma Smith (D&C 25:7); he told women in the Relief Society that he intended to make of them 'a kingdom of priests'; and he welcomed women to receive temple endowments, including the wearing of a garment that symbolized priesthood authority."[46]

Historical accounts are staples of feminist Mormon blogs. For instance, Feminist Mormon Housewives regularly featured podcasts and blog posts that explored historical narratives meant to buttress feminist causes, sometimes written as responses to Mormon leaders or spokespeople who questioned feminist activity. One such post identified one of church patriarch Brigham Young's daughters, Susa Young Gates, as an ally with the national women's rights movement and established her as a precedent for modern LDS feminists doing the same.[47]

The attempt to locate feminism in church history marks a particular strategy for co-opting memory: "Memory selects and distorts in the service of present interests. The present interest may be narrowly defined—memory may be called up and shaped in an instrumental fashion to support some current strategic end."[48] The location of feminist identities in Mormon history is strategic as a means of both legitimating feminist ideology and signaling belonging for Mormon feminists in the church today.

Testimony as Defensive Communication Strategy

The second narrative strategy that marks Mormon feminists' commitment to community involves a reliance on the Mormon ritual of bearing testimony as a way of grounding their identities within the ritual community. This is a way of declaring themselves faithful and co-opting that identity, in effect further marginalizing the experiences of many heterodox feminists by aligning the movement with orthodoxy as a defensive communicative strategy.

At the height of online Mormon feminist activity, several vocal (yet unofficial) leaders of the movement emerged, including the founder of Feminist Mormon Housewives, Lisa Butterworth, and its myriad bloggers; Joanna Brooks, an academic and self-styled spokesperson for heterodox Mormonism; and Kate Kelly, a prominent proponent of women's ordination to the Mormon priesthood and cofounder of the activist group Ordain Women in 2013. These figureheads crafted narratives about what a Mormon feminist looks like, believes, and does. This narrative was summed up by Brooks.

> Here is the central idea of Mormon feminism: the Mormon movement founded by Joseph Smith offers some very powerful truths that promote the dignity and equality of all people.... But there are also aspects of the church—its bureaucracy, or some aspects of the temple—that some Mormons feel do not affirm the equality or dignity of all people. And when we encounter these, we encounter contradictions at the heart of our faith. The way we deal with these contradictions is going to be very personal to every Mormon woman. Every woman must find her own answers. But to be a Mormon feminist is to support your sisters without judging their paths. Mormon feminism is solidarity. And it's knowledge.[49]

Mormon feminism, then, is a faithful proposition designed to help bring Smith's church in line with his own teachings. Not only that, but it builds on Mormon doctrinal norms around personal revelation, agency, and obtaining a personal testimony about truth ("Every woman must find her own answers" parallels the oft-repeated Mormon dictum "Everyone must receive a testimony for themselves"). Even as this statement of essential Mormon feminism echoes third-wave secular feminism, it reflects Mormon feminists' tendency to use doctrine itself to assimilate themselves into Mormon community—just as orthodox Mormons and the institution use doctrine to marginalize them.

Similarly, the website "I'm a Mormon Feminist" (mormonfeminist.org) was built as a counterpoint to the church's "I'm a Mormon" campaign website, the now-defunct mormon.org, visually mimicking the latter's series of profiles highlighting particular Mormons and their stories. "I'm a Mormon Feminist" includes a frequently asked questions section, with one question concerning whether Mormon feminists sustain their leaders, and offers this response: "Yes, we do sustain our leaders. Mormon feminists love being Mormon. As members of the Church of Jesus Christ of Latter-day Saints, we also have a testimony of the Restored Gospel. Because of this, we do believe that our current leaders were divinely placed and do receive modern revelation."[50] The spokeswoman for a feminist action group known as Women Advocating for Voice and Equality (WAVE) explained her group's framing choices: "We're trying very hard to be viewed as faithful members trying to contribute, rather than some evil feminists."[51]

This pervasive narrative depicts Mormon feminism as a faithful movement and implicitly defines *faithful* in ways that resonate with hegemonic Mormon identities. But my interviews and ethnographic work in social networks highlighted a different reality: a significant number of feminist Mormons I studied did not believe the church's historical claims, doctrinal claims, or claims of authority. All these discrepancies are points of departure that most orthodox Mormons, including most bishops and other leaders with disciplinary power, would consider decidedly *unfaithful*. Like any narrative bent on highlighting similarities and banishing difference, the feminist-as-faithful narrative built an ethos that, while enticing, obscured the actual lived realities of many Mormon feminists. But crafting a narrative that could potentially influence the culture or teachings of the church required that Mormon feminists self-consciously allude to their own faithfulness.

This tactic was on full display during the Pants Day event, when the *Washington Post*'s *OnFaith* blog featured an editorial proclaiming, "Mormon women wearing pants love the gospel." The author, herself a member of the movement, explained that the feminists involved in All Enlisted were "active, faithful members of the church" with "strong testimonies of the Gospel of Jesus Christ and a desire to serve God and His children by, among other things, attending church meetings and fulfilling callings."[52] But in my interviews, cross-referenced with publicly available blog and Facebook posts, I learned that many participants and organizers were inactive, and some had ceased believing years ago. Many participants attended their wards for the first time in years to do so wearing pants.

The contradiction between the framing of Mormon feminism as faithful and the recognition that not all LDS feminists are faithful according to cultural and institutional definitions of that term is the Achilles' heel of Mormon feminist identity. Interestingly, the framing of Mormon feminism as faithful mirrors that time-honored Mormon defensive communicative strategy, discussed in chapter 2, employed by the church and regularly criticized by progressive Mormons: obfuscating some important things to focus on other important things, with the basic motivation that the audience of a difficult message may not be prepared to understand the whole truth.

Ordain Women and the Boundaries of Tolerable Dissent

If Pants Day seemed a small and timid feminist action, another movement just months later would test the limits of Mormon feminism as a cohesive effort. Building on the efforts of prior internet-based petitions, in March 2013 human rights lawyer Kate Kelly and several other prominent Mormon feminists organized Ordain Women (OW), an organization specifically calling on the LDS church to open its all-male priesthood to women's ordination. The group's website originally featured a dozen or so profiles of feminists voicing their support for ordination and quickly gained momentum. When the website first launched, the issue of women's ordination was considered radical, and most Mormon feminists were unwilling or unable to publicly align with its goals for fear of backlash or because they simply did not agree with its goals.

In October 2013, Kelly organized the group's first mass action: a march on Temple Square itself during the biannual General Conference priesthood session, a significant annual ritual set aside for men only. The group requested standby tickets for admission to the priesthood session and were turned away. The group repeated their action the following spring, requesting advance tickets to attend the priesthood session in April. Their request was denied, and in an unusual move, the online Mormon Newsroom posted a public memorandum to the group's leaders (naming them individually) and chastised their ongoing efforts.

> Women in the Church, by a very large majority, do not share your advocacy for priesthood ordination for women and consider that position to be extreme. Declaring such an objective to be non-negotiable, as you have done, actually detracts from the helpful discussions that Church leaders have held as they seek to listen to the thoughts, concerns, and hopes of women inside and outside the Church leadership. Ordination of women to the priesthood is a matter of doctrine that is contrary to the Lord's revealed organization for His Church.
>
> Your organization has again publicized its intention to demonstrate on Temple Square.... Activist events like this detract from the sacred environment of Temple Square and the spirit of harmony sought at General Conference. Please reconsider.[53]

By directly calling out the organizers and invoking the Mormon values of cohesion and submission, the institution directly refuted OW's efforts and its participants.

Kelly and other participants moved forward with their plans but were again denied entrance. Within a month, Kelly had been placed on informal probation by her local leaders, and in June she was excommunicated. While some cultural norms around gender, like appropriate Sunday dress, have some leeway, the gendered division at the root of the patriarchal order proved too central to withstand the threat of rebellion. Yet despite the clear and present danger in supporting women's ordination, OW succeeded in making the issue a topic of bloggernacle-wide conversation, obliterating the taboo that had surrounded it for the whole of Mormon history, and increasing the number of visible supporters from a dozen to several thousand.[54] Since that time, this issue that was once the most divisive in Mormon feminist circles has become normalized. It is no longer considered extreme for a Mormon feminist to believe that women should receive priesthood ordination.

Feminisms on the Mediated Margins

Evolving doctrine and cultural norms provide structural constraints and outline a complex picture of the possibilities for acceptable Mormon womanhood. For many LDS women, this constraint provides purpose and fulfillment. Some orthodox Mormon women say they find power in their roles as wives and mothers; others say they have no concern with power but believe that God's design for the traditional family provides the only path to real happiness in this life. These women rely on church narratives regarding the importance of structure and hierarchy to understand their position vis-à-vis male leadership.

For feminist Mormons, community online serves to reinforce progressive ideologies while increasing dissatisfaction with scripted roles. These women often find offline expression of their heterodox views problematic or dangerous and attend their local wards as closeted feminists. Those who out themselves in their wards as outspoken feminists use narrative tropes to strategically locate themselves within the ritual community. These tropes mark LDS identity as centered on community loyalty over and above individual rights.

Many Mormon women who believe the church is led by God through his prophets still feel uncomfortable with their role within its structure but hesitate to name themselves feminists. These women use discursive strategies to avoid associating themselves with the negative emic connotations of the feminist label while still quietly harboring hopes for changes within the church. Cognizant of the social sanctions at risk when adopting the label or openly advocating for change in the church, some Mormon women reject the term altogether to obfuscate their deeply held feminist sentiments.

The fallout around Ordain Women illustrated the very real risk that Mormon feminists undertake by stirring up contention in the Mormon universe. Taking care not to "rock the boat," as one Mormon woman told me, feminist Mormons choose their battles carefully on Sunday, surrounded by their fellow Saints. But outside their wards and behind the computer screen, feminist Mormons form communities online where they advocate eloquently for change within their church. Sometimes, they use an anonymous screen name.

6

Identity Shifts in a Mormon Moment

> Mormons' continued eagerness to be accepted as fully American, as "mainstream," may seem a little desperate. But it is also testament to the enduring appeal of an idealized America that lives up to its pluralistic creed. Even as Mormons recognize their continued, unwilling exile from that America, we are affirming those ideals by learning, haltingly, to cope with our own messy history and to tolerate, albeit imperfectly, difference and dissent within the faith.
>
> —Kristine Haglund, "What the 'Mormon Moment' Actually Accomplished"

> Though they seem to invoke an origin in a historical past with which they continue to correspond, actually identities are about questions of using the resources of history, language, and culture in the process of becoming rather than being: not "who we are" or "where we came from," so much as what we might become, how we have been represented and how that bears on how we might represent ourselves. Identities are therefore constituted within, not outside representation.... They arise from the narrativization of the self, but the necessarily fictional nature of this process in no way undermines its discursive, material or political effectivity, even if the belongingness, the "suturing into the story" through which identities arise is, partly, in the imaginary (as well as the symbolic) and therefore, always, partly construed in fantasy, or at least within a fantasmatic field.
>
> —Stuart Hall, "Who Needs Identity?"

As the smoke cleared from the 2012 Mormon moment, the Church of Jesus Christ of Latter-day Saints emerged arguably more a part of the American mainstream than at any time in its 182-year history. Its public relations campaigns, combined with extensive (often excessive) media coverage of Mitt Romney's Mormonism, feminist activism, and wildly proliferating heterodox voices, demystified the faith, offering Mormons an unprecedented place at the table of American society. But the church that emerged thus victoriously was, in many ways, an altogether different church: one that made significant concessions to this internal and external scrutiny and one in which fractures and fissures belied its narrative of global unity and community.

Shifts within the policies, practices, and rhetoric of the Church of Jesus Christ of Latter-day Saints and Mormon identity itself are easy to overlook. In this vast, bureaucratic system, change never happens all at once; it slowly evolves in increments, through small moments that often seem insignificant to outsiders and often to Mormons themselves. It happens in moments that mark minute discursive shifts, moments that are negotiated and circulated. These eventually gain social sanction and ever so slowly shift cultural norms and official policy. Recent changes in Mormon discourse—from the muddled clarification of the church's stance on caffeine to the role of political ideology in a conservative faith; from the roles of orthodoxy and orthopraxy in determining legitimate Mormon identity to shifting discourses on the roles of women in the faith—mark responses to pressure from both inside the organization and outside scrutiny and signal adaptation in an increasingly digital world. This evolution in LDS identity—so visible in the Mormon moment—hinted at broader cultural shifts in America toward nuanced and gradually deinstitutionalized religious identities, thanks largely to the competing structural nodes present in digital culture and expression.

Thus far this book has detailed how Mormons appropriated digital space during the Mormon moment to reimagine Mormon community: by debating and pushing back against cultural norms (chapter 2), by challenging long-standing stereotypes about political identities (chapter 3), by remapping borders of acceptable identity vis-à-vis orthodoxy and orthopraxy (chapter 4), and by questioning and challenging gendered expectations and roles through organized social action (chapter 5). In this final chapter, I rely on the data from the previous chapters to argue that the pressures and features of a mediated Mormon moment in the digital age kickstarted incremental yet significant structural changes within the Church of Jesus Christ of Latter-day Saints—changes made possible and necessary by the flattening, opening power of the internet.

This is not an argument without controversy. The Church of Jesus Christ of Latter-day Saints is built on the twin doctrines of priesthood authority and continuing revelation (discussed in detail in chapters 1, 2, and 5). Together, these doctrines insist that changes in policies and doctrines of the church do not and cannot come from external or internal pressures but only through direct divine revelation to the church's all-male hierarchy in Salt Lake City. Recent shifts in doctrine and practice, coming on the heels of such external and internal pressures and made so visible by the affordances of the internet, required the institution to double down in other areas of orthodoxy and orthopraxy to combat the perception that the church's hand (read: God's hand) could be forced by the whims of social action and popular opinion.

Thus, in arguing that the context of a Mormon moment in the digital age forced change on the institution, I am also paradoxically arguing that media attention and the digital environment also reinforce continuity in the institution. Change is often a pendulum, after all, as some conservative impulses are reaffirmed for every small change that threatens the integrity of the institution—a sort of battening down of the sacred hatches. In this way, some of the strongest evidence for change in Mormonism over the last decade is its on-again, off-again institutional retrenchment and policing of its members.

In the following pages, I use institutional discourse around one highly circulated shift regarding rhetoric on race to illustrate how a digitally connected world forces institutional narratives into alignment with emerging public discourse. Then I discuss the relationship between shifting discourses more broadly and the rash of church discipline and excommunications that closed out the Mormon moment, both of which I argue signal strategic institutional efforts to accommodate a broader cultural reformation.

Media and Mormon Community

Media have always been central to the extension across space and maintenance in time of Mormon institutional narratives. Of course, Mormonism has not always had the exacting, organized bureaucratic structure of today from which to extend cohesive narratives in the first place. As described in chapter 1, as the LDS church expanded globally in the late nineteenth and early twentieth centuries, increasing decentralization made the whole enterprise unwieldy. Church auxiliaries operated independently and manuals, lesson plans, and local practices varied geographically. Because this decentralization threatened institutional authority and the potential for cohesion among its many congregations,[1] church-wide correlation efforts beginning in the 1960s intentionally streamlined all church media—scriptures, handbooks, manuals, lesson plans, tracts, videos, and more—with single-purpose messaging. The prophetic voice became the mediated and correlated voice.

In the decades that followed, Mormon leaders at both institutional and local levels cultivated fear of uncorrelated media, both implicitly and explicitly. The most dangerous of these were labeled "anti-Mormon literature," typically print material containing claims and arguments against the veracity of the Mormon faith or against its historical narratives. Because anti-Mormon literature does not promote itself as such, faithful Mormons shunned, at the behest of their leaders, all non-church-approved publications on topics related to Mormonism (sometimes including history, philosophy, and other related subjects) for fear of confronting anti-Mormon literature with its power to beguile and deceive. As one Mormon who grew up prior to the internet explained in an interview, when faithful Mormons had questions, or if they sought ammunition to defend their faith from detractors, or as they prepared materials for church talks and lessons, they relied exclusively on information published by the church. They did not turn to the local library or the religious section of local bookstores. These unmoderated sources were understood to pose a real spiritual threat to the reader, an ability to plant seeds of doubt in the guise of scientific or rational "truth."

Correlation begat a global Mormon imagined community, homogenizing Mormon culture and teachings across dispersed geographic regions and communicating these back through media. Before the internet, correlation efforts ensured that church media synchronized Mormon narratives across space and time. The legacy of correlation is also responsible for a black-and-white bifurcation of media: church-approved sources were and are "official" and thus right; all other sources, being "unofficial," are wrong. Thus, print (and later audiovisual) media provided a semblance of imagined community for Mormons worldwide beginning in the mid-twentieth century; today, new media pose an unprecedented threat to this media-induced unification.

The Challenge of the Internet

The church still attempts to correlate its message with its own sophisticated appropriation of the internet, born from its proselytizing emphasis and its need to connect with an increasingly global membership. From its public relations campaigns, search engine optimization, advanced market research techniques, interactive church websites (with user-generated content and the now-defunct "Chat with a Missionary" feature on mormon.org), and ubiquitous presence on social networking sites such as Facebook and Twitter, the institution has invested millions of dollars in staying up to date with current new media trends. The church's own websites provide streamlined access to "official," church-approved texts at the click of a mouse, which, coupled with its often-militant policing of members' blogging and social media activities (often done at a local level), enforces the legacy of correlation in a new media environment.

In an April 2008 church-wide address, Second Counselor in the First Presidency Dieter Uchtdorf praised new technologies for their ability to advance the church's message: "New technologies such as [the internet] make it possible for the gospel message to be spread throughout the world. The Church Web sites are good examples of how you can use this technology as a wonderful resource of inspiration, help, and learning." However, despite the internet's potential to spread Mormon ideology, the church remains ambivalent about it, as Uchtdorf explained: "Be cautious. These same technologies can allow evil influences to cross the threshold of your homes. These dangerous traps are only a mouse click away. Pornography, violence, intolerance, and ungodliness destroy families, marriages, and individual lives."[2]

Moral panics around new media are a common religious response, but Mormon institutional ambivalence about the internet reflects more nuanced concerns. Unlike the more clearly delineated threats of pornography or violence, the church's attitudes toward the internet in this period reflects its grappling with more surreptitious threats: easy access to information that challenges its core narratives. Indeed, the church's own problematic history is also "a mouse click away."

This understanding—that the internet contains a vast and dangerous trove of anti-Mormon information—is deeply ingrained in Mormon culture. My earliest experiences studying Mormonism in 2009 illustrate this point. During a lesson with missionaries, where we discussed Joseph Smith and the Restoration, a missionary offered to recommend some good books (he mentioned Mormon historian Richard Bushman's *Rough Stone Rolling*) or bring me further church-published reading materials if I was interested in learning more. "But," he cautioned, "don't Google 'Joseph Smith.'" His warning stemmed from a knowledge of the fraught nature of online texts, which are potentially challenging to Mormon orthodoxy. He explained that there is so much "garbage" online and that most sources are unreliable and "just want to attack" (true enough).

Of course, I did Google "Joseph Smith" that very day. (What student of media and religion could help it?) The search results spanned a wide range, from the official website of the Church of Jesus Christ of Latter-day Saints at the top, to information from Utah Lighthouse Ministry on Joseph Smith's history of fraud and his criminal record, to message boards at exmormon.org describing the LDS founder as an emotionally abusive pedophile who used threats of eternal damnation to lure his plural wives into bed.

While the internet has long been rife with this type of challenging information for those who knew where to look, many Mormons encountered it for the first time during the Mormon moment of 2012–13. This period just preceded the church's stepped-up efforts to optimize its web pages to better conform to search engine algorithms and ensure that faithful results are plentiful when searching for information on Mormonism. At that time, a searching Mormon (or non-Mormon) would instead be directed to blogs, wikis, and online communities addressing every potentially controversial point of Mormon doctrine or history.

These digital texts created an endless challenge to the LDS narrative and were, in many ways, comparable to Martin Luther's pamphleteering to arouse popular sentiment against the church authority. To outsiders, the ubiquity of this kind of information likely comes as no surprise; information is the purpose of the internet, after all. But seeing this information laid out online, complete with citations, jarred many Mormons who had dedicated their lives to the church and faithfully and ritualistically avoided anti-Mormon information. One former Mormon told me in an interview in 2012 that he first read about scientific research debunking the Book of Mormon's claims about the ancient world while browsing the internet in preparation for a Sunday School lesson: "One minute, I was a true believer, and a moment later, I was sobbing on the floor, repeating over and over, 'It's all a hoax! What are we going to do?"

Certainly, not all reactions are this visceral and immediate. More common in my interviews was a tendency for contradictory information to build up over time on what participants repeatedly referred to as a mental shelf where they would store anything they were afraid to think too deeply about for fear of upending their long-held beliefs and, in many cases, threatening their place as a member of a Mormon family and community. For many Mormons, the contents of the shelf eventually became too heavy; as their cognitive dissonance became unbearable, their shelves would collapse. Their belief in the church became unsupportable.

One website, MormonThink, gained notoriety in this period.[3] A compendium of historical and academic resources that orthodox church members decidedly viewed as antichurch literature, the site at first remained anonymous due to its owners fear of reprisal. Still, the content posted to MormonThink—lengthy and thoroughly cited commentaries on contentious issues from church history, practice, and policy—was widely trusted and cited among critical and former Mormons and other church critics. It is probably no surprise that in 2012, MormonThink editor David Twede was threatened with excommunication (he elected to resign from the website and from the LDS church).

While some Mormons dismissed websites like MormonThink as anti-Mormon and unreliable, others found them disconcerting. Even faithful, lifelong Mormons often had not heard about many topics—from details of specific archaeological finds that refute the Book of Mormon's historicity and authorship to evidence of child marriage and polyandry among early church members—that are explored in detail on MormonThink. While the website's stated goal was to neutrally examine the facts, the historical and scientific evidence it provided challenged vital aspects of the church's narrative. One man told me that after his brush with MormonThink, he adjusted his belief in the Book of Mormon to view it as "inspired but not historical." Others encountering similar information said they felt betrayed, embarrassed, or angry and told me they left the church altogether.

As this information became more widespread among Mormons, church leaders acknowledged that members—particularly the younger, tech-savvy generations—were leaving at an unprecedented rate. Some observers attributed this exodus to the internet. Marlin Jensen, emeritus General Authority and official Church Historian and Recorder from 2005 to 2012, shared that his own daughter once came to him and asked, "Dad, why didn't you ever tell me that Joseph Smith was a polygamist?" He further explained, "Everything's out there for [the younger generation] to consume if they want to Google it."[4] Over a dozen Mormons I interviewed said the first time they encountered information that threatened the church's narrative was online; of those, more than half ultimately lost faith altogether. This tally doesn't include innumerable such accounts from my online participant observation, where these stories are ubiquitous but hard to quantify, as they likely reflect the self-selection bias of the heavy internet users who populate these spaces.

While all traditionally closed belief systems are challenged by the open text of the internet, Mormonism's historical model of top-down communication faces unique challenges, since its authority structure is divinely designed and the prophetic voice inerrant. With threats to orthodoxy only a mouse click away, the complex consequences of new media convergence increasingly force the church to make concessions and accommodations to its tightfisted grasp on the Mormon narrative.

These accommodations come about in emerging institutional positions on various current issues of social concern, which have the power to alter the church at the structural level. In other words, the Mormon Church is using the internet to counter the internet—by offering up new, negotiated narratives to counteract the information that Mormons and others will inevitably encounter online. In one recent and markedly high-profile instance of this renegotiation, the church confronted historical narratives vis-à-vis race and institutional exclusion.

The Priesthood Ban Catches Up with the Church

The modern LDS church fosters an inclusive, "global church" image: while Mormonism is an American-born religion with a distinctly American narrative and headquartered in the western United States, church growth statistics claim 150 percent more members living outside than inside the United States today.[5] Mormon promotional materials, like the "I'm a Mormon" campaign and the *Meet the Mormons* film, released in select theaters in October 2014, routinely featured images and stories of international Mormons alongside their American counterparts. But this image of a diverse global church welcoming to all is threatened by the historical record, which shows a very different image of a church with racist policies and doctrines. In addition to impeding international growth by thwarting proselytizing efforts among specific ethnic and racial groups, this record raises important questions for faithful Mormons about the nature of doctrine and authority in a church where doctrine changes and authority can be wrong.

Racial differentiation and exclusion are built into the structure of Mormonism. The Book of Mormon is, at its foundation, a racially charged narrative. The plot centers on ongoing battles between two Native American tribes, the Lamanites and the Nephites. In one instance, God curses the once "white, and exceedingly fair and delightsome" Lamanites with "a skin of blackness" for their unbelief to ensure that they would "not be enticing" to the righteous, pale Nephite tribe.[6] Later, they are promised that they might turn "white and delightsome" after conversion.[7] As recently as the 1970s, brown-skinned Native people from across the Western Hemisphere (including North and South America, Mexico, Hawaii, Tonga, Samoa, and New Zealand) were routinely referred to as "Lamanites."[8] Although this term has fallen out of favor in recent decades (I have never heard it used by anyone under age fifty or so, except as a poor attempt at humor), in my ethnographic work I heard this term used repeatedly by older faithful Mormons to describe their Native friends and acquaintances and twice by Mormons who have Native ancestry and consider themselves Lamanites.[9]

Regardless of terminology, Native people continue to attract a particular flavor of Mormon missionary fervor, rooted in the Book of Mormon's prophecies that the Lamanites will ultimately join the faith. This missionary zeal reached its apex in the infamous LDS Indian Student Placement Program, which officially began in 1954 (though it had been in operation unofficially since 1947) and lasted through 2000, removing baptized Hopi and Navajo children from their reservation homes to place them in white LDS foster homes during the school year for "educational and spiritual enrichment."[10]

This preoccupation with Native people, with its paternalistic racism, is just one part of Mormonism's racial sticking points. Over the past decade, especially during the Mormon moment, critical media coverage homed in on the church's historic teachings and practices regarding Black people. With the known exception of two or three Black men ordained in its early years, from its founding, the church excluded men of African descent from the priesthood held by all otherwise worthy men over the age of twelve.[11] Black men and women were also excluded from temple participation,[12] which meant that anyone with dark skin and African or indeterminable descent was excluded from all church leadership roles and from many temple ordinances. This includes the endowment and celestial marriage, rites that are essential to Mormon exaltation in the afterlife. In keeping with Mormon belief, these policies effectively barred Black people from the highest levels of heaven itself.

For over a hundred years, this exclusion was enforced and justified by church leaders such as Brigham Young, Wilford Woodruff, and John Taylor, who variously explained the priesthood ban as a result of the curse of Cain or the behavior of Black souls in the preexistence.[13] In the first explanation, God punished Cain, the first murderer in the book of Genesis, and all his descendants with dark skin. The second explanation builds on Mormon doctrine concerning the war in heaven, when premortal souls chose between Jesus's and Lucifer's plans for the salvation of humanity: a third of the souls sided with Lucifer and became demons without mortal bodies, and the remaining two-thirds became humans who would be rewarded or punished in mortality for their degree of devotion to Christ. According to this explanation, less-valiant souls who did not take sides or were "fence-sitters" were born into mortality as Black people. Both explanations describe dark skin itself as the outward curse marking an inward ill. Brigham Young, who succeeded Joseph Smith as church president and prophet, stated, "Shall I tell you the law of God in regard to the African race? If the white man who belongs to the chosen seed mixes his blood with the seed of Cain, the penalty, under the law of God, is death on the spot. This will always be so."[14] In practice and in policy, racial lineage became one barometer for measuring worthiness.

As the civil rights movement challenged American social norms vis-à-vis race and integration, the LDS church held fast to its stance on people of African descent, even excommunicating some white members who dared protest the policy. But shifting cultural tides catch up to the shore when change becomes an institutional survival mechanism; in 1978, missionary expansion in Brazil was hampered by the indeterminate racial lineage of many dark-skinned Brazilians. The First Presidency received a revelation and lifted the priesthood ban.[15] Conversion rates skyrocketed, both in South America and across the newly opened African continent.[16]

Since lifting the priesthood ban, the church has shied away from officially addressing its history, leaving opaque the origin of the ban in the first place and never offering any statement or direction to thwart folk explanations—and certainly never offering any form of official or unofficial apology. In 1981, an updated version of the Book of Mormon changed the passage regarding dark-skinned Native converts from "white and delightsome" to "pure and delightsome," though the verse describing the original curse placed on the Lamanites, 2 Nephi 5:21, remains unchanged: "Wherefore, as they were white, and exceedingly fair and delightsome, that they might not be enticing unto my people the Lord God did cause a skin of blackness to come upon them." The idea that the priesthood ban had somehow originated with unrighteousness and a curse from God ran as a quiet undercurrent in various books and pamphlets, largely "anti-Mormon literature" written by Evangelicals or former members as exposés to challenge the authority of the church. Historians published important books on the subject, but lacking the imprimatur of the church, they were largely unread by the lay membership. The church's official teaching manuals and publications rarely explored the issue beyond mentioning the lifting of the ban as a glorious time for the church and an answer to the long-suffering prayers of its leaders, a day many faithful members said they had always believed would come.

In 2012, the issue of race in the church came to a head in large part due to the national spotlight on Mormonism during Mitt Romney's presidential bid. Several media outlets, both on and offline, began mining the issue along with other titillating topics like polygamy and church finances. As discussed briefly in chapter 2, on February 28, the *Washington Post* ran a feature on race and the LDS church quoting a popular religion professor at Brigham Young University regarding the origins of the priesthood ban. Citing the historical Mormon teaching both that Black people descended from Cain and that they were less valiant in the preexistence as potential explanations for the ban, Randy Bott also opined that withholding the priesthood from Blacks was a blessing in disguise.

> "What is discrimination?" Bott asks. "I think that is keeping something from somebody that would be a benefit for them, right? But what if it wouldn't have been a benefit to them?" Bott says that the denial of the priesthood to blacks on Earth—although not in the afterlife—protected them from the lowest rungs of hell reserved for people who abuse their priesthood powers. "You couldn't fall off the top of the ladder, because you weren't on the top of the ladder. So, in reality the blacks not having the priesthood was the greatest blessing God could give them."[17]

The article quickly circulated on social media and blogs, and the idea that racism is embedded in Mormon beliefs began to cross into political discussions around Romney's viability as a candidate, making it relevant to many non-Mormons and Mormons alike.[18] The church's racial past was no longer a boutique interest of historians and former Mormons; now, thanks to the internet's power of dissemination, the record was open to the world.

Because Bott's statements drew public attention to an embarrassing corner of the Mormon past, the church was forced to respond. The LDS Newsroom responded immediately with an "official" statement, strongly denouncing Bott's comments and insisting that they "absolutely do not represent the teachings and doctrines" of the church, that the church does not "tolerate racism in any form," that the origins and meaning of the "restriction" are unknown, and that the church "condemns any and all past racism by individuals both inside and outside the Church."[19] The statement, although it came from a public relations website and not from the First Presidency, marked an important shift in the official narrative about the priesthood ban. As opaque as it was, for the first time, the church had labeled its own past statements and teachings as racist.

Just one month later, Provo's *Daily Herald* announced Bott's impending retirement from BYU. His son went on record in the *Herald*, stating retirement had been Bott's "plan for at least the last year."[20] Although the timing may have been a coincidence, speculation swirled in online Mormon communities over whether the public condemnation he received from his leaders may have precipitated his retirement or, alternately, if his pending retirement may have loosened his lips in the first place, making Bott more comfortable sharing his perspective with the *Washington Post* regardless of the fallout. Notably, most of these conversations suggested that Bott's retirement came as a direct result of his daring to speak about an embarrassing and divisive, but not unusual, Mormon teaching. Despite the speculative nature of these conversations, the sheer plausibility (and, from this writer's perspective, likelihood) that there may have been more to this story than coincidence speaks to the well-established nature of Mormon authority and the precariousness of individuals speaking out in the church.

Toward Transparency: The Gospel Topics Essays

That Newsroom statement proved to be the first small step in a gradual institutional disavowal of the ban and a move toward greater historical transparency. Beginning in November 2013, the church gradually opened some aspects of its historical record for inspection, expanding and thus shifting its own explanations of this and other controversial topics. Unceremoniously on November 20, a section of the church's website called Gospel Topics was restructured with new content. Previously, this page had hosted an alphabetized topical encyclopedia of dozens of selected keywords in Mormon teachings, policies, and history, from Aaronic Priesthood to Zion, with a paragraph or so of information per topic.[21] The new Gospel Topics page included, at first, just five articles. Three of these, "Jesus Christ," "Gospel Learning," and "Christmas," were brief, faith-promoting articles that drew on LDS scripture and quotes and were not so different from content one might find in a General Conference address or *Ensign* article.[22]

The other two, "Are 'Mormons' Christian?" and "First Vision Accounts," were quite unlike any content the church had previously sponsored, especially the latter.[23] Observers quickly noted that these new topical essays offered "more complete and detailed information on doctrinal beliefs, practices, and historical events of the church than at any other time in its history."[24] Compared to the previous Gospel Topics page and the church's broader approach to controversial topics, these articles were so extensive and open that some Mormons on social media questioned whether the church's website had been hacked and these were actually anti-Mormon literature.

Every few months for the remainder of 2013 and 2014, a new Gospel Topics essay appeared on the website, for a total of fourteen articles ranging from one thousand to four thousand words (exclusive of footnotes), covering several of Mormonism's most controversial topics. While some have few citations or cite only the official church canon (the Standard Works), such as "Plural Marriage in the Church of Jesus Christ of Latter-day Saints," others have extensive citations and endnotes, most notably "Peace and Violence among 19th-Century Latter-day Saints," which has forty-seven.[25] While the articles had no byline, they were written in a decidedly academic style and ended with the words "The Church acknowledges the contribution of historians and scholars to the historical context set forth in this article, whose contribution is used with their permission." The historians were never named, but most Mormons who were skeptical about the Gospel Topics essays accepted them wholeheartedly when they learned that the essays were "official" and church sponsored. The imprimatur of the LDS website suggests another significant shift in Mormonism, the shift to a digital prophetic voice. The faithful trust the disembodied, invisible webmaster as if it were a hand etching divine commands in stone.

At the time of their launch, the polygamy articles received particular attention in the media for their unprecedented openness and clarity—especially for the fact that they admit openly that Joseph Smith had as many as thirty-five wives, some of them as young as fifteen and some of them already married to other men. The church was, for the first time in modern history, owning and defending the controversial details that had long been the fodder of "anti-Mormons" to denounce and embarrass the faith instead of sweeping these facts under the rug. While each of the Gospel Topics essays is apologetic in nature and by no means unbiased (speculating, for instance, that Smith never consummated his more controversial marriages), they took the unprecedented tack of challenging many long-held teachings and folk doctrines many adult members had been taught and have themselves taught to others.

On December 6, 2013, a new article, "Race and the Priesthood," appeared on the site.[26] This nearly two-thousand-word article is an attempt to put the priesthood ban in historical context, proposing that the church's establishment during a time of racial tension in American history contributed to the priesthood ban—in other words (words that the essay does not use), that the church's policies were racist because American society was racist. It also acknowledges that the complexities of tracing genealogies of converts in South America to prove or disprove their African descent contributed to the lifting of the restriction. While the article's tone is decidedly faith-promoting, it marked the first time the church addressed the reasons behind the ban in any substantive, public way.

This significant shift in Mormon discourse about the meaning and origin of the priesthood ban for the first time disavowed not only racist justifications for the ban but the ban itself by suggesting (obliquely) that it was never doctrinal in the first place. Such a suggestion absolves the institution of blame for its racist past, placing that blame squarely on the shoulders of a broader racist American culture. But this shirking of responsibility creates a new problem: admitting that LDS leaders can be wrong on important issues—in this case, for more than one hundred years.

The premiere of these in-depth Gospel Topics essays was unprecedented, but it was also unnoticed by most Mormons. Unlike prophetic pronouncements in days past, read at General Conference by LDS leaders or over the pulpit in local congregations, these articles were posted quietly on a back page of a dense website. Despite the impetus that led to the articles in the first place, they were not broadly circulated or publicized among LDS congregations. Repeatedly, Mormons reported that their local leaders, including bishops and stake presidents, remained unaware of the Newsroom and the Gospel Topics essays. Some have explained this reticence as the result of an institutional effort to walk a tightrope between explaining these difficult issues for people experiencing crises of faith while not *creating* crises of faith for others.[27] For at least some people I spoke with, the articles seemed to backfire in this way, creating an awareness of difficult issues before the reader was prepared to deal with them.

In fact, it was many months before the main page at www.lds.org/topics linked directly to the essays; prior to that, these important articles could only be located with a direct link or by searching the page for a specific title or keyword, and these extra steps made the articles difficult to find. Web-savvy Mormons and those connected to the broader Mormon web learned about the essays primarily by seeing them linked on blogs and Facebook feeds, but no press releases or announcements on official church social media were forthcoming. Their unheralded arrival, coupled with the erratic timing between each essay's publication, suggested institutional experimentation, as if the church (its public relations department? its historical department? the General Authorities?) was testing the waters of LDS response.

That hesitancy was not ill founded. Even when members did encounter the Gospel Topics essays, some remained resistant to their messages, which often contradicted the narratives they had learned in previous years. Almost a year after the appearance of the "Race and the Priesthood" article was posted, one Sunday School teacher in Hawaii learned this lesson the hard way: after he used the church's essay to answer his students' questions about the priesthood ban, Brian Dawson's local church leaders removed him from his teaching assignment and told him that Black history was not a subject fit for church discussion. The *Salt Lake Tribune* reported, "The essay on race, says Tamu Smith, co-author of *Diary of Two Mad Black Mormons*, is not all that familiar to the LDS faithful and, often, their congregational leaders. 'The majority of the church doesn't know about it,' says Smith, who has traveled the country for book signings and speaking events. 'My former stake president in Provo would not have known about it, either, if I hadn't called it to his attention.' ... It's 'great' that the essay is on the church website, Smith says, 'but people don't believe it.'"[28]

Eventually, a year after the articles first began to appear, the church issued a statement via its online Newsroom to explain the need for these essays: "We live in a world where there is so much information available on every topic. And particularly in the age of the internet, there are both good and bad sources of information. As a Church, it's important for us to research and provide official, reputable, historically accurate information about our history and doctrine."[29]

As of this writing, the Gospel Topics essays remain on the church's website,[30] but they are difficult to find from the home page or from the library page that features other resources. One page introduces the history of the Gospel Topics essay initiative, ending with this exhortation: "The Church places great emphasis on knowledge and on the importance of being well informed about Church history, doctrine, and practices.... We again encourage members to study the *Gospel Topics* essays cited in the links below as they 'seek learning, even by study and also by faith.'" There are no links below that text.[31]

Regardless of why these essays were not broadly publicized by the church and why leaders did not continue to publish similar historical content, they have become a convenient way for the church to show that it has addressed controversial issues while doing so in a way many members will never encounter. This confers an element of plausible deniability if the church is accused of obfuscating its more controversial history (an accusation that was at the fore of John Dehlin's critiques of the church, as discussed in chapter 4). Some have described these articles and other institutional efforts toward greater historical transparency as an attempt to inoculate members against the shock of learning the truth suddenly; some seminary and institute courses (for high school– and college-aged members) have begun to incorporate the essays into their curriculum.[32] By gradually and casually introducing these controversial elements of Mormon history, the institution might outrun the issues before members and investigators discover them online.

And Back to Opacity: Institutional Surveillance and Censure

LDS institutional efforts toward greater transparency are just one face of an institution ambivalent about the internet age. While simultaneously releasing the Gospel Topics essays that seemed to encourage inquiry and hard questions, the institution worked quickly to surveil, censure, and silence many of its most formidable online critics. Within its own ranks, prominent excommunications and disciplinary meetings ironically attempted to silence the very critics who had long argued for institutional accountability and transparency on many issues addressed in the Gospel Topics essays in the first place.

In June 2014, prominent feminist and Ordain Women founder Kate Kelly (discussed in chapter 5) was excommunicated. The following February, vocal critic and *Mormon Stories* founder John Dehlin (discussed in chapter 4) also faced a disciplinary council and was excommunicated. Because these two Mormons were figureheads of heterodoxy, these excommunications sent shock waves through their communities. It was clear that certain voices were not welcome within the ranks. In letters posted online and circulated widely, both Kelly's and Dehlin's local leaders explained that their respective excommunications were the results of "conduct contrary to the laws and order of the Church." Kelly's bishop went on to say, "The difficulty, Sister Kelly, is not that you say you have questions or even that you believe that women should receive the priesthood. The problem is that you have persisted in an aggressive effort to persuade other Church members to your point of view and that your course of action has threatened to erode the faith of others. You are entitled to your views, but you are not entitled to promote them and proselyte others to them while remaining in full fellowship in the Church."[33]

While the focus of Kelly's teachings differed from Dehlin's, he too was told that it was his online activism, not the content of his personal beliefs, that crossed the line from tolerable to intolerable dissent. In his excommunication letter, his stake president explained, "You have spread these teachings widely via the Internet to hundreds of people in the past and have shared with me... that you will continue to do so. I want you to know, Brother Dehlin, that this action was not taken against you because you have doubts or because you were asking questions about Church doctrine. Rather, this decision has been reached because of your categorical statements opposing the doctrine of the Church, and their wide dissemination via your Internet presence, which has led others away from the Church."[34] For both Kelly and Dehlin, the internet was their undoing. According to these documents, it was not their doubt or questions that endangered their membership; it was their equivalent of modern-day pamphleteering, in classic Lutheran fashion, that threatened the institution's authority.

After Kelly's and Dehlin's excommunications, other disciplinary actions were taken against particularly vocal heterodox and feminist Mormons across the States. Marisa and Carson Calderwood were excommunicated in May 2015 for publicly stating online that they did not believe in the Book of Mormon.[35] Kirk and Lindsay Van Allen, who were threatened with discipline and ultimately chose to resign, were called into question over Kirk's blog, where he wrote that he did not believe the doctrine of polygamy was inspired by God.[36] While some disciplinary councils were discussed in blogs and podcasts, many others went under the radar of media scrutiny. In my interviews and observations, I found evidence for a relatively large uptick in the number of disciplinary meetings held over issues of heterodoxy. In several cases, members' social media or blogging activities were reported to a bishop, then those members were called in for interviews with their local leaders and, less often, asked to attend disciplinary councils.

Because these meetings are initiated at the local level (involving bishops and stake presidents but, according to official church policy, not instigated by General Authorities or the First Presidency) and because they are considered confidential by the institution, it is difficult to say with certainty whether or not there is a growing institutional trend toward silencing vocal critics; observers such as myself only hear the stories of those who self-report by posting online, and it is easy to see that a self-selection bias might misrepresent the ubiquity of this trend. But because my embedded participant observation in Mormon online circles predated these excommunications, I noted a clear change in tone and atmosphere in online Mormon spaces. Prior to Kelly's and Dehlin's excommunications, there was a general feeling in the bloggernacle that the LDS church had moved beyond this type of banishment and was more interested in cultivating an open, big-tent approach to community, encouraging questions and even—as reflected in the Gospel Topics initiative—actively pursuing answers to difficult ones. The sudden uptick in disciplinary actions at the end of the Mormon moment put that ease in check, reminding heterodox Mormons that the institution has a vested interest in maintaining control over its narrative.

Dehlin's excommunication was particularly paradoxical considering the recent Gospel Topics initiative, as his *Mormon Stories* efforts had long sought to encourage openness about LDS history, and he had on several occasions made public appeals to the LDS church to open its historical record and teach investigators and youths the hard truths about Mormon history and practice. In fact, in interviews and across the Mormon bloggernacle, many individuals commented that the Gospel Topics initiative was a likely response to the advocacy work of Dehlin and others like him. Just as Kelly's excommunication paradoxically led to greater institutional efforts toward women's equality (see chapter 5), by forcing Dehlin and others out of the organization, strategic LDS efforts toward transparency appear less reactionary and more revelatory—features that are at the heart of the Mormon organization.

Prophetic Voice in the Digital Age

Pressures and exposure from social media catalyzed these and other institutional responses. The web is a record-keeper, providing unprecedented ability for Mormons and others to discover dissonant narratives about the church's past, forcing the institution to respond to contemporary cultural currents by altering its own discursive strategies and in some cases, like the issue of race, markedly altering its stance altogether. While the issue of race is paradigmatic, discourses around other key issues are also subtly changing—the question of caffeine, the role of polygamy in Mormon history, and the question of whether homosexuality is an inborn trait or a choice. As each narrative shift occurs, critics and insiders alike wonder about the role of the internet in these shifting discourses. If this seems like a rather underwhelming Reformation, remember that small steps like this, small shifts in discourse, are how change happens incrementally in top-down social systems. As slow as this change may seem, the internet is pushing these issues at a far faster rate than at any other time in Mormonism's past.

Shifting modern Mormon identities offer a useful model for considering how traditional authority structures change as a response to narrative discontinuity on the internet and how people make sense of identity in a digital, increasingly decentralized world. In religions that have traditionally valued the role of authority to normalize discourse around appropriate belief or behavior, the internet has confounded what it means to belong by offering new perspectives and challenging long-standing cultural paradigms. By providing a platform for instantaneous interaction across geographical space and by providing a semblance of anonymity, the internet gives voice to competing perspectives of the Mormon faith and its appropriate performance.

Imagined through print and audiovisual cultures, LDS community—as an ideal of homogeneity and cohesion worldwide—is now debunked by internet communication. The church continues to battle to correlate its message online. But the open text of the internet and the social practices that develop around it are beyond correlation, and so the church must adapt its emerging positions—an adaptation seen in the release of the Gospel Topics essays, in expanded roles for women, and in the increasing delegation of both public relations and internal communication to the online LDS Newsroom. But maintaining its authoritarian structure in the face of this flattening dynamic of the internet necessitates a strict disciplinary hand, shoring up the boundaries of the religious community. Simultaneously, Mormon vernacular communities re-create, subvert, and negotiate LDS social structures, creating disjointed and disorganized interpretive communities—communities that function as disembodied churches in their own right.

I began collecting data for this book in 2012, when the LDS church had not yet clarified—then unclarified—its stance on caffeine; when the "I'm a Mormon" campaign was new; when Mitt Romney was a candidate for president of the United States; when Mormon feminists had not yet collectively worn pants to church as a mass action or publicly petitioned for tickets to the priesthood session of General Conference; and when rumors were circulating of a mysterious online "hit piece" or "exposé," depending on one's perspective, of John Dehlin's various online activities by one Gregory Smith. Since then, the institution and vernacular communities have engaged in a virtual dance in historic Mormon fashion: expand, then contract; concede, then retreat. Each movement shifts the Mormon Overton window—that range of possibilities for life as a Mormon—and these shifts threaten cohesion and institutional control in unprecedented ways.

It has become commonplace among scholars, journalists, and interested observers to compare the modern-day effects of internet-based digital culture on religious belief and practice to the massive paradigm shifts of the sixteenth century.[37] Indeed, I myself have made and continue to make this comparison, which is rife with useful parallels to our modern situation: primarily, that sudden, ubiquitous access to information challenges religious institutions' interpretive authority and privileges the development of idiosyncratic, niche sects united through a textual imagined community. The Reformation, of course, resulted in a schism that divided Catholicism and instituted first one, then many new branches of Christianity. With today's shifts, this internet Reformation in Mormonism, the natural question arises: Will there be a Mormon schism? Will there be a grand split between orthodox and heterodox Mormon communities, resulting in new institutional organizations?

Perhaps a formal schism is unnecessary. Online communities, after all, provide catharsis and community for heterodox members unsatisfied with the narratives offered in their churches. In effect, the schisms have already occurred. The creation, for instance, of an online community for feminist Mormons is, in my view, schismatic in both cause and effect. Heterodox (and extremely orthodox) groups do not need a physical meetinghouse or an official IRS sanction to effectively be churches in many important ways (though many of these groups do meet in person on occasion, and many are tax-exempt nonprofit organizations). They have tenets of faith, scriptural texts, hierarchies of leadership, rules of engagement, and orientations to the cosmos and to one another. Individuals mark themselves as members in ritualistic ways, engage in ritualistic patterns of sharing, and recite narrative credos. They even engage in passionate proselytizing.

The institution's response to the threat of the internet's affordances is to broaden its narrative and broaden its discourses about what it means to be Mormon. And the vernacular response to the open text of the internet includes a negotiation of belonging, challenging orthodoxy and encouraging heterodoxy and new expressions of faithfulness. Whether or not this sea change in Mormonism from Web 2.0 is an unmitigated good is up for debate. It is a slow shift toward "big-tent Mormonism," allowing for the inclusion of many who a generation past might have chosen to leave or even might have been excommunicated. This shift is one that many heterodox Mormons applaud and some orthodox Mormons bemoan.[38]

In the digital age, structure still constrains Mormon identity, defining the limits for acceptable identity narratives for members. But while Mormons and others embedded within a social system are constrained by the discourses of that institution, the internet allows shifts in the borders of belonging—stretching possibilities and reimagining constraints, altering the social system at the structural level.

Notes

Introduction

1 According to the Pew Forum on Religion and Public Life's 2014 Religious Landscape Survey, American religious life is fluid: 34 percent of adults do not affiliate with the religious traditions in which they were raised. For more detailed analyses of America's religious composition, see Pew Research Center, "America's Changing Religious Landscape," May 12, 2014, https://www.pewforum.org/2015/05/12/americas-changing-religious-landscape/.
2 It must be noted that the church does not officially recognize self-described fundamentalists and insists that anyone who practices polygamy is not properly Mormon, another important example of the modern institution's effort to police Mormon identity.
3 Pew Research Center, "Romney's Mormon Faith Likely a Factor in Primaries, Not in a General Election," November 23, 2011, https://www.pewresearch.org/religion/2011/11/23/romneys-mormon-faith-likely-a-factor-in-primaries-not-in-a-general-election/.
4 Krista Tippett, "Mormon Demystified: Interview with Joanna Brooks," *On Being*, National Public Radio, October 20, 2011.
5 Jacques Derrida, "Différence," in *Identity: A Reader*, ed. Paul du Guy, Jessica Evans, and Peter Redman (Thousand Oaks: Sage, 2004), 87.
6 Derrida, "Différence," 89.
7 Derrida, 90.
8 Ferdinand de Saussure, *Writings in General Linguistics*, trans. Roy Harris, ed. Charles Bally and Albert Sechehaye (Oxford: Oxford University Press, 2006).
9 Roland Barthes, *Mythologies* (New York: Hill and Wang, 1972).
10 Louis Althusser, "Ideology Interpellates Individuals as Subjects," in *Identity: A Reader*, ed. Paul du Guy, Jessica Evans, and Peter Redman (Thousand Oaks: Sage, 2004), 31–38.
11 Louis Althusser, *For Marx* (London: Penguin, 1969).
12 Charles Taylor, *Modern Social Imaginaries* (Durham: Duke University Press, 2003).
13 Anthony Giddens, *Modernity and Self-Identity: Self and Society in the Late Modern Age* (Stanford: Stanford University Press, 1991), 82.
14 John Dewey, *Democracy and Education* (New York: Macmillan, 1916), 5.
15 Peter L. Berger and Thomas Luckmann, *The Social Construction of Reality: A Treatise in the Sociology of Knowledge* (Garden City, NY: Anchor Books, 1966).
16 James Carey, *Communication as Culture: Essays on Media and Society* (New York: Routledge, 1989), 18.
17 Erving Goffman, *The Presentation of Self in Everyday Life* (New York: Doubleday, 1959); Victor Turner, *The Ritual Process: Structure and Anti-Structure* (New York: Aldine, 1969).
18 Martin Buber, *I and Thou*, trans. Walter Kauffman (New York: Scribner, 2011).
19 Jürgen Habermas, *The Structural Transformation of the Public Sphere: An Inquiry into a Category of Bourgeois Society*, trans. Thomas Burger (Cambridge, MA: MIT Press, 1991), 49.

20 Albert O. Hirschman, *Exit, Voice, and Loyalty: Responses to Decline in Firms, Organizations, and States* (Cambridge, MA: Harvard University Press, 1970).
21 William I. Thomas and Dorothy Thomas, *The Child in America*, 2nd ed. (New York: Alfred Knopf, 1929), 572.
22 Clifford Geertz, *Interpretation of Cultures* (New York: Basic Books, 1966), 90.
23 Rom. 10:9–10, King James Bible.
24 Susan Friend Harding, *The Book of Jerry Falwell: Fundamentalist Language and Politics* (Princeton University Press, 2000), 34.
25 Harding, *Book of Jerry Falwell*, 37.
26 Catherine Bell, *Ritual: Perspectives and Dimensions* (New York: Oxford University Press, 1997), 139.
27 Turner, *Ritual Process*, 14.
28 Bruce Lincoln, "Mythic Narrative and Cultural Diversity in American Society," in *Myth and Method*, ed. Laurie L. Patton and Wendy Doniger (Charlottesville: University Press of Virginia, 1996), 166.
29 Erving Goffman, *Interaction Ritual: Essays on Face-to-Face Behavior* (New York: Anchor Books, 1967).
30 Rodney Stark, "Why Religious Movements Succeed or Fail: A Revised General Model," *Journal of Contemporary Religion* 11, no. 2 (1996): 133–46.
31 See, for example, Howard Reingold, *The Virtual Community: Homesteading on the Electronic Frontier* (Reading, MA: Addison-Wesley, 1993); and Sherry Turkle, *Life on the Screen: Identity in the Age of the Internet* (New York: Simon & Schuster, 1995).
32 See, for example, Erika Pearson, "All the World Wide Web's a Stage: The Performance of Identity in Online Social Networks," *First Monday* 14, no. 3 (2009), https://firstmonday.org/ojs/index.php/fm/article/view/2162/2127.
33 For a discussion of how these patterns manifest in online dating, see Nicole Ellison, Rebecca Heino, and Jennifer Gibbs, "Managing Impressions Online: Self-Presentation Processes in the Online Dating Environment," *Journal of Computer-Mediated Communication* 11, no. 2 (2006): 415–41, https://onlinelibrary.wiley.com/doi/full/10.1111/j.1083-6101.2006.00020.x. For discussions of online friendships more generally, see danah boyd, "Friends, Friendsters, and Top 8: Writing Community into Being on Social Network Sites," *First Monday* 11, no. 12 (2006), https://firstmonday.org/ojs/index.php/fm/article/view/1418/1336.
34 See, for example, Manuel Castells, *The Rise of the Network Society: The Information Age: Economy, Society, and Culture*, vol. 1, 2nd ed. (New York: Wiley Blackwell, 2010).
35 Hua Qian and Craig R. Scott, "Anonymity and Self-Disclosure on Weblogs," *Journal of Computer-Mediated Communication* 12 (2007): 1428–51.
36 See Tom Brignall, "The New Panopticon: The Internet Viewed as a Structure of Social Control," *Theory & Science* 3, no. 1 (2002): n.p.; and John Edward Campbell and Matt Carlson, "Panopticon.com: Online Surveillance and the Commodification of Privacy," *Journal of Broadcasting and Electronic Media* 46, no. 4 (2002): 586–606.
37 While this is explored in detail in the following chapters, one example worth mentioning here is the church's teaching that gender is a binary and is an external characteristic of the individual, which erases the experiences of gender-nonconforming Mormons.
38 Giddens, *Modernity*.
39 See Michael Holquist, *Dialogism: Bakhtin and His World*, 2nd ed. (New York: Routledge, 2002).

40 Robert Darnton, "It Happened One Night," *New York Review of Books*, June 24, 2004. https://www.nybooks.com/articles/2004/06/24/it-happened-one-night/.
41 Susanna Kim, "Is the Word 'Mormon' Really Trademarked?," ABC News, June 4, 2014, https://abcnews.go.com/Business/church-day-saints-trademark-word-mormon/story?id=23988596.

Chapter 1

1 For excellent overviews of the First Vision and Book of Mormon translation, see Richard L. Bushman, *Joseph Smith: Rough Stone Rolling* (New York: Vintage, 2007).
2 For an interesting account of copyright laws and processes vis-à-vis the Book of Mormon, see Nathaniel Hinckley Wadsworth, "Copyright Laws and the 1830 Book of Mormon," *BYU Studies* 45, no. 3 (2006): 77–95. Wadsworth suggests that while historians generally agree on an 1830 copyright, Smith may have failed to meet complex statutory requirements to obtain full legal protection. Questions about proper ownership of the sacred narrative are echoed in ongoing concerns over Mormon identity.
3 Matthew Bowman, *The Mormon People: The Making of an American Faith* (New York: Random House, 2012).
4 Bushman, *Joseph Smith*; Bowman, *Mormon People*.
5 Jan Shipps, *Sojourner in the Promised Land: Forty Years among the Mormons* (Urbana: University of Illinois Press, 2000); Jared Farmer, *Mormons in the Media, 1930–2012* (ebook), 2012, https://www.dropbox.com/s/7mmp40swqoujz3x/2012-Farmer-Mormons-in-the-Media.pdf?dl=0.
6 Mark Twain, *Roughing It* (Hartford, CT: American Publishing Company, 1872), 89; Sir Arthur Conan Doyle, *A Study in Scarlet* (New York: Penguin Books, 1995).
7 Dennis L. Lythgoe, "The Changing Image of Mormonism," *Dialogue: A Journal of Mormon Thought* 3, no. 4 (1968): 45–58; Shipps, *Sojourner*.
8 Chiung Chen and Ethan Yorgason, "'Those Amazing Mormons': The Media's Construction of Latter-day Saints as Model Minority," *Dialogue: A Journal of Mormon Thought* 32, no. 2 (1999): 107–28; Shipps, *Sojourner*.
9 Pew Research Center, "Romney's Mormon Faith Likely a Factor in Primaries, Not in a General Election," November 23, 2011, https://www.pewresearch.org/religion/2011/11/23/romneys-mormon-faith-likely-a-factor-in-primaries-not-in-a-general-election/.
10 Bowman, *Mormon People*, 194.
11 Jerry Rose, "The Correlation Program of the Church of Jesus Christ of Latter-Day Saints during the Twentieth Century" (master's thesis, Brigham Young University, 1973), 10, https://scholarsarchive.byu.edu/etd/5085.
12 LDS, "Growth into a Worldwide Church," *Church History in the Fulness of Times: Student Manual* (Salt Lake City: Church of Jesus Christ of Latter-day Saints, 2002), chap. 42, https://www.churchofjesuschrist.org/study/manual/church-history-in-the-fulness-of-times/chapter-forty-two.
13 Armand Mauss, *The Angel and the Beehive: The Mormon Struggle with Assimilation* (Chicago: University of Illinois Press, 1994); Bowman, *Mormon People*, 191.
14 Benedict Anderson, *Imagined Communities: Reflections on the Origin and Spread of Nationalism* (New York: Verso, 1991).
15 Mauss, *Angel*.
16 Peggy Fletcher Stack, "Sunstone: Designer Recalls History of LDS Church's 'Visual

Identity,'" *Salt Lake Tribune*, July 27, 2012, https://archive.sltrib.com/article.php?id=54575040&itype=CMSID.

17 Carrie A. Moore, "New LDS Ad Campaign Touts the 'Truth Restored,'" *Deseret News*, April 4, 2008, https://www.thechurchnews.com/2008/4/4/23231915/new-lds-ad-campaign-touts-the-truth-restored.

18 Jessica Lynn Skinner, "Awareness and Perceptions of Church Advertising: Student Reactions to the Mormon Church's Advertising Campaign" (master's thesis, University of Kansas, 2008), https://www.proquest.com/docview/275671975.

19 Gary C. Lawrence, *How Americans View Mormonism: Seven Steps to Improve Our Image* (Orange, CA: Parameter Foundation, 2008).

20 Joel Campbell, "Mormon Ad Campaign Draws Attention in 9 U.S. Markets," *Deseret News*, August 21, 2010, https://www.deseret.com/2010/8/21/20135975/mormon-ad-campaign-draws-attention-in-9-u-s-markets.

21 For instance, one ad concludes with its featured member saying, "I am fun. I am spontaneous yet disciplined. I am the mother of three beautiful little girls. My name is Cassandra Barney, and I am a Mormon."

22 During my primary research period, the church hosted two main websites: lds.org was a hub of information for members, and mormon.org was a missionary website for curious non-Mormons (sometimes called "investigators" in Mormon parlance). The bifurcation of online communications through insider and outsider sites mirrors broader institutional communicative strategies. These URLs have been updated in recent years in keeping with newer institutional strategies to move away from the terms *LDS* and *Mormon*. At the time of this writing, the former lds.org redirects to churchofjesuschrist.org, and mormon.org redirects to churchofjesuschrist.org/comeuntochrist; the digital insider/outsider bifurcation remains.

23 The internal process for screening profile submissions, which was opaque and never explicitly disclosed, often took many months; some Mormons I interviewed expressed disapproval that, in their words, college-aged men (that is, missionaries) mediated and sanitized the voices of "real" Mormons before they were fit to be presented to the world.

24 Jaweed Kaleem, "Hundreds of Mormon Ads Launched in New York City," Huffington Post, June 22, 2011, https://www.huffpost.com/entry/mormon-ads-new-york_n_881834.

25 Shira Telushkin, "The Facebook of Mormon," *Atlantic*, January 31, 2014, https://www.theatlantic.com/technology/archive/2014/01/the-facebook-of-mormon/283467/.

26 Peter Applebome, "A Mormon Spectacle, Way Off Broadway," *New York Times*, July 13, 2011, https://www.nytimes.com/2011/07/14/nyregion/hill-cumorah-pageant-offers-mormon-spectacle-way-off-broadway.html; Walter Kirn, "The Mormon Moment," *Newsweek*, June 5, 2011, https://www.newsweek.com/mormon-moment-67951; Michael de Groote, "Being Mormon in a Mormon Moment," *Deseret News*, September 4, 2011, https://www.deseret.com/2011/9/4/20213788/being-mormon-in-a-mormon-moment; *Newsweek*, "A Mormon Moment," September 9, 2001, https://www.newsweek.com/mormon-moment-152121.

27 In September 1993, six Mormon academics were excommunicated or disfellowshipped (i.e., excluded from key ritual practices such as temple attendance) for variously challenging, undermining, or reinterpreting church teachings on issues like Heavenly Mother, the history of polygamy in the church, and interpretations of end times prophecy. These disciplinary actions were seen by some as evidence of anti-intellectualism in the church and the church's efforts to quash divergent points of view.

28 Shipps, *Sojourner*; Terryl L. Givens, *People of Paradox: A History of Mormon Culture* (New York: Oxford University Press, 2007); Douglas J. Davies, "The Invention of Sacred Tradition: Mormonism," in *The Invention of Sacred Tradition*, ed. James R. Lewis and Olav Hammer (New York: Cambridge University Press, 2011), 56–75; Bowman, *Mormon People*.

29 For just a few examples, see Richard Bushman, "I Have a Question: What Is the Difference between the American Revolution of 1776 and the Rebellions in Our Own Time?," *Ensign* (June 1976), https://www.churchofjesuschrist.org/study/ensign/1976/06/i-have-a-question/what-is-the-difference-between-the-american-revolution-of-1776-and-the-rebellions-in-our-own-time; Newsroom, "Approaching Latter-day Saint Doctrine," Church of Jesus Christ of Latter-day Saints, May 4, 2007, https://newsroom.churchofjesuschrist.org/article/approaching-mormon-doctrine; Church of Jesus Christ of Latter-day Saints, "Bishops See National Trend in Mormon Congregations," Newsroom, February 28, 2008, https://newsroom.churchofjesuschrist.org/article/bishops-see-national-trend-in-mormon-congregations; Church of Jesus Christ of Latter-day Saints, "The Religious Experience of Mormonism," Newsroom, June 1, 2008, http://www.mormonnewsroom.org/article/the-religious-experience-of-mormonism; and Church of Jesus Christ of Latter-day Saints, "'In One Heavenly Family': Scholar Terryl Givens on Proxy Baptism," Newsroom, July 31, 2012, https://newsroom.churchofjesuschrist.org/article/proxy-baptism-terryl-givens.

30 See, for example, Kent P. Jackson, "Book Review: Richard Lyman Bushman, Joseph Smith: Rough Stone Rolling," *Mormon Historical Studies* 7 no. 2 (2006): 133–47.

31 Mauss, *Angel*.

32 Rosabeth M. Kanter, "Commitment and Social Organization: A Study of Commitment Mechanisms in Utopian Communities," *American Sociological Review* 33 (1968): 499–517. See also her monograph, *Commitment and Community: Communes and Utopias in Sociological Perspective* (Cambridge, MA: Harvard University Press, 1972).

33 Robert R. King and Kay A. King, "The Effect of Mormon Organizational Boundaries on Group Cohesion," *Dialogue: A Journal of Mormon Thought* 7, no. 1 (1972): 60–75.

34 Givens, *People*.

35 Shipps, *Sojourner*, 98.

36 Shipps, 7.

37 Newsroom, "Facts and Statistics," Church of Jesus Christ of Latter-day Saints, 2022, https://newsroom.churchofjesuschrist.org/facts-and-statistics/.

Chapter 2

1 Michel Foucault, *The History of Sexuality*, vol. 1 (New York: Penguin, 1990).

2 CIA, "United States: People and Society," *The World Factbook 2023* (Washington, DC: Central Intelligence Agency, 2023), https://www.cia.gov/the-world-factbook/countries/united-states/#people-and-society; Newsroom, "Facts and Statistics," Church of Jesus Christ of Latter-day Saints, 2022, https://newsroom.churchofjesuschrist.org/facts-and-statistics/.

3 As a rite of passage, Mormons receive individual "patriarchal blessings" that declare, among other things, their individual lineage from the house of Israel—that is, from the biblical Abraham and a particular ancient Israeli tribe; for a more thorough explanation of this teaching, see Daniel H. Ludlow, "Of the House of Israel," *Ensign* (January 1991).

4 Some scholars and critics argue that the church grossly overestimates its membership, sometimes through reported practices such as "baseball baptisms" (whereby some missionaries have been said to increase their baptism rates by inviting young boys to participate in sports activities and yet requiring them to be baptized first) and by counting inactive members, even those who have not attended since childhood, until they reach 110 years old.

5 For a pictorial guide to media representations of Mormonism from 1830 to 2012 highlighting Mormons' outsider status in largely Christian America, see Jared Farmer, *Mormons in the Media, 1930–2012* (ebook), 2012, https://www.dropbox.com/s/7mmp40swq0ujz3x/2012-Farmer--Mormons-in-the-Media.pdf?dl=0.

6 The LDS doctrine of continuing revelation is summarized in the Ninth Article of Faith: "We believe all that God has revealed, all that He does now reveal, and we believe that He will yet reveal many great and important things pertaining to the Kingdom of God" (Articles of Faith 1:9, Pearl of Great Price).

7 See Doctrine and Covenants 132:6.

8 LDS, "Prophet, Seer, and Revelator." Church of Jesus Christ of Latter-day Saints, n.d., https://history.churchofjesuschrist.org/content/prophet-seer-and-revelator.

9 *Investigator* is an emic term for anyone who is asking questions about the LDS faith with the perceived potential to convert; it is often used to describe those who engage with missionaries about church history and practice.

10 Along with the Doctrine and Covenants, the Pearl of Great Price is also considered a sacred, open-canon LDS text.

11 Robert J. Woodford, "Doctrine and Covenants Editions," in *Encyclopedia of Mormonism*, ed. Daniel H. Ludlow (Macmillan, 1992), 425–27.

12 Clifford Geertz, *Interpretation of Cultures* (New York: Basic Books, 1966); Roy Rappaport, *Ritual and Religion in the Making of Humanity* (New York: Cambridge University Press, 1999); Samuel Heilman, *The People of the Book: Drama, Fellowship, and Religion* (Livingston, NJ: Transaction, 2001).

13 See Doctrine and Covenants 26:2 and 107:27:31.

14 Paul B. Pixton, "Common Consent," in Ludlow, *Encyclopedia of Mormonism*, 297–99.

15 Rappaport, *Ritual.*

16 Rappaport.

17 For an organizational flowchart of current General Authorities, see LDS, "General Authorities and General Officers of the Church of Jesus Christ of Latter-day Saints," Church of Jesus Christ of Latter-day Saints, October 2023, https://assets.churchofjesuschrist.org/09/80/0980519967b511ee882feeeeac1e6623c39e93bf/general_authority_chart_november_2023_eng.pdf.

18 Robert R. King and Kay A. King, "The Effect of Mormon Organizational Boundaries on Group Cohesion," *Dialogue: A Journal of Mormon Thought* 7, no. 1 (1972): 60–75.

19 See Ludlow, "Of the House"; and Joseph W. Sitati, "Blessings of the Gospel Available to All," General Conference address, Church of Jesus Christ of Latter-day Saints, October 4, 2009, https://www.churchofjesuschrist.org/study/general-conference/2009/10/blessings-of-the-gospel-available-to-all. Note that the use of the word *Gentile* is another self-imposed linkage between Mormonism and Judaism; it has been said that only in Mormonism can a Jew be referred to as a Gentile.

20 M. Russell Ballard, "Prepare for the Blessings of the Temple," *Ensign* (October 2010).

21 Differentiating between knowledge versus mere belief or faith is a major narrative strategy distinguishing true insiders; see my earlier work, "Seeing the Light: Mormon

Conversion and Deconversion Narratives in Off- and Online Worlds," *Journal of Media and Religion* 12, no. 1 (2013): 16–24.

22 Douglas J. Davies, "The Invention of Sacred Tradition: Mormonism," in *The Invention of Sacred Tradition*, ed. James R. Lewis and Olav Hammer (New York: Cambridge University Press, 2011), 56–75.

23 Hyrum Smith, "The Word of Wisdom," *Times and Seasons* 3, no. 15 (1 June 1842): 800, https://www.josephsmithpapers.org/paper-summary/times-and-seasons-1-june-1842/2.

24 Willard Richards, "Journal, 1842–43: President Joseph Smith's Journal 1843 as Kept by Willard Richards," in *An American Prophet's Record: The Diaries and Journals of Joseph Smith*, ed. Scott Faulring (Salt Lake City, Utah: Signature Books in Association with Smith Research Associates, 1989), 331.

25 Matthew Bowman, *The Mormon People: The Making of an American Faith* (New York: Random House, 2012), 170.

26 Joseph Fielding McConkie and Craig J. Ostler, *Revelations of the Restoration: A Commentary on the Doctrine and Covenants and Other Modern Revelations* (Salt Lake City: Deseret Books, 1964).

27 Bowman, *Mormon People*, 170.

28 Rosabeth M. Kanter, "Commitment and Social Organization: A Study of Commitment Mechanisms in Utopian Communities," *American Sociological Review* 33 (1968): 499–517. See also King and King, "Effect of Mormon Organizational Boundaries," 60–75.

29 Kanter, "Commitment," 500.

30 Doctrine and Covenants 89:6.

31 Sterling W. Sill, "The Strait Gate," *Ensign* (July 1980), https://www.churchofjesuschrist.org/study/ensign/1980/07/the-strait-gate.

32 Thomas J. Boud, "The Energy Drink Epidemic," *Ensign* (December 2008), https://www.lds.org/ensign/2008/12/the-energy-drink-epidemic.

33 Mary Douglas, *Purity and Danger: An Analysis of the Concepts of Pollution and Taboo* (New York: Routledge, 1996), 134.

34 The Newsroom website was originally located at www.newsroom.lds.org. By 2012, when this statement was issued, it had been relocated to www.mormonnewsroom.org; at the time of this writing, it is located at newsroom.churchofjesuschrist.org.

35 This tagline remained on the website in June 2013, after the events in this story; however, the tagline has since been deleted, though it is generally understood that organizations' online newsrooms are meant to serve public and media relations functions.

36 While the original statement has since been removed from the Newsroom website, it was also reported by Ben Winslow, "LDS Church Clarifies Caffeine Use for Faithful," FOX 13 Online News, August 30, 2012, https://www.fox13now.com/2012/08/30/lds-blog-post-says-caffeine-ok-for-mormons.

37 Peggy Fletcher Stack, "OK, Mormons, Drink Up—Coke and Pepsi Are OK," *Salt Lake Tribune*, August 31, 2012, https://archive.sltrib.com/article.php?id=54797595&itype=CMSID.

38 Several days later, the entry was marked with an asterisk that indicated, "This posting has been updated since it was originally published."

39 Newsroom, "Mormonism in the News: Getting It Right," Church of Jesus Christ of Latter-day Saints, August 29, 2012, https://newsroom.churchofjesuschrist.org/article/mormonism-news--getting-it-right-august-29; emphasis mine.

40 Peggy Fletcher Stack, "Just Dew It: BYU Students Pushing for Caffeinated Colas,"

Salt Lake Tribune, September 14, 2012, https://archive.sltrib.com/article.php?id=54875621&itype=CMSID.

41 Mike Buzalka, "Mission Accomplished at BYU Dining," *Food Management*, March 1, 2009, https://www.food-management.com/fm-innovators/mission-accomplished-byu-dining.

42 Fletcher Stack, "Just Dew It."

43 Stephanie Graff, "'No Demand' for Caffeine at BYU?," *Digital Universe*, September 11, 2012, https://universe.byu.edu/2012/09/11/no-demand-for-caffeine-at-byu/.

44 Fletcher Stack, "Just Dew It"; Ben Winslow, "BYU Caffeine Movement Fizzles," FOX 13 Online News, September 13, 2012, https://www.fox13now.com/2012/09/13/byu-caffeine-movement-fizzles.

45 Crystal Myler, "Caffeine Protest Stopped on BYU's Brigham Square," *Digital Universe*, September 14, 2012, https://universe.byu.edu/2012/09/14/caffeine-policy-protest-stopped-in-brigham-square/.

46 Austin Mills, "Offer Caffeinated Beverages on Campus," Change.org petition, October 11, 2016, https://www.change.org/p/brigham-young-university-offer-caffeinated-beverages-on-campus.

47 Dieter F. Uchtdorf, "O How Great the Plan of Our God!," General Conference address, Church of Jesus Christ of Latter-day Saints, October 2016, https://www.churchofjesuschrist.org/study/general-conference/2016/10/o-how-great-the-plan-of-our-god.

48 Terryl L. Givens, *People of Paradox: A History of Mormon Culture* (New York: Oxford University Press, 2007).

49 Newsroom, "Approaching Latter-day Saint Doctrine," Church of Jesus Christ of Latter-day Saints, May 4, 2007, https://newsroom.churchofjesuschrist.org/article/approaching-mormon-doctrine.

50 Lee A. Palmer, ed., "Ward Teaching," *Improvement Era* 48, no. 6 (1945): 354, http://archive.org/stream/improvementera4806unse#page/n35/mode/2up/search/palmer.

51 Neil L. Andersen, "Trial of Your Faith," General Conference address, Church of Jesus Christ of Latter-day Saints, October 2012, https://www.churchofjesuschrist.org/study/general-conference/2012/10/trial-of-your-faith.

52 LDS, "The Family: A Proclamation to the World," Church of Jesus Christ of Latter-day Saints, 1995, https://www.lds.org/topics/family-proclamation.

53 Aaron Shafovaloff, "Mormonism, Officiality, and Plausible Deniability," Mormonism Research Ministry, 2009, https://www.mrm.org/official-doctrine; Eric Johnson, "The Mormon Taqiyya," *Mormonism Researched*, July–August 2013, https://www.mrm.org/lying-for-lord.

54 Brigham Young, "The Persecution of the Saints, Etc.," in *Journal of Discourses* 10, no. 25 (Salt Lake City: Deseret Book, 1974, 1863).

55 Daymon Mickel Smith, *The Last Shall Be First and the First Shall Be Last: Discourse and Mormon History (a Dissertation)* (CreateSpace Independent Publishing, 2010).

56 For an example of this type of apologetic defense, see Gregory Smith, "Polygamy, Prophets, and Prevarication: Frequently and Rarely Asked Questions about the Initiation, Practice, and Cessation of Plural Marriage in the Church of Jesus Christ of Latter-day Saints," Foundation for Apologetic Information and Research, 2005, https://www.fairlatterdaysaints.org/archive/publications/polygamy-prophets-and-prevarication.

57 Gordon B. Hinckley, quoted in David van Biema, "Kingdom Come," *Time*, August 4,

1997, https://content.time.com/time/subscriber/article/0,33009,986794-7,00.html; ellipsis in original.

58 Jamie Reno, "Exclusive: Brigham Young's Great-Great-Granddaughter on Mormonism and Mitt Romney," Daily Beast, August 7, 2012, https://www.thedailybeast.com/exclusive-brigham-youngs-great-great-granddaughter-on-mormonism-and-mitt-romney.

59 Claudia Bushman, "Women's Agency in the Contemporary LDS Church: Popular Perspectives," panel presented at the Women and the LDS Church Conference, University of Utah, Salt Lake City, August 25, 2012.

60 Armand Mauss, *The Angel and the Beehive: The Mormon Struggle with Assimilation* (Chicago: University of Illinois Press, 1994), 125.

61 Jason Horowitz, "The Genesis of a Church's Stand on Race," *Washington Post*, February 28, 2012, https://www.washingtonpost.com/politics/the-genesis-of-a-churchs-stand-on-race/2012/02/22/gIQAQZXyfR_story.html.

62 Newsroom, "Church Statement regarding 'Washington Post' Article on Race and the Church," Church of Jesus Christ of Latter-day Saints, February 29, 2012, https://newsroom.churchofjesuschrist.org/article/racial-remarks-in-washington-post-article.

63 Geertz, *Interpretation*, 90.

64 James E. Faulconer, "Why a Mormon Won't Drink Coffee but Might Have a Coke: The Atheological Character of the Church of Jesus Christ of Latter-day Saints," *Element* 2, no. 2 (2006): 21–37.

65 Scott Gordon, "Journeys of Faith on the Internet," panel discussion, the Mormonism and the Internet Conference, Utah Valley University, Orem, March 29, 2012.

66 Howard W. Hunter, "Your Temple Recommend," *New Era* (April 1995), https://www.churchofjesuschrist.org/study/new-era/1995/04/your-temple-recommend.

67 Alan Hurst, "Of Caffeine and Covenants," *Peculiar People* (blog), September 19, 2012, https://www.patheos.com/blogs/peculiarpeople/2012/09/of-caffeine-and-covenants/.

68 Givens, *People*, 1.

69 Stuart Hall, "Encoding/Decoding," in *Media and Cultural Studies*, ed. Meenakshi Gigi Durham and Douglas M. Kellner (Malden, MA: Blackwell, 2001), 170.

70 Jacques Derrida, "Difference," in *Identity: A Reader*, ed. Paul du Guy, Jessica Evans, and Peter Redman (Thousand Oaks: Sage, 2004), 87, 89.

71 Derrida, 90.

Chapter 3

1 David Corn, "Secret Video: Romney Tells Millionaire Donors What He Really Thinks of Obama Voters," *Mother Jones*, September 17, 2012, https://www.motherjones.com/politics/2012/09/secret-video-romney-private-fundraiser/.

2 Jill Lawrence, "Will Mormon Faith Hurt Bid for White House? Mitt Romney Says His Religion Isn't a Factor, but Some Voters Say It Is," *USA Today*, February 13, 2007, 1A; Wesley Pruden, "Then It's Agreed: They're Sorry," *Washington Times*, December 14, 2007, A04.

3 Michael Fletcher, "S.C. Economy Trumps Other Concerns in GOP Primary," *Washington Post*, July 9, 2011, A01; Christina Lamb, "Gloves Are off as Obama Hits at 'Weird' Mitt; a Worried Presidential Team Has Seized on the Mormon Faith of His Biggest Republican Rival," *Sunday Times* (London), October 23, 2011, 36; Lisa Miller, "Mitt

Romney's Hard-Hearted Twist on the Mormon Work Ethic," *Washington Post*, September 20, 2012, B02.

4 Harold Bloom, *The American Religion*, 2nd ed. (New York: Chu Hartley, 2006); Simon Critchley, "Why I Love Mormonism," *Opinionator* (blog), September 16, 2012, https://archive.nytimes.com/opinionator.blogs.nytimes.com/2012/09/16/why-i-love-mormonism/; Richard T. Hughes, "The Mormon Faith and the Romney Doctrine of American Exceptionalism," *Huffington Post Blog*, September 12, 2012, https://www.huffpost.com/entry/mormon-faith-and-the-romney-doctrine-of-american-exceptionalism_b_1874881?utm_hp_ref=religion; Matthew Bowman, *The Mormon People: The Making of an American Faith* (New York: Random House, 2012).

5 Bloom, *American*, 96.

6 See 1 Nephi 13:14, Book of Mormon; 3 Nephi 11:8, Book of Mormon; and Doctrine and Covenants 84:2–3.

7 See 1 Nephi 13:12, Book of Mormon; 1 Nephi 13:17–19, Book of Mormon; and Richard Bushman, "I Have a Question: What Is the Difference between the American Revolution of 1776 and the Rebellions in Our Own Time?," *Ensign* (June 1976), https://www.churchofjesuschrist.org/study/ensign/1976/06/i-have-a-question/what-is-the-difference-between-the-american-revolution-of-1776-and-the-rebellions-in-our-own-time.

8 Doctrine and Covenants 101:80; see also Dallin H. Oaks, "The Divinely Inspired Constitution," *Ensign* (February 1992), https://www.churchofjesuschrist.org/study/ensign/1992/02/the-divinely-inspired-constitution.

9 See, for example, D. Michael Stewart, "I Have a Question: What Do We Know about the Purported Statement of Joseph Smith That the Constitution Would Hang by a Thread and That the Elders Would Save It?," *Ensign* (June 1976), https://www.churchofjesuschrist.org/study/ensign/1976/06/i-have-a-question/did-joseph-smith-say-that-the-constitution-would-hang-by-a-thread-and-that-the-elders-would-save-it?/.

10 Lydia Saad, "In U.S., 22% Are Hesitant to Support a Mormon in 2012," Gallup, June 20, 2011, https://news.gallup.com/poll/148100/hesitant-support-mormon-2012.aspx.

11 Amy Sullivan, "Mitt Romney's Evangelical Problem," *Washington Monthly*, September 2005, https://washingtonmonthly.com/2005/09/01/mitt-romneys-evangelical-problem/.

12 Pew Research Center, "Romney's Mormon Faith Likely a Factor in Primaries, Not in a General Election," November 23, 2011, https://www.pewresearch.org/religion/2011/11/23/romneys-mormon-faith-likely-a-factor-in-primaries-not-in-a-general-election/.

13 Terryl L. Givens, *The Viper on the Hearth: Mormons, Myths, and the Construction of Heresy* (New York: Oxford University Press, 1997), 22.

14 Ernst Anton Jentsch, *On the Psychology of the Uncanny*, trans. and ed. Roy Sellars (Basingstoke: Palgrave Macmillan, 2009); Sigmund Freud, *The Uncanny*, trans. David McClintock (London: Penguin Books, 2003).

15 Article VI, paragraph 3.

16 Michele Dillon, "Can Post-secular Society Tolerate Religious Differences?," *Sociology of Religion* 71, no. 2 (2010): 139–56.

17 For a fascinating discussion of this movement and its ties to ideas about religious and sexual purity, see Sara Moslener, *Virgin Nation: Sexual Purity and American Adolescence* (New York: Oxford University Press, 2015).

18 Clyde Wilcox and Carin Robinson, *Onward Christian Soldiers? The Religious Right in American Politics*, 4th ed. (Boulder: Westview, 2010).

19 Pew Research Center, "The Media, Religion and the 2012 Campaign for President,"

December 14, 2012, https://www.pewresearch.org/journalism/2012/12/14/media-religion-and-2012-campaign-president/.

20 CNN Political Unit, "Perry Supporter Says Romney's Religion 'a Cult,'" CNN, October 7, 2011, https://www.cnn.com/2011/10/08/politics/perry-response-mormonism/index.html.

21 Robert Jeffress, "Video of Pastor Robert Jeffress at Values Voter Summit," *Deseret News*, October 8, 2011, https://www.deseret.com/2011/10/8/20221616/video-of-pastor-robert-jeffress-at-values-voters-summit.

22 Richard A. Oppel Jr. and Erik Eckholm, "Prominent Pastor Calls Romney's Church a Cult," *New York Times*, October 7, 2011, https://www.nytimes.com/2011/10/08/us/politics/prominent-pastor-calls-romneys-church-a-cult.html.

23 Michael Otterson, "Michael Otterson: How Do Mormons Answer 'Not Christian' Claims?," *Deseret News*, October 23, 2011, https://www.deseret.com/2011/10/23/20224969/how-do-mormons-answer-not-christian-claims.

24 See, for example, Stephanie Condon, "Billy Graham's Organization Removes Mormonism from Its List of Cults," CBS News, October 18, 2012, https://www.cbsnews.com/news/billy-grahams-organization-removes-mormonism-from-its-list-of-cults/; Colleen Curry, "Billy Graham's Website Removes 'Mormonism' from Cult List," ABC News, October 18, 2012, https://abcnews.go.com/blogs/politics/2012/10/billy-grahams-website-removes-mormonism-from-cult-list; and Abby Ohlheiser, "Bill Graham Is No Longer Saying Mormonism Is a Cult for Some Reason," *Slate*, October 16, 2012, https://slate.com/news-and-politics/2012/10/billy-graham-website-scrubbed-of-mormonism-cult-reference-after-endorsement.html.

25 Billy Graham Evangelistic Association, "Looking for Answers: What Is a Cult?," BillyGraham.org, 2010, retrieved via Internet Archive at http://web.archive.org/web/20100605052727/http://www.billygraham.org/articlepage.asp?ArticleID=2072.

26 Dennis L. Lythgoe, "The Changing Image of Mormonism," *Dialogue: A Journal of Mormon Thought* 3, no. 4 (1968): 45–58; Jan Shipps, *Sojourner in the Promised Land: Forty Years among the Mormons* (Urbana: University of Illinois Press, 2000).

27 Pew Research Center, "Romney's Mormon Faith."

28 Harold Bloom, "Will This Election Be the Mormon Breakthrough?," *New York Times*, November 12, 2011, https://www.nytimes.com/2011/11/13/opinion/sunday/will-this-election-be-the-mormon-breakthrough.html.

29 Sally Denton, "Romney and the White Horse Prophecy," Salon, January 29, 2012, https://www.salon.com/2012/01/29/mitt_and_the_white_horse_prophecy/.

30 Penn Jillette, "Mitt's Magical Mormon Undies: Penn Jillette's Rant Redux," Big Think, September 18, 2012, https://www.youtube.com/watch?v=_qJDd-2tM-A.

31 Margaret Doris, "Mitt's Magic Underwear and the Granny Ass Dance," *Esquire* (blog), August 30, 2012, https://www.esquire.com/news-politics/news/a15568/mitt-romney-mormon-underwear-12188879/.

32 Archon Fung, "Infotopia: Unleashing the Democratic Power of Transparency," *Politics and Society* 41, no. 2 (2013): 185.

33 Christopher Hitchens, "Mitt Romney and the Weird and Sinister Beliefs of Mormonism," *Slate*, October 17, 2011, https://slate.com/news-and-politics/2011/10/is-mormonism-a-cult-who-cares-its-their-weird-and-sinister-beliefs-we-should-be-worried-about.html.

34 Lane Williams, "Mormon Media Observer: Time to End the Secrecy Allegation against Mormons," *Deseret News*, August 27, 2012, https://www.deseret.com/2012/

8/27/20505941/mormon-media-observer-time-to-end-the-secrecy-allegation-against-mormons/.

35 "Media, Religion."

36 For example, see Joseph D. Becker, "Romney's Religion: Should It Matter?," *Commonweal Magazine*, May 31, 2012, https://www.commonwealmagazine.org/romneys-religion.

37 Guy Raz, "'Ask Mormon Girl' Discusses Mitt Romney's Candidacy," *All Things Considered*, National Public Radio, December 2, 2011, http://www.npr.org/2011/12/02/143063003/ask-mormon-girl-discusses-mitt-romneys-candidacy.

38 Randall Balmer, "Why Mitt Romney Needs to Talk Openly about His Mormon Faith," *New Republic*, February 6, 2012, http://www.newrepublic.com/article/politics/100375/romney-mormon-election-religion#primary-form.

39 Hitchens, "Mitt Romney."

40 Stacey Solie, "Jim Lehrer: Ask Mitt Romney If He Stands by Mormonism's Views of Women," Daily Beast, October 2, 2012, https://www.thedailybeast.com/jim-lehrer-ask-mitt-romney-if-he-stands-by-mormonisms-views-of-women.

41 Amy Sullivan, "The De Facto Religious Test in Presidential Politics," *Time*, October 21, 2011, https://swampland.time.com/2011/10/21/the-de-facto-religious-test-in-presidential-politics/.

42 Tim Rutten, "A Religious 'Test' for Mitt Romney," *Los Angeles Times*, June 1, 2011, https://www.latimes.com/opinion/la-xpm-2011-jun-01-la-oe-0601-rutten-20110601-story.html.

43 Shmuley Boteach, "Are Mormons Any Weirder Than the Rest of Us?," *Jerusalem Post*, November 28, 2011, https://www.huffpost.com/entry/are-mormons-any-weirder-t_b_1116390.

44 Sheryl Gay Stolberg, "For Romney, a Role of Faith and Authority," *New York Times*, October 15, 2011, https://www.nytimes.com/2011/10/16/us/politics/for-romney-a-role-of-faith-and-authority.html.

45 McKay Coppins, "What's with Mitt's Mormon Money?," BuzzFeedNews, January 24, 2012, https://www.buzzfeednews.com/article/mckaycoppins/whats-with-mitts-mormon-money; McKay Coppins, "Mitt Skips the Mormon Moment," BuzzFeedNews, January 13, 2012, https://www.buzzfeednews.com/article/mckaycoppins/mitt-skips-the-mormon-moment; McKay Coppins, "A Brief Guide to 'Mormon Underwear,'" BuzzFeedNews, January 25, 2012, https://www.buzzfeednews.com/article/mckaycoppins/a-brief-guide-to-mormon-underwear.

46 McKay Coppins, "A Mormon Reporter on the Romney Bus," BuzzFeedNews, November 14, 2012, https://www.buzzfeednews.com/article/mckaycoppins/a-mormon-reporter-on-the-romney-bus.

47 Pew Research Center, "Americans Learned Little about the Mormon Faith, but Some Attitudes Have Softened," December 14, 2012, https://www.pewresearch.org/religion/2012/12/14/attitudes-toward-mormon-faith/.

48 See, for example, Kristi Keck, "Romney Takes Leap of Faith with Religion Speech," CNN Politics, December 6, 2007, https://www.cnn.com/2007/POLITICS/12/05/romney.speech/; and Scott Neuman and Barbara Bradley Hagerty, "Romney Seeks to Allay Concerns about His Faith," NPR, December 6, 2007, https://www.npr.org/2007/12/06/16970082/romney-delivers-speech-on-faith.

49 Mitt Romney, "Faith in America" (speech), George H. W. Bush Presidential Library,

College Station, Texas, December 6, 2007, https://www.npr.org/templates/story/story.php?storyId=16969460.

50 Keck, "Romney Takes Leap."

51 The original statement, "Political Neutrality," from the Newsroom of Church of Jesus Christ of Latter-day Saints (February 4, 2012) can be viewed via the Internet Archive at https://web.archive.org/web/20120204165855/http://www.mormonnewsroom.org/official-statement/political-neutrality; see the latest at Newsroom, "Political Neutrality and Participation," Church of Jesus Christ of Latter-day Saints, June 1, 2023, https://newsroom.churchofjesuschrist.org/official-statement/political-neutrality. While the IRS requires religious organizations to remain "politically neutral" to qualify for tax-exempt, 501(c)(3) status, the church often engaged in politics as an institution, dating back to the first prominent Mormon to campaign for the presidency: in 1844, Joseph Smith himself ran on an independent platform, sending ambassadors to all twenty-six states to simultaneously campaign and preach the gospel; see Arnold K. Garr, "Joseph Smith: Campaign for President of the United States," *Ensign* (February 2009), https://www.churchofjesuschrist.org/study/ensign/2009/02/joseph-smith-campaign-for-president-of-the-united-states.

52 Emily Schultheis, "Mormon Church Runs Search Ads on Romney's Name," Politico, November 5, 2012, https://www.politico.com/blogs/burns-haberman/2012/09/mormon-church-runs-search-ads-on-romneys-name-134567.

53 Coppins, "Mormon Reporter."

54 Coppins.

55 Jessica Ravitz, "The Making of Mitt Romney: A Look at His Faith Journey," originally published via *CNN Belief Blog*, October 27, 2012, excerpted in Mark, "Mitt Romney's Faithful Life," *Get Religion* (blog), November 13, 2011, https://www.getreligion.org/getreligion/2011/11/mitt-romneys-faithful-life.

56 Coppins, "Mormon Reporter." I have frequently heard the same argument to explain why Heavenly Father is venerated and discussed specifically and often but not Heavenly Mother: she is too sacred. If she were discussed openly, she too might be dragged through the mud.

57 Glenn Beck, "Polygamy? Magic Underwear? People on Bikes? Glenn Discusses Mormon Myths in TheBlaze TV Special!," TheBlaze TV, September 6, 2012, https://www.glennbeck.com/2012/09/06/polygamy-magic-underwear-people-on-bikes-glenn-discusses-mormon-myths-in-theblaze-tv-special/.

58 Scott Taylor, "Mormons & Media: A Presidential Spin, Thanks to Romney, Huntsman," *Deseret Morning News*, February 1, 2011, https://www.deseret.com/2011/2/1/20170901/mormons-media-a-presidential-spin-thanks-to-romney-huntsman.

59 Jamshid Ghazi Askar, "Analysis: How a Mormon Can Be U.S. President," *Deseret Morning News*, February 1, 2011, https://www.deseret.com/2011/2/1/20170921/analysis-how-a-mormon-can-be-u-s-president.

60 Richard Larsen, "Comparing Obama, Romney on Religion," *Idaho State Journal*, March 22, 2008.

61 Quoted in Mandy Morgan, "BYU Students Energized by Alum Mitt Romney's Presidential Bid," *Deseret News*, November 6, 2012, https://www.deseret.com/2012/11/6/20509346/byu-students-energized-by-alum-mitt-romney-s-presidential-bid.

62 Thomas Burr, "Harry Reid: Mitt Romney Is Not the Face of Mormonism," *Salt Lake Tribune*, September 24, 2012. https://archive.sltrib.com/article.php?id=54958981&itype=CMSID.

63 Lane Williams, "Mormon Media Observer: What Mitt Might Have Said," *Deseret News*, September 4, 2012, https://www.deseret.com/2012/9/4/20506233/mormon-media-observer-what-mitt-might-have-said.
64 Pat Bagley, "Thanks to Mitt Romney, Mormonism Is under the Microscope," *Salt Lake Tribune*, September 8, 2012, https://archive.sltrib.com/article.php?id=54851585&itype=CMSID.
65 Linda Eyre and Richard Eyre, "The Mormon Speech We Wish Romney Would Give," *Deseret News*, August 2, 2012, https://www.deseret.com/2012/8/28/20505976/the-mormon-speech-we-wish-romney-would-give.
66 Balmer, "Why Mitt Romney Needs to Talk Openly."
67 Daymon Mickel Smith, *The Last Shall Be First and the First Shall Be Last: Discourse and Mormon History (a Dissertation)* (CreateSpace Independent Publishing, 2010).
68 Gregory A. Prince, "Mitt Romney Is *Not* the Face of Mormonism," *Huffington Post Blog*, September 19, 2012. https://www.huffpost.com/entry/mitt-romney-is-not-the-face-of-mormonism_b_1897404.
69 Burr, "Harry Reid."
70 Miller, "Mitt Romney's Hard-Hearted Twist."
71 Peggy Fletcher Stack, "Memo to Mitt: Mormons Make Up That 47% on Assistance, Too," *Salt Lake Tribune*, September 25, 2012, https://archive.sltrib.com/article.php?itype=CMSID&id=54965674.
72 Gina Colvin, "Should Romney Repent? 'Yes!', Says the Prophet Mormon," *Patheos* (blog), September 20, 2012, https://www.patheos.com/blogs/kiwimormon/2012/09/should-romney-repent-yes-says-the-prophet-mormon/.
73 Jana Riess, "Mormon Throwdown: Harry Reid Goes Mano-a-Mano with Mitt Romney," *Religion News Service* (blog), September 24, 2012. Retrieved via Internet Archive at https://web.archive.org/web/20140928091649/https://archives.religionnews.com/blogs/jana-riess/mormon-throwdown-harry-reid-goes-mano-a-mano-with-mitt-romney.
74 Joanna Brooks, "Is Romney's Foreign Policy Problem a Product of His Mormonism?," *Religion Dispatches* (blog), September 17, 2012, https://religiondispatches.org/is-romneys-foreign-policy-problem-a-product-of-his-mormonism/.
75 Joanna Brooks, "My Take: Hard Truths Matter; I'm Mormon, and I'm Voting for Obama," *CNN Belief Blog*, October 18, 2012, retrieved via Internet Archive at https://web.archive.org/web/20121021040640/http://religion.blogs.cnn.com/2012/10/18/my-take-hard-truths-matter-im-mormon-and-im-voting-for-obama/.
76 For a discussion of factive versus commissive performatives, see Roy Rappaport, *Ritual and Religion in the Making of Humanity* (New York: Cambridge University Press, 1999).
77 While his nomination suggests that he had enough support in the Republican party to serve as the nominee, whether his bid for presidency ultimately failed because of his faith remains unclear.

Chapter 4

1 Faithful Answers, Informed Response (FAIR), https://www.fairlatterdaysaints.org. In 2013, the organization's name was changed to FairMormon; in 2021, it was renamed FAIR, retooling the acronym as Faithful Answers, Informed Response.
2 https://www.mormonstories.org/.
3 These discussions took place in many forums, most notably the bulletin board–style

message boards at www.mormondiscussions.com (now https://discussmormonism.com/) and www.exmormon.org as well as in private Facebook groups.

4 For example, Gregory L. Smith, "Shattered Glass: The Traditions of Mormon Same-Sex Marriage Advocates Encounter Boyd K. Packer," *Mormon Studies Review* 23, no. 1 (2011): 61–85, https://scholarsarchive.byu.edu/cgi/viewcontent.cgi?article=1835&context=msr.

5 Gregory L. Smith, "Introduction," in *An Open Letter to Dr. Michael Coe*, Foundation for Apologetic Information and Research, 2011, https://www.fairlatterdaysaints.org/archive/publications/an-open-letter-to-dr-michael-coe.

6 Smith, "Shattered Glass."

7 Gregory L. Smith, "Dubious 'Mormon' Stories: A Twenty-First Century Construction of Exit Narratives," *Interpreter: A Journal of Mormon Thought*, February 23, 2013, https://journal.interpreterfoundation.org/wp-content/uploads/2013/02/SMITH1-Review-Mormon-Stories.pdf.

8 BYU, "A New Beginning for the *Mormon Studies Review*," Neal A. Maxwell Institute for Religious Scholarship, July 23, 2012, https://scholarsarchive.byu.edu/insights/vol32/iss3/4/.

9 Daniel Peterson, personal email to Gerald Bradford, June 14, 2012, https://www.reddit.com/r/mormon/comments/v5zwt/very_seriously_yours_daniel_c_peterson/.

10 Daniel Peterson, conference remarks, August 3, 2012.

11 *Interpreter: A Journal of Mormon Thought*, https://journal.interpreterfoundation.org/journal/.

12 Bryan King to John Dehlin, February 9, 2015, in John Dehlin, press release, February 10, 2015, https://www.mormonstories.org/wp-content/uploads/2015/01/JohnDehlinDisciplinaryCouncilPressRelase-FinalV4.pdf.

13 For instance, when some prominent (and heterodox) Mormon academics questioned Dehlin's account of the reasons for his disciplinary council (in particular, his insistence that his LGBT advocacy was the impetus), he responded by describing them as apologists—denoting to his supporters that their allegiance is with the institution rather than with truth.

14 Dissent communities range from sympathetic forums for progressive Mormons like New Order Mormon (http://forum.newordermormon.org/) and the public Facebook group for LGBT allies Mormons Building Bridges (https://www.facebook.com/groups/mormonsbuildingbridges/) to hostile communities for former members like Facebook's closed group Ex Mormons Worldwide (https://www.facebook.com/groups/70210653951/) and the bulletin board–style communities Post-Mormon (http://postmormon.org) and Recovery from Mormonism (http://exmormon.org).

15 In my ethnographic work, I've seen evidence that the turnover in these and other heterodox Mormon groups online follows a pattern reflecting the gradual dissociation of leave-takers from Mormonism as their primary social sphere. The pattern of awareness of issues, immersion in heterodox groups, and construction of a new identity is loosely reflected in my work on deconversion narratives (see Avance "Seeing the Light: Mormon Conversion and Deconversion Narratives in Off- and Online Worlds," *Journal of Media and Religion* 12, no. 1 [2013]: 16–24); many subjects then become less active and eventually leave these communities, presumably because their social needs are eventually met elsewhere, though more work needs to be done to understand whether they replace their involvement in online communities with other groups, return to Mormon orthodoxy, or engage in something else entirely.

16 Avery Cardinal Dulles, *A History of Apologetics*, 2nd ed (San Francisco: Ignatius Press, 2005).

17 James R. Clark, *Messages of the First Presidency of the Church of Jesus Christ of Latter-day Saints*, vol. 2 (Salt Lake City: Bookcraft, 1965), 239.

18 LDS, "Internet," in *Handbook 2: Administering the Church*, 21.1.22 (Salt Lake City: Church of Jesus Christ of Latter-day Saints, 2010), 183, https://www.churchofjesuschrist.org/bc/content/shared/content/english/pdf/language-materials/08702_eng.pdf?lang=eng. The inclusion or exclusion of such a disclaimer on any given Mormon's website or blog is often a telling first clue as to the level of orthodoxy represented there; nearly every orthodox blog and website I studied includes this disclaimer.

19 B. H. Roberts, *Studies of the Book of Mormon*, ed. Brigham D. Madsen (Urbana: University of Illinois Press, 1985).

20 Boyd Jay Peterson, *Hugh Nibley: A Consecrated Life* (Draper, UT: Greg Kofford Books, 2002).

21 LDS, "FARMS Becomes Part of BYU," *Ensign* (January 1998), https://www.lds.org/ensign/1998/01/news-of-the-church/farms-becomes-part-of-byu.

22 Scott Gordon, interview, September 20, 2012.

23 Gordon, interview.

24 Steve Densley, interview, September 17, 2012.

25 Fawn Brodie, *No Man Knows My History: The Life of Joseph Smith*, 2nd ed. (New York: Vintage, 1995).

26 See, for example, Jerald Tanner and Sandra Tanner, *Mormonism: Shadow or Reality?* (Modern Microfilm); and Jerald Tanner and Sandra Tanner, *Evolution of the Mormon Temple Ceremony: 1842–1990* (Salt Lake City: Utah Lighthouse Ministry, 1990).

27 David G. Bromley, "The Social Construction of Contested Exit Roles: Defectors, Whistleblowers, and Apostates," in *The Politics of Religious Apostasy: The Role of Apostates in the Transformation of Religious Movements*, ed. David G. Bromley (Westport, CT: Praeger, 1998), 19.

28 Neal A. Maxwell, "The Net Gathers of Every Kind," General Conference address, Church of Jesus Christ of Latter-day Saints, October 1980, https://www.churchofjesuschrist.org/study/general-conference/1980/10/the-net-gathers-of-every-kind.

29 Neal A. Maxwell, "Becometh as a Child," General Conference address, Church of Jesus Christ of Latter-day Saints, April 1996, https://www.churchofjesuschrist.org/study/general-conference/1996/04/becometh-as-a-child.

30 Neal A. Maxwell, "Remember How Merciful the Lord Hath Been," General Conference address, Church of Jesus Christ of Latter-day Saints, April 2004. https://www.churchofjesuschrist.org/study/general-conference/2004/04/remember-how-merciful-the-lord-hath-been.

31 Densley, interview.

32 Densley, interview.

33 Neil L. Andersen, "Trial of Your Faith," General Conference address, Church of Jesus Christ of Latter-day Saints, October 2012, https://www.churchofjesuschrist.org/study/general-conference/2012/10/trial-of-your-faith.

34 See Religious News Service, "Mormon Church Said to Be Keeping Files on Dissenters," *Times-News*, August 13, 1992, 5B; D. Michael Quinn, *The Mormon Hierarchy: Extensions of Power* (Salt Lake City: Signature Books, 1997), 311; FAIR, "Question: What Is the Strengthening Church Members Committee?," Faithful Answers, Informed Response, 2014, https://www.fairlatterdaysaints.org/answers/Mormonism_and_Church_discipline/Strengthening_Church_Members_Committee.

35 https://www.fairlatterdaysaints.org.
36 Michael Otterson, "Anti-Church Material," interview with Ruth Todd (Salt Lake City: Church of Jesus Christ of Latter-day Saints, July 2, 2012), https://www.youtube.com/watch?v=JSUvFTQu5nY.
37 Densley, interview.
38 John Dehlin, interview, October 4, 2012.
39 These include the podcasts *The Gift of the Mormon Faith Crisis, A Thoughtful Faith, Mormon Mental Health, and Mormon Matters* as well as the websites stayLDS.org, gaymormonstories.org, and openstoriesfoundation.org. Now-defunct affiliated projects include the *Mormon Stories Sunday School* podcast and the websites mormonresearchfoundation.org (which became defunct in 2012) and mormonstoriesgermany.org (which is still hosted but has not been updated since 2018).
40 Originally Dehlin organized regional support groups for those in faith transitions or crises, but when the tone of some of these groups became increasingly hostile and local conferences and meetings became difficult to oversee—there were reports of drunken revelry and marital infidelity—Dehlin distanced himself from official affiliation with any groups but his own, which he closely monitors and oversees.
41 His popularity is not unquestioned among heterodox and dissenting Mormons, however; some feel that he takes his ownership of his podcast communities too seriously, censures members too authoritarian, fails to create a safe space for women and feminism, and reproduces the hierarchical structure of the church that he criticizes.
42 Rosalynde Welch, "The Odd Couple: Story and Community," *Patheos* (blog), June 28, 2012, https://www.patheos.com/latter-day-saint/odd-couple-rosalynde-welch-06-29-2012.
43 Dehlin, interview.
44 Rosemary Avance, "Seeing the Light: Mormon Conversion and Deconversion Narratives in Off- and Online Worlds," *Journal of Media and Religion* 12, no. 1 (2013): 16–24.
45 Elizabeth E. Brusco, *The Reformation of Machismo: Evangelical Conversion and Gender in Columbia* (Austin: University of Texas Press, 1995), 129.
46 For an excellent overview of Mormonism's embodiment of American ideals for masculinity as a way of attempting to mainstream with the broader culture, see Elizabeth Ruchti, "The Performance of Normativity: Mormons and the Construction of an American Masculinity," *Journal of Men, Masculinities, and Spirituality* 1, no. 2 (2007): 137–54.
47 Joan Acker, "Hierarchies, Jobs, Bodies: A Theory of Gendered Organizations," *Gender & Society* 4, no. 2 (1990): 139–58.
48 For more on LDS expectations for women's deferral to men's priesthood authority, see LDS, *Latter-day Saint Woman*, vol. 1 (Salt Lake City: Church of Jesus Christ of Latter-day Saints, 2000), 93–96.
49 For example, see Ezra Taft Benson, "Worthy Fathers, Worthy Sons," General Conference address, Church of Jesus Christ of Latter-day Saints, October 1985, https://www.churchofjesuschrist.org/study/general-conference/1985/10/worthy-fathers-worthy-sons; Kim Crenshaw Sorenson, "A Latter-day Father's Guidebook," *Ensign* (February 1995), https://www.churchofjesuschrist.org/study/ensign/1995/02/a-latter-day-fathers-guidebook.
50 David Knowlton, "On Mormon Masculinity," *Sunstone* 88 (1992), 24, https://sunstone.org/wp-content/uploads/sbi/articles/088-19-31.pdf.
51 Jonathan Max Wilson, "Announcing the 1st Semiannual LDS Friends & Foes

Rendezvous," *Millennial Star* (blog), February 13, 2014, https://www.millennialstar.org/announcing-the-1st-semiannual-lds-friends-foes-rendezvous/.

52 Victor Turner, *The Ritual Process: Structure and Anti-Structure* (New York: Aldine, 1969).

53 Jason Horowitz, "The Genesis of a Church's Stand on Race," *Washington Post*, February 28, 2012, https://www.washingtonpost.com/politics/the-genesis-of-a-churchs-stand-on-race/2012/02/22/gIQAQZXyfR_story.html.

54 King, letter.

Chapter 5

1 The All Enlisted Facebook page, which was created in December 2012, has since been deleted; I last accessed it in December 2017 at https://www.facebook.com/groups/479498132093781/.

2 Stephanie Lauritzen, "The Dignity of Your Womanhood," *Mormon Child Bride* (blog), December 5, 2012, https://mormonchildbride.blogspot.com/2012/12/the-dignity-of-your-womanhood.html.

3 Although fMhs has over 3,700 members, it is a closed, private group. Members must be approved by moderators and agree to a code of confidentiality to join, and I was honored to be trusted as a member of the page while I learned about what it means to be a Mormon feminist. Throughout this chapter, out of respect for participants' privacy, I only cite information I obtained or substantiated from interviews or other sources (on- or offline) and/or received explicit permission to share.

4 *Feminist Mormon Housewives* blog, https://www.feministmormonhousewives.org/.

5 All Enlisted Facebook page.

6 LDS, "250: We Are All Enlisted," *Hymns of the Church of Jesus Christ of Latter-day Saints* (Salt Lake City: Church of Jesus Christ of Latter-day Saints, 2002), https://www.churchofjesuschrist.org/music/library/hymns/we-are-all-enlisted.

7 Carol Mattingly, *Appropriate[ing] Dress: Women's Rhetorical Style in Nineteenth-Century America* (Carbondale: Southern Illinois University Press, 2002).

8 LDS, "Policies and Procedures," *New Era* (August 1971), Church of Jesus Christ of Latter-day Saints, https://www.churchofjesuschrist.org/study/new-era/1971/08/policies-and-procedures.

9 Peggy Fletcher Stack, "Mormon Women Plan 'Wear Pants to Church Day,'" *Salt Lake Tribune*, December 11, 2012, https://archive.sltrib.com/article.php?id=55445256&itype=cmsid.

10 Diana Douglas, "Mormon Women Dare to Wear Pants to Church," *Weekend Edition*, National Public Radio, December 16, 2012, https://www.npr.org/2012/12/16/167284923/mormon-women-dare-to-wear-pants-to-church; Timothy Pratt, "Mormon Women Set Out to Take a Stand, in Pants," *New York Times*, December 19, 2012, https://www.nytimes.com/2012/12/20/us/19mormon.html; Katie J. M. Baker, "Mormon Feminists under Fire for Encouraging Women to Wear Pants to Church," Jezebel, December 12, 2012, https://jezebel.com/mormon-feminists-under-fire-for-encouraging-women-to-we-5967794; Sadie Whitelocks, "Mormon Women Launch 'Wear Pants to Church Day' in Backlash over Strict Dress Code," *Daily Mail*, December 13, 2012, https://www.dailymail.co.uk/femail/article-2247550/Mormon-women-launch-wear-pants-church-day-backlash-strict-dress-code.html; Sadie Whitelocks, "'I Hadn't Worn Pants to Church for 37 Years': Mormon Women Ditch Strict Dress Code

in Push for Gender Equality," *Daily Mail*, December 17, 2012, https://www.dailymail.co.uk/femail/article-2249477/I-hadnt-worn-pants-church-37-years-Mormon-women-ditch-strict-dress-code-push-gender-equality.html.

11 Erin Ann McBride, "Pants in Church: A Feminist Movement," *The Church* (blog), Meridian Magazine, December 13, 2012, https://latterdaysaintmag.com/article-1-11915/.

12 3 Nephi 11:28–29, Book of Mormon.

13 Nineveh Dinha, "Group Encourages LDS Women to Wear Pants to Church," FOX 13 News (broadcast television), Salt Lake City, December 11, 2012, https://www.fox13now.com/2012/12/11/group-encourages-lds-women-to-wear-pants-to-church.

14 See, for example, Stephanie Lauritzen, "It Feels Right," *Mormon Child Bride* (blog), April 4, 2012, https://mormonchildbride.blogspot.com/2012/04/it-feels-right.html.

15 Cathy McKitrick, "Mormon Women Wear Pants to Church despite Objections," *Salt Lake Tribune*, December 17, 2012, https://archive.sltrib.com/article.php?id=55477393&itype=cmsid; Brittany Green-Miner and Ashton Goodell, "Mormon Women Wear Pants to Church," FOX 13 News (broadcast television), Salt Lake City, December 16, 2012. https://www.fox13now.com/2012/12/16/mormon-women-wear-pants-to-church-for-equality.

16 See, for example, DefyGravity, "Wearing Pants to Church," *Exponent II* (blog), December 12, 2012, https://exponentii.org/blog/wearing-pants-to-church-2/; Brent, "45: A Mormon in the Cheap Seats: Pants-Wearing Women Running Wild," *Doves & Serpents* (blog), December 12, 2012, https://www.dovesandserpents.org/wp/2012/12/45-mcs-women-running-wild/; and hannahwheelwright, "Pantsgate 2012," *Young Mormon Feminists* (blog), December 13, 2012, https://youngmormonfeminists.org/2012/12/13/pantsgate-2012/.

17 Lawrence Foster, "From Frontier Activism to Neo-Victorian Domesticity: Mormon Women in the Nineteenth and Twentieth Centuries," *Journal of Mormon History* 6 (1979): 3–21.

18 See Linda P. Wilcox, "The Imperfect Science: Brigham Young on Medical Doctors," *Dialogue: A Journal of Mormon Thought* 12 (1979): 26–36.

19 Thomas G. Alexander, "An Experiment in Progressive Legislation: The Granting of Woman Suffrage in Utah in 1870," *Utah Historical Quarterly* 38, no. 1 (1970): 20–30; Joan Iversen, "Feminist Implications of Mormon Polygyny," *Feminist Studies* 10, no. 3 (1984): 505–22.

20 Foster, "From Frontier Activism."

21 Quoted in Mary Jane Woodger, "Elaine Anderson Cannon, Young Women General President: Innovations, Inspiration, and Implementations," *Journal of Mormon History* 40, no. 4 (2014): 192.

22 LDS, "The Family: A Proclamation to the World," Church of Jesus Christ of Latter-day Saints, 1995, https://www.lds.org/topics/family-proclamation.

23 LDS, "How Does the Church Define Gender?," Church of Jesus Christ of Latter-day Saints, 2021, https://www.churchofjesuschrist.org/topics/transgender/understanding; LDS, "Transgender Individuals," in *General Handbook*, 38.6.23 (Salt Lake City: Church of Jesus Christ of Latter-day Saints, 2021), https://www.churchofjesuschrist.org/study/manual/general-handbook/38-church-policies-and-guidelines.

24 LDS, *Young Women Manual 1* (Salt Lake City: Church of Jesus Christ of Latter-day Saints, 2002), 56.

25 Richard G. Scott, "The Sanctity of Womanhood," *New Era* (November 2008), https://www.churchofjesuschrist.org/study/new-era/2008/11/the-sanctity-of-womanhood.

26 Dean L. Larsen, "Marriage and the Patriarchal Order," *Ensign* (September 1982), https://www.churchofjesuschrist.org/study/ensign/1982/09/marriage-and-the-patriarchal-order; Brent A. Barlow, "Strengthening the Patriarchal Order in the Home," *Ensign* (February 1973), https://www.churchofjesuschrist.org/study/ensign/1973/02/strengthening-the-patriarchal-order-in-the-home; Cree-L Kofford, "Marriage in the Lord's Way, Part One," *Ensign* (June 1998), https://www.churchofjesuschrist.org/study/ensign/1998/06/marriage-in-the-lords-way-part-one. In January 2022, the Barlow article was updated with a disclaimer that states, "Articles in the magazines archive may reflect practices and language of an earlier time." Again, the institution gives itself a convenient rhetorical pass by offering a vague disclaimer that does not explain which aspects of the article are outdated and which are not.

27 So central are marriage and childbirth in Mormonism that those who cannot or do not marry in this life are sealed in marriage posthumously through esoteric temple rituals on their behalf; Mormon teachings also suggest that women have the opportunity (if not the obligation) to bear children throughout eternity.

28 Within these priesthood orders are many hierarchically organized offices such as deacon, teacher, bishop, elder, seventy, and so on, further illustrating the Mormon commitment to hierarchy.

29 Ellis T. Rasmussen, *A Latter-day Saint Commentary on the Old Testament* (Salt Lake City: Deseret Book, 2004), 17.

30 See, for example, Mary Farrell Bednarowski, "Widening the Banks of the Mainstream: Women Constructing Theologies," in *Women's Leadership in Marginal Religions: Explorations outside the Mainstream*, ed. Catherine Wessinger (Chicago: University of Illinois Press, 1993), 13.

31 While the church's total assets and worth are unknown largely because of its tax-exempt status, its for-profit holdings alone are estimated at around $100 billion; see Lauren Frias, "Mormon-Church-Linked Investment Fund Amassed $100 Billion in Tax-Free Money and Claimed It Was Being Stored in Preparation for 'the Second Coming of Christ,' According to a Whistleblower Complaint," *Business Insider*, December 17, 2019, https://www.insider.com/mormon-church-ensign-100-billion-in-tax-exempt-accounts-whistleblower-2019-12.

32 Joanna Brooks, "Why the Women's Ordination Question Will Shape the Future of Mormonism," *Religion Dispatches* (blog), September 30, 2013, https://religiondispatches.org/why-the-womens-ordination-question-will-shape-the-future-of-mormonism/.

33 Michel Foucault, *The History of Sexuality*, vol. 1 (New York: Penguin, 1990).

34 See Sonia Johnson, *From Housewife to Heretic* (New York: Doubleday, 1981).

35 See Carrel Hilton Sheldon Carrel, "Launching Exponent II," *Exponent II* 22, no. 4 (1999), https://exponentii.org/history/.

36 See, for example, Taylor Petrey, "Issues in Mormon Feminism," *Patheos* (blog), January 7, 2013, https://www.patheos.com/blogs/peculiarpeople/2013/01/issues-in-mormon-feminism/.

37 Jessica Finnigan and Nancy Ross, "'I'm a Mormon Feminist': How Social Media Revitalized and Enlarged a Movement," *Interdisciplinary Journal of Research on Religion* 9, no. 12 (2013): 10.

38 "All Are Alike Unto God," What Women Know, 2012, http://whatwomenknow.org/all_are_alike/.
39 Boyd K. Packer, "All-Church Coordinating Council," Church of Jesus Christ of Latter-day Saints, May 18, 1993, retrieved via Internet Archive at https://archive.org/details/coordinating_council_1993_boyd_k_packer/page/n3/mode/2up.
40 See, for example, LDS, "About Patriarchal Blessings," *New Era* (March 2004), https://www.churchofjesuschrist.org/study/new-era/2004/03/about-patriarchal-blessings.
41 Rosemary Avance, "Seeing the Light: Mormon Conversion and Deconversion Narratives in Off- and Online Worlds," *Journal of Media and Religion* 12, no. 1 (2013): 22.
42 The complex relationship between historical narrative and modern Mormon identity underscores a paradox inherent in a tradition that at once reifies its historical foundations as a pure past (a conservative impulse) and valorizes the concept of continual revelation and evolving doctrine (a progressive impulse). While Joseph Smith's infant church and Mormon pioneer ancestry are valorized as the purest example of Mormon identity, the doctrine of continuing revelation problematizes an easy categorization of LDS faith as conservative.
43 Caroline Kline, "Good Mormon Feminists vs. Bad Mormon Feminists: The Dividing Line," *Feminism and Religion* (blog), July 4, 2011, https://feminismandreligion.com/2011/07/04/good-mormon-feminists-vs-bad-mormon-feminists-the-dividing-line/.
44 Linda King Newell, "A Gift Given, a Gift Taken: Washing, Anointing, and Blessing the Sick among Mormon Women," *Sunstone* 44 (1981), https://ldsseminary.files.wordpress.com/2018/02/a-gift-given-a-gift-taken-linda-newell.pdf; Linda King Newell, "The Historical Relationship of Mormon Women and Priesthood," *Dialogue: A Journal of Mormon Thought*, 18, no. 23(1985), https://www.dialoguejournal.com/wp-content/uploads/sbi/articles/Dialogue_V18N03_23.pdf.
45 Of the six, three were disfellowshipped (what the church now refers to as "formal membership restrictions") or excommunicated (now called "withdrawal of membership") due to their public feminist teachings: Lynne Kanavel Whitesides, who was disfellowshipped for both her public teachings on Mother in Heaven and making televised comments on the church's mistreatment of women; Maxine Hanks, who published *Women and Authority: Re-emerging Mormon Feminism* the year before her excommunication; and Lavina Fielding Anderson, who coedited a history of Mormon women and published a list of intellectuals targeted by the church. Then as now, institutional discipline for feminist Mormons is often reserved for those who dare proselytize their feminist worldview through media.
46 Brooks, "Why the Women's."
47 Kimberly, "Keep Busy in the Face of Discouragement," *Feminist Mormon Housewives* (blog), January 21, 2013, https://www.feministmormonhousewives.org/2013/01/keep-busy-in-the-face-of-discouragement/.
48 Michael Schudson, "Dynamics of Distortion in Collective Memory," in *Memory Distortion: How Minds, Brains, and Societies Reconstruct the Past*, ed. Daniel L. Schacter (Cambridge, MA: Harvard University Press, 1997), 351.
49 Joanna Brooks, "Ask Mormon Girl: I'm a 31 Year Old Mexican Mormon and… Feminist. Help?," *AskMormonGirl* (blog), February 4, 2013, https://askmormongirl.wordpress.com/2013/02/04/ask-mormon-girl-im-a-31-year-old-mexican-mormon-and-feminist-help/.
50 "Home," I'm a Mormon Feminist, 2013. https://mormonfeminist.org/.
51 Quoted in Eric S. Peterson, "New Mormon-Feminist Group Lobbies LDS Church,"

City Weekly, September 21, 2010, https://www.cityweekly.net/utah/new-mormon-feminist-group-lobbies-lds-church/Content?oid=2149312.

52 Catherine Jeppsen, "Mormon Women Wearing Pants Love the Gospel," *OnFaith* (blog), December 14, 2012, retrieved via Internet Archive at https://web.archive.org/web/20140611011241/http://www.faithstreet.com/onfaith/2012/12/14/mormon-women-wearing-pants-love-the-gospel/11140.

53 Newsroom, "Church Asks Activist Group to Reconsider Plans to Protest at General Conference," Church of Jesus Christ of Latter-day Saints, March 17, 2014, retrieved via Internet Archive at http://web.archive.org/web/20140723033743/http://www.mormonnewsroom.org/article/church-asks-activist-group-to-reconsider-general-conference-protest-plans.

54 At the time of this writing, the website features hundreds of supporter profiles and is still accepting and publishing new submissions. The group's Facebook page has more than 6,800 publicly viewable "likes" and 6,300 followers.

Chapter 6

1 Matthew Bowman, *The Mormon People: The Making of an American Faith* (New York: Random House, 2012), 194.

2 Dieter F. Uchtdorf, "A Matter of a Few Degrees," General Conference address, Church of Jesus Christ of Latter-day Saints, April 5, 2008, https://www.churchofjesuschrist.org/study/ensign/2008/05/a-matter-of-a-few-degrees.

3 MormonThink, http://www.mormonthink.com/.

4 Peter Henderson and Kristina Cooke, "Special Report: Mormonism Besieged by the Modern Age," Reuters, January 31, 2012, https://www.reuters.com/article/2012/01/31/us-mormonchurch-idUSTRE80T1CM20120131/.

5 In 2022, the church reported a total worldwide membership of 17 million, with just over 6.8 million members in the United States; see Newsroom, "Facts and Statistics," Church of Jesus Christ of Latter-day Saints, 2022, https://newsroom.churchofjesuschrist.org/facts-and-statistics/.

6 "And he had caused the cursing to come upon them, yea, even a sore cursing, because of their iniquity. For behold, they had hardened their hearts against him, that they had become like unto a flint; wherefore, as they were white, and exceedingly fair and delightsome, that they might not be enticing unto my people the Lord God did cause a skin of blackness to come upon them" (2 Nephi 5:21, Book of Mormon).

7 "And then shall they rejoice; for they shall know that it is a blessing unto them from the hand of God; and their scales of darkness shall begin to fall from their eyes; and many generations shall not pass away among them, save they shall be a white and a delightsome people" (2 Nephi 30:6, Book of Mormon; pre-1981).

8 See LDS, "People and Places," *New Era* (August 1971), https://www.churchofjesuschrist.org/study/new-era/1971/08/people-and-places.

9 Considering the lack of genetic evidence linking modern-day Native tribes to Israel, some LDS scholars favor a limited geography model, suggesting that not all Native American tribes are descended from the canonic Lamanites. Folk teaching and vernacular use of the term *Lamanite*, however, is not nearly as nuanced.

10 See Steve Pavlik, "Of Saints and Lamanites: An Analysis of Navajo Mormonism," *Wicazo Sa Review* 8, no. 1 (1992): 21–30.

11 Elijah Abel and Walker Lewis are two examples of Black men ordained as elders during this period. LDS historians have only recently begun to circulate these men's stories as evidence that the church's founder may not have been as exclusory as his church became after his death.

12 Note that this was decades before the exclusion was articulated in policy; see W. Paul Reeve, *Religion of a Different Color: Race and the Mormon Struggle for Whiteness* (New York: Oxford University Press, 2015).

13 See First Presidency, "Statement by the First Presidency of the Church of Jesus Christ of Latter-day Saints on the Negro Question, August 17, 1951," in *Mormonism and the Negro*, Bookmark, 1967, 16–18.

14 Brigham Young, "The Persecution of the Saints, Etc.," in *Journal of Discourses* 10, no. 25 (Salt Lake City: Deseret Book, 1974, 1863).

15 Mark Grover, "The Mormon Priesthood Revelation and the São Paulo, Brazil Temple," *Dialogue: A Journal of Mormon Thought* 23, no. 1 (1990): 39–53.

16 LDS, *Saints: The Story of the Church of Jesus Christ in the Latter Days*, vol. 3, *Boldly, Nobly, and Independent, 1893–1955* (Salt Lake: Church of Jesus Christ of Latter-day Saints, 2022).

17 Jason Horowitz, "The Genesis of a Church's Stand on Race," *Washington Post*, February 28, 2012, https://www.washingtonpost.com/politics/the-genesis-of-a-churchs-stand-on-race/2012/02/22/gIQAQZXyfR_story.html.

18 For a timeline of the incident, see Kent Larsen, "The Bott Gaffe: A Chronology," *Times and Seasons* (blog), March 6, 2012, http://archive.timesandseasons.org/2012/03/the-bott-gaffe-a-chronology/.

19 Newsroom, "Church Statement regarding 'Washington Post' Article on Race and the Church," Church of Jesus Christ of Latter-day Saints, February 29, 2012, https://newsroom.churchofjesuschrist.org/article/racial-remarks-in-washington-post-article.

20 "BYU Religion Prof Bott Retiring in June," *Daily Herald*, March 22, 2012, https://www.heraldextra.com/news/2012/mar/22/byu-religion-prof-bott-retiring-in-june/.

21 Originally located at https://www.lds.org/topics, as of this writing, the Gospel Topics page can be found at https://www.churchofjesuschrist.org/study/manual/gospel-topics/intro. See the original via Internet Archive at https://web.archive.org/web/20110613170338/http://lds.org/study/topics.

22 LDS, "Jesus Christ," Gospel Topics, Church of Jesus Christ of Latter-day Saints, November 2013, retrieved via Internet Archive at https://web.archive.org/web/20131204200008/http://www.lds.org/topics/jesus-christ; LDS, "Gospel Learning," Gospel Topics, Church of Jesus Christ of Latter-day Saints, November 2013, retrieved via Internet Archive at https://web.archive.org/web/20131222032903/http://www.lds.org/topics/gospel-study; LDS, "Christmas," Gospel Topics, Church of Jesus Christ of Latter-day Saints, November 2013, retrieved via Internet Archive at https://web.archive.org/web/20131223193230/http://www.lds.org/topics/christmas.

23 LDS, "Are 'Mormons' Christian?" Gospel Topics, Church of Jesus Christ of Latter-day Saints, November 2013, retrieved via Internet Archive at https://web.archive.org/web/20131213140552/http://www.lds.org/topics/christians; LDS, "First Vision Accounts," Gospel Topics, Church of Jesus Christ of Latter-day Saints, November 2013, retrieved via Internet Archive at https://web.archive.org/web/20131206175257/http://www.lds.org/topics/first-vision-accounts.

24 Genelle Pugmire, "LDS Church Working on Online Topics Project," *Daily Herald*, January 17, 2014, retrieved via Internet Archive at https://web.archive.org/web/

20140117031250/http://www.heraldextra.com/news/local/lds-church-working-on-online-topics-project/article_4afdfb8d-8cdc-5a4e-8477-7cf21de7d7e7.html.

25 LDS, "Plural Marriage in the Church of Jesus Christ of Latter-day Saints," Gospel Topics, Church of Jesus Christ of Latter-day Saints, 2014, https://www.churchofjesuschrist.org/study/manual/gospel-topics-essays/plural-marriage-in-the-church-of-jesus-christ-of-latter-day-saints; LDS, "Peace and Violence among 19th-Century Latter-day Saints," Gospel Topics, Church of Jesus Christ of Latter-day Saints, 2014, https://www.churchofjesuschrist.org/study/manual/gospel-topics-essays/peace-and-violence-among-19th-century-latter-day-saints.

26 LDS, "Race and the Priesthood," Gospel Topics, Church of Jesus Christ of Latter-day Saints, December 6, 2013, retrieved via Internet Archive at https://web.archive.org/web/20131216073826/http://www.lds.org/topics/race-and-the-priesthood.

27 Walch, "Polygamy."

28 Peggy Fletcher Stack, "This Mormon Sunday School Teacher Was Dismissed for Using Church's Own Race Essay in Lesson," *Salt Lake Tribune*, May 5, 2015, https://archive.sltrib.com/article.php?id=2475803&itype=CMSID.

29 Newsroom, "Church Provides Context for Recent Media Coverage on Gospel Topics Pages," Church of Jesus Christ of Latter-day Saints, 2014, https://newsroom.churchofjesuschrist.org/article/church-provides-context-gospel-topics-pages.

30 LDS, "Gospel Topics Essays: Contents," Church of Jesus Christ of Latter-day Saints, https://www.churchofjesuschrist.org/study/manual/gospel-topics-essays.

31 LDS, "Gospel Topics Essays," Church of Jesus Christ of Latter-day Saints, https://www.churchofjesuschrist.org/study/manual/gospel-topics-essays/essays.

32 Tad Walch, "Polygamy Essays Provide Information about Early LDS Church—and Current Leadership," *Deseret News*, October 25, 2014, https://www.deseret.com/2014/10/25/20551279/polygamy-essays-provide-information-about-early-lds-church-and-current-leadership.

33 Mark M. Harrison to Kathleen Marie Kelly, June 17, 2014, in Tad Walch, "Ordain Women Founder's Recruitment Efforts Result in Excommunication from LDS Church," *Deseret News*, June 23, 2014, https://www.deseret.com/2014/6/23/20543750/ordain-women-founder-s-recruitment-efforts-result-in-excommunication-from-lds-church.

34 Bryan King to John Dehlin, February 9, 2015, in John Dehlin, press release, February 10, 2015, https://www.mormonstories.org/wp-content/uploads/2015/01/JohnDehlinDisciplinaryCouncilPressRelase-FinalV4.pdf.

35 The Calderwoods were active in online communities for heterodox and doubting Mormons, particularly Carson, who blogged at rationalfaiths.com, a blog devoted to difficult questions about Mormonism. John Dehlin and the *Mormon Stories* community offered public support to the Calderwoods during the disciplinary process, and the Calderwoods participated in a podcast after their excommunication. See John Dehlin, "Marisa and Carson Calderwood Discuss Their Excommunication," *Mormon Stories* podcast, episode 544, May 24, 2015, https://www.mormonstories.org/portfolio-items/marisa-and-carson-calderwood-discuss-their-excommunication/.

36 Van Allen's personal blog is now obsolete; the original post was housed at mormonverse.com (http://mormonverse.com/2015/02/02/dc-132-a-revelation-of-men-not-god/). He and Lindsay were also featured on *Mormon Stories*; see John Dehlin, "Kirk and Lindsay Van Allen—Facing Church Discipline for Rejecting Polygamy (D&C 132)," *Mormon Stories*, episode 530, April 8, 2015, https://www.mormonstories.org/portfolio

-items/kirk-and-lindsay-van-allen-facing-church-discipline-for-rejecting-polygamy-dc-132/.

37 For example, see Aleida Assmann, "The Printing Press and the Internet: From a Culture of Memory to a Culture of Attention," in *Globalization, Cultural Identities, and Media Representations*, ed. Natasha Gentz and Stefan Kramer (New York: SUNY Press, 2012), 11–14; David Bawden and Lyn Robinson, "A Distant Mirror? The Internet and the Printing Press," *Aslib Proceedings*. 52, no. 2 (2000): 51–57; James A. Dewar, *The Information Age and the Printing Press: Looking Backward to See Ahead* (Santa Monica: RAND Corporation, 1998), https://www.rand.org/pubs/papers/P8014.html; Greg Peterson, "The Internet and Christian and Muslim Communities," in *Religion and Popular Culture in America*, ed. Bruce David Forbes and Jeffery H. Mahan (Los Angeles: University of California Press, 2000), 123–38; and Aleks Krotoski, "What Effect Has the Internet Had on Religion?," *Guardian*, April 16, 2011, https://www.theguardian.com/technology/2011/apr/17/untangling-web-aleks-krotoski-religion.

38 The flattening dynamics of the internet signal an unprecedented democratization in religion, but it is not without exception. The availability of these publishing platforms still biases information in favor of the young and highly educated. Many Mormons—particularly those who are older than fifty, those who are less educated, and those who do not spend as much time online—are unaware of the existence of internet communities. For the most part, these Mormons also seem to be largely unaware of the counter-narratives available on the internet.

Bibliography

Acker, Joan. "Hierarchies, Jobs, Bodies: A Theory of Gendered Organizations." *Gender & Society* 4, no. 2 (1990): 139–58.

Albrecht, Stan L. "The Consequential Dimension of Mormon Religiosity." In *Latter-day Saint Social Life: Social Research on the LDS Church and Its Members*, edited by James T. Duke, 253–92. Religious Studies Center. Provo, UT: Brigham Young University, 1998.

Alexander, Thomas G. "An Experiment in Progressive Legislation: The Granting of Woman Suffrage in Utah in 1870." *Utah Historical Quarterly* 38, no. 1 (1970): 20–30.

Alexander, Thomas G. *Mormonism in Transition: A History of the Latter-day Saints, 1890–1930*. Champaign: University of Illinois Press, 1996.

Althusser, Louis. *For Marx*. London: Penguin, 1969.

Althusser, Louis. "Ideology Interpellates Individuals as Subjects." In *Identity: A Reader*, edited by Paul du Guy, Jessica Evans, and Peter Redman, 31–38. Thousand Oaks: Sage, 2004.

Andersen, Neil L. "Trial of Your Faith." General Conference address. Church of Jesus Christ of Latter-day Saints, October 2012. https://www.churchofjesuschrist.org/study/general-conference/2012/10/trial-of-your-faith.

Anderson, Benedict. *Imagined Communities: Reflections on the Origin and Spread of Nationalism*. New York: Verso, 1991.

Applebome, Peter. "A Mormon Spectacle, Way Off Broadway." *New York Times*, July 13, 2011. https://www.nytimes.com/2011/07/14/nyregion/hill-cumorah-pageant-offers-mormon-spectacle-way-off-broadway.html.

Askar, Jamshid Ghazi. "Analysis: How a Mormon Can Be U.S. President." *Deseret Morning News*, February 1, 2011. https://www.deseret.com/2011/2/1/20170921/analysis-how-a-mormon-can-be-u-s-president.

Assmann, Aleida. "The Printing Press and the Internet: From a Culture of Memory to a Culture of Attention." In *Globalization, Cultural Identities, and Media Representations*, edited by Natasha Gentz and Stefan Kramer, 11–14. New York: SUNY Press, 2012.

Atkinson, Rowland, and John Flint. "Accessing Hidden and Hard-to-Reach Populations: Snowball Research Strategies." *Social Research Update* 33 (2001). https://sru.soc.surrey.ac.uk/SRU33.PDF.

Avance, Rosemary. "Seeing the Light: Mormon Conversion and Deconversion Narratives in Off- and Online Worlds." *Journal of Media and Religion* 12, no. 1 (2013): 16–24.

Bagley, Pat. "Thanks to Mitt Romney, Mormonism Is under the Microscope." *Salt Lake Tribune*, September 8, 2012. https://archive.sltrib.com/article.php?id=54851585&itype=CMSID.

Baker, Katie J. M. "Mormon Feminists under Fire for Encouraging Women to Wear Pants to Church." Jezebel, December 12, 2012. https://jezebel.com/mormon-feminists-under-fire-for-encouraging-women-to-we-5967794.

Ballard, M. Russell. "Beware of False Prophets and False Teachers." *Ensign* (October 1999).

https://www.lds.org/general-conference/1999/10/beware-of-false-prophets-and-false-teachers.

Ballard, M. Russell. "Prepare for the Blessings of the Temple." *Ensign* (October 2010). https://www.lds.org/ensign/2010/10/prepare-for-the-blessings-of-the-temple?lang=eng.

Balmer, Randall. "Why Mitt Romney Needs to Talk Openly about His Mormon Faith." *New Republic*, February 6, 2012. https://newrepublic.com/article/100375/romney-mormon-election-religion#primary-form.

Barlow, Brent A. "Strengthening the Patriarchal Order in the Home." *Ensign* (February 1973). https://www.churchofjesuschrist.org/study/ensign/1973/02/strengthening-the-patriarchal-order-in-the-home.

Barthes, Roland. *Mythologies*. New York: Hill and Wang, 1972.

Bawden, David, and Lyn Robinson. "A Distant Mirror? The Internet and the Printing Press." *Aslib Proceedings* 52, no. 2 (2000): 51–57.

Beck, Glenn. "Polygamy? Magic Underwear? People on Bikes? Glenn Discusses Mormon Myths in TheBlaze TV Special!" TheBlaze TV, September 6, 2012. https://www.glennbeck.com/2012/09/06/polygamy-magic-underwear-people-on-bikes-glenn-discusses-mormon-myths-in-theblaze-tv-special/.

Becker, Joseph D. "Romney's Religion: Should It Matter?" *Commonweal Magazine*, May 31, 2012. https://www.commonwealmagazine.org/romneys-religion.

Bednarowski, Mary Farrell. "Widening the Banks of the Mainstream: Women Constructing Theologies." In *Women's Leadership in Marginal Religions: Explorations outside the Mainstream*, edited by Catherine Wessinger, 211–32. Chicago: University of Illinois Press, 1993.

Beer, David. "Social Network(ing) Sites… Revisiting the Story So Far: A Response to danah boyd & Nicole Ellison." *Journal of Computer-Mediated Communication* 13, no. 2 (2008): 516–29.

Bell, Catherine. *Ritual: Perspectives and Dimensions*. New York: Oxford University Press, 1997.

Benson, Ezra Taft. "Worthy Fathers, Worthy Sons." General Conference address. Church of Jesus Christ of Latter-day Saints, October 1985. https://www.churchofjesuschrist.org/study/general-conference/1985/10/worthy-fathers-worthy-sons.

Berger, Peter L., and Thomas Luckmann. *The Social Construction of Reality: A Treatise in the Sociology of Knowledge*. Garden City, NY: Anchor Books, 1966.

Billy Graham Evangelistic Association. "Looking for Answers: What Is a Cult?" BillyGraham.org, 2010. Retrieved via Internet Archive at http://web.archive.org/web/20100605052727/http://www.billygraham.org/articlepage.asp?ArticleID=2072.

Bloom, Harold. *The American Religion*. 2nd ed. New York: Chu Hartley, 2006.

Bloom, Harold. "Will This Election Be the Mormon Breakthrough?" *New York Times*, November 12, 2011. https://www.nytimes.com/2011/11/13/opinion/sunday/will-this-election-be-the-mormon-breakthrough.html.

Boellstorff, Tom, Bonnie Nardi, Celia Pearce, and T. L. Taylor. *Ethnography and Virtual Worlds: A Handbook of Method*. Princeton University Press, 2012.

Boteach, Shmuley. "Are Mormons Any Weirder Than the Rest of Us?" *Jerusalem Post*,

November 28, 2011. https://www.huffpost.com/entry/are-mormons-any-weirder-t_b_1116390.

Boud, Thomas J. "The Energy Drink Epidemic." *Ensign* (December 2008). https://www.lds.org/ensign/2008/12/the-energy-drink-epidemic?lang=eng.

Bowman, Matthew. *The Mormon People: The Making of an American Faith*. New York: Random House, 2012.

boyd, danah. "Friends, Friendsters, and Top 8: Writing Community into Being on Social Network Sites." *First Monday* 11, no. 12 (2006). https://firstmonday.org/ojs/index.php/fm/article/view/1418/1336.

Brent. "45: A Mormon in the Cheap Seats: Pants-Wearing Women Running Wild." *Doves & Serpents* (blog), December 12, 2012. https://www.dovesandserpents.org/wp/2012/12/45-mcs-women-running-wild/.

Brignall, Tom. "The New Panopticon: The Internet Viewed as a Structure of Social Control." *Theory & Science* 3, no. 1 (2002): n.p.

Brodie, Fawn. *No Man Knows My History: The Life of Joseph Smith*. 2nd ed. New York: Vintage, 1995.

Bromley, David G. "The Social Construction of Contested Exit Roles: Defectors, Whistleblowers, and Apostates." In *The Politics of Religious Apostasy: The Role of Apostates in the Transformation of Religious Movements*, edited by David G. Bromley, 19–48. Westport, CT: Praeger, 1998.

Brooks, Joanna. "Ask Mormon Girl: I'm a 31 Year Old Mexican Mormon and… Feminist. Help?" *AskMormonGirl* (blog), February 4, 2013. https://askmormongirl.wordpress.com/2013/02/04/ask-mormon-girl-im-a-31-year-old-mexican-mormon-and-feminist-help/.

Brooks, Joanna. "Does Mormonism Encourage LDS People to Lie?" *Religion Dispatches* (blog), August 9, 2012. https://religiondispatches.org/does-mormonism-encourage-lds-people-to-lie/.

Brooks, Joanna. "Is Romney's Foreign Policy Problem a Product of His Mormonism?" *Religion Dispatches* (blog), September 17, 2012. https://religiondispatches.org/is-romneys-foreign-policy-problem-a-product-of-his-mormonism/.

Brooks, Joanna. "My Take: Hard Truths Matter; I'm Mormon, and I'm Voting for Obama." *CNN Belief Blog*, October 18, 2012. Retrieved via Internet Archive at https://web.archive.org/web/20121021040640/http://religion.blogs.cnn.com/2012/10/18/my-take-hard-truths-matter-im-mormon-and-im-voting-for-obama/.

Brooks, Joanna. "Should Mormon Women Be Ordained? Or Are They Already Priesthood Holders?" *AskMormonGirl* (blog), June 28, 2013. https://askmormongirl.wordpress.com/2013/06/28/should-mormon-women-be-ordained-or-are-they-already-priesthood-holders/.

Brooks, Joanna. "Why the Women's Ordination Question Will Shape the Future of Mormonism." *Religion Dispatches* (blog), September 30, 2013. https://religiondispatches.org/why-the-womens-ordination-question-will-shape-the-future-of-mormonism/.

Brusco, Elizabeth E. *The Reformation of Machismo: Evangelical Conversion and Gender in Columbia*. Austin: University of Texas Press, 1995.

Buber, Martin. *I and Thou*. Translated by Walter Kauffman. New York: Scribner, 2011.

Burke, Kenneth. *Rhetoric of Religion: Studies in Logology*. Berkeley: University of California Press, 1970.

Burr, Thomas. "Harry Reid: Mitt Romney Is Not the Face of Mormonism." *Salt Lake Tribune*, September 24, 2012. https://archive.sltrib.com/article.php?id=54958981&itype=CMSID.

Bushman, Claudia. "Women's Agency in the Contemporary LDS Church: Popular Perspectives." Panel presented at the Women and the LDS Church Conference, University of Utah, Salt Lake City, August 25, 2012.

Bushman, Richard L. "I Have a Question: What Is the Difference between the American Revolution of 1776 and the Rebellions in Our Own Time?" *Ensign* (June 1976). https://www.churchofjesuschrist.org/study/ensign/1976/06/i-have-a-question/what-is-the-difference-between-the-american-revolution-of-1776-and-the-rebellions-in-our-own-time.

Bushman, Richard L. *Joseph Smith: Rough Stone Rolling*. New York: Vintage, 2007.

Buzalka, Mike. "Mission Accomplished at BYU Dining." *Food Management*, March 1, 2009. https://www.food-management.com/fm-innovators/mission-accomplished-byu-dining.

BYU. "A New Beginning for the *Mormon Studies Review*." Neal A. Maxwell Institute for Religious Scholarship, July 23, 2012. https://scholarsarchive.byu.edu/insights/vol32/iss3/4/.

Campbell, Heidi. *When Religion Meets New Media*. New York: Routledge, 2010.

Campbell, Joel. "Mormon Ad Campaign Draws Attention in 9 U.S. Markets." *Deseret News*, August 21, 2010. https://www.deseret.com/2010/8/21/20135975/mormon-ad-campaign-draws-attention-in-9-u-s-markets.

Campbell, John Edward. *Getting It On Online: Cyberspace, Gay Male Sexuality, and Embodied Identity*. New York: Harrington Park Press, 2004.

Campbell, John Edward, and Matt Carlson. "Panopticon.com: Online Surveillance and the Commodification of Privacy." *Journal of Broadcasting and Electronic Media* 46, no. 4 (2002): 586–606.

Carey, James. *Communication as Culture: Essays on Media and Society*. New York: Routledge, 1989.

Castells, Manuel. *The Rise of the Network Society: The Information Age: Economy, Society, and Culture*. Vol. 1. 2nd ed. New York: Wiley Blackwell, 2010.

Castronovo, Russ. *Necro Citizenship: Death, Eroticism, and the Public Sphere in the Nineteenth-Century United States*. Durham, NC: Duke University Press, 2001.

Chen, Chiung Hwang, and Ethan Yorgason. "'Those Amazing Mormons': The Media's Construction of Latter-day Saints as Model Minority." *Dialogue: A Journal of Mormon Thought* 32, no. 2 (1999): 107–28.

Chick, Jack. *The Visitors*. Chick Publications, 1984. https://www.chick.com/reading/tracts/0061/0061_01.asp.

Christofferson, D. Todd. "The Doctrine of Christ." General Conference address. Church of Jesus Christ of Latter-day Saints, April 2012. https://www.churchofjesuschrist.org/study/general-conference/2012/04/the-doctrine-of-christ.

CIA. "United States: People and Society." *The World Factbook 2023*. Washington, DC: Central

Intelligence Agency, 2023. https://www.cia.gov/the-world-factbook/countries/united-states/#people-and-society.

Clark, James R. *Messages of the First Presidency of the Church of Jesus Christ of Latter-day Saints*. Vol. 2. Salt Lake City: Bookcraft, 1965.

CNN Political Unit. "Perry Supporter Says Romney's Religion 'a Cult.'" CNN, October 7, 2011. https://www.cnn.com/2011/10/08/politics/perry-response-mormonism/index.html.

Colvin, Gina. "Should Romney Repent? 'Yes!', Says the Prophet Mormon." *Patheos* (blog), September 20, 2012. https://www.patheos.com/blogs/kiwimormon/2012/09/should-romney-repent-yes-says-the-prophet-mormon/.

Condon, Stephanie. "Billy Graham's Organization Removes Mormonism from Its List of Cults." CBS News, October 18, 2012. https://www.cbsnews.com/news/billy-grahams-organization-removes-mormonism-from-its-list-of-cults/.

Coppins, McKay. "A Brief Guide to 'Mormon Underwear.'" BuzzFeedNews, January 25, 2012. https://www.buzzfeednews.com/article/mckaycoppins/a-brief-guide-to-mormon-underwear.

Coppins, McKay. "Mitt Skips the Mormon Moment." BuzzFeedNews, January 13, 2012. https://www.buzzfeednews.com/article/mckaycoppins/mitt-skips-the-mormon-moment.

Coppins, McKay. "A Mormon Reporter on the Romney Bus." BuzzFeedNews, November 14, 2012. https://www.buzzfeednews.com/article/mckaycoppins/a-mormon-reporter-on-the-romney-bus.

Coppins, McKay. "What's with Mitt's Mormon Money?" BuzzFeedNews, January 24, 2012. https://www.buzzfeednews.com/article/mckaycoppins/whats-with-mitts-mormon-money.

Corn, David. "Secret Video: Romney Tells Millionaire Donors What He Really Thinks of Obama Voters." *Mother Jones*, September 17, 2012. https://www.motherjones.com/politics/2012/09/secret-video-romney-private-fundraiser/.

Critchley, Simon. "Why I Love Mormonism." *Opinionator* (blog), September 16, 2012. https://archive.nytimes.com/opinionator.blogs.nytimes.com/2012/09/16/why-i-love-mormonism/.

Curry, Colleen. "Billy Graham's Website Removes 'Mormonism' from Cult List." ABC News, October 18, 2012, https://abcnews.go.com/blogs/politics/2012/10/billy-grahams-website-removes-mormonism-from-cult-list.

Daily Herald. "BYU Religion Prof Bott Retiring in June." March 22, 2012. https://www.heraldextra.com/news/2012/mar/22/byu-religion-prof-bott-retiring-in-june/.

Darnton, Robert. "It Happened One Night." *New York Review of Books*, June 24, 2004. https://www.nybooks.com/articles/2004/06/24/it-happened-one-night/.

Davies, Douglas J. "The Invention of Sacred Tradition: Mormonism." In *The Invention of Sacred Tradition*, edited by James R. Lewis and Olav Hammer, 56–75. New York: Cambridge University Press, 2011.

Davies, Douglas J. *The Mormon Culture of Salvation: Force, Grace, and Glory*. Farnham: Ashgate, 2000.

Decker, Ed, and Dave Hunt. *The God Makers: A Shocking Expose of What the Mormon Church Really Believes*. Eugene, OR: Harvest House, 1984.

DefyGravity. "Wearing Pants to Church." *Exponent II* (blog), December 12, 2012. https://exponentii.org/blog/wearing-pants-to-church-2/.

de Groote, Michael. "Being Mormon in a Mormon Moment." *Deseret News*, September 4, 2011. https://www.deseret.com/2011/9/4/20213788/being-mormon-in-a-mormon-moment.

Dehlin, John. "Kirk and Lindsay Van Allen—Facing Church Discipline for Rejecting Polygamy (D&C 132)." *Mormon Stories* podcast, episode 530, April 8, 2015. https://www.mormonstories.org/portfolio-items/kirk-and-lindsay-van-allen-facing-church-discipline-for-rejecting-polygamy-dc-132/.

Dehlin, John. "Marisa and Carson Calderwood Discuss Their Excommunication." *Mormon Stories* podcast, episode 544, May 24, 2015. https://www.mormonstories.org/portfolio-items/marisa-and-carson-calderwood-discuss-their-excommunication/.

Densley, Steve. "Is Defending the Church against Church Doctrine?" *FAIR* (blog), September 18, 2012. https://www.fairlatterdaysaints.org/blog/2012/09/17/is-defending-the-church-against-church-doctrine.

Denton, Sally. "Romney and the White Horse Prophecy." Salon, January 29, 2012. https://www.salon.com/2012/01/29/mitt_and_the_white_horse_prophecy/.

Derrida, Jacques. "Difference." In *Identity: A Reader*, edited by Paul du Guy, Jessica Evans, and Peter Redman, 87–93. Thousand Oaks: Sage, 2004.

de Saussure, Ferdinand. *Writings in General Linguistics*. Translated by Roy Harris. Edited by Charles Bally and Albert Sechehaye. Oxford: Oxford University Press, 2006.

Dewar, James A. *The Information Age and the Printing Press: Looking Backward to See Ahead*. Santa Monica: RAND Corporation, 1998. https://www.rand.org/pubs/papers/P8014.html.

Dewey, John. *Democracy and Education*. New York: Macmillan, 1916.

Dillon, Michele. "Can Post-secular Society Tolerate Religious Differences?" *Sociology of Religion* 71, no. 2 (2010): 139–56.

Dinha, Nineveh. "Group Encourages LDS Women to Wear Pants to Church." FOX 13 News (broadcast television), Salt Lake City, December 11, 2012. https://www.fox13now.com/2012/12/11/group-encourages-lds-women-to-wear-pants-to-church.

"Doctor Scratch." "DCP Responds to Getting Fired from the Review." DiscussMormonism (Previously Mormon Discussions) discussion board, June 16, 2012. https://discussmormonism.com/viewtopic.php?t=124378.

Doris, Margaret. "Mitt's Magic Underwear and the Granny Ass Dance." *Esquire* (blog), August 30, 2012. https://www.esquire.com/news-politics/news/a15568/mitt-romney-mormon-underwear-12188879/.

Douglas, Dianna. "Mormon Women Dare to Wear Pants to Church." *Weekend Edition*, National Public Radio, December 16, 2012. https://www.npr.org/2012/12/16/167284923/mormon-women-dare-to-wear-pants-to-church.

Douglas, Mary. *Purity and Danger: An Analysis of the Concepts of Pollution and Taboo*. New York: Routledge, 1996.

Doyle, Arthur Conan. *A Study in Scarlet*. New York: Penguin Books, 1995.

Dulles, Avery Cardinal. *A History of Apologetics*. 2nd ed. San Francisco: Ignatius Press, 2005.

Eisenstein, Elizabeth. *The Printing Revolution in Early Modern Europe*. Cambridge: Cambridge University Press, 1983.

Ellison, Nicole, Rebecca Heino, and Jennifer Gibbs. "Managing Impressions Online: Self-Presentation Processes in the Online Dating Environment." *Journal of Computer-Mediated Communication* 11, no. 2 (2006): 415–41. https://onlinelibrary.wiley.com/doi/full/10.1111/j.1083-6101.2006.00020.x.

Emerson, Robert, Rachel Fretz, and Linda Shaw. *Writing Ethnographic Fieldnotes*. Chicago: University of Chicago Press, 1995.

Eyre, Linda, and Richard Eyre. "The Mormon Speech We Wish Romney Would Give." *Deseret News*, August 2, 2012. https://www.deseret.com/2012/8/28/20505976/the-mormon-speech-we-wish-romney-would-give.

FAIR. "Question: What Is the Strengthening Church Members Committee?" Faithful Answers, Informed Response, 2014. https://www.fairlatterdaysaints.org/answers/Mormonism_and_Church_discipline/Strengthening_Church_Members_Committee.

Farmer, Jared. *Mormons in the Media, 1930–2012*. Ebook, 2012. https://www.dropbox.com/s/7mmp40swq0ujz3x/2012-Farmer--Mormons-in-the-Media.pdf?dl=0.

Faulconer, James E. "Why a Mormon Won't Drink Coffee but Might Have a Coke: The Atheological Character of the Church of Jesus Christ of Latter-day Saints." *Element* 2, no. 2 (2006): 21–37.

Feller, Gavin. *Eternity in the Ether: A Mormon Media History*. Champaign: University of Illinois Press, 2023.

Ferguson, John E., III, Benjamin R. Knoll, and Jana Riess. "The Word of Wisdom in Contemporary American Mormonism: Perceptions and Practice." *Dialogue: A Journal of Mormon Thought* 51, no. 1 (2018): 39–78.

Finnigan, Jessica, and Nancy Ross. "'I'm a Mormon Feminist': How Social Media Revitalized and Enlarged a Movement." *Interdisciplinary Journal of Research on Religion* 9, no. 12 (2013): 1–25.

First Presidency. "Statement by the First Presidency of the Church of Jesus Christ of Latter-day Saints on the Negro Question, August 17, 1951." In *Mormonism and the Negro*, edited by John J. Stewart and William E. Berrett, 16–18. Orem, UT: Bookmark, 1967.

Flake, Kathleen. "An Enduring Contest: American Christianities and the State." In *American Christianities: A History of Dominance and Diversity*, edited by Catherine A. Brekus and W. Clark Gipin, 491–508. Chapel Hill: University of North Carolina Press, 2011.

Flake, Kathleen. "'Not to Be Riten': The Mormon Temple Rite as Oral Canon." *Journal of Ritual Studies* 9, no. 2 (1995): 1–21.

Flake, Kathleen. "Rendering to the Corporation: A Personal Ecclesiology." *Sunstone* (1994): 23–28.

Fletcher, Michael. "S.C. Economy Trumps Other Concerns in GOP Primary." *Washington Post*, July 9, 2011, A01.

Fletcher Stack, Peggy. "Just Dew It: BYU Students Pushing for Caffeinated Colas." *Salt Lake Tribune*, September 14, 2012. https://archive.sltrib.com/article.php?id=54875621&itype=CMSID.

Fletcher Stack, Peggy. "Memo to Mitt: Mormons Make Up That 47% on Assistance, Too."

Salt Lake Tribune, September 25, 2012. https://archive.sltrib.com/article.php?itype=CMSID&id=54965674.

Fletcher Stack, Peggy. "Mormon Women Plan 'Wear Pants to Church Day.'" *Salt Lake Tribune*, December 11, 2012. https://archive.sltrib.com/article.php?id=55445256&itype=cmsid.

Fletcher Stack, Peggy. "OK, Mormons, Drink Up—Coke and Pepsi Are OK." *Salt Lake Tribune*, August 31, 2012. https://archive.sltrib.com/article.php?id=54797595&itype=CMSID.

Fletcher Stack, Peggy. "Sunstone: Designer Recalls History of LDS Church's 'Visual Identity.'" *Salt Lake Tribune*, July 27, 2012. https://archive.sltrib.com/article.php?id=54575040&itype=CMSID.

Fletcher Stack, Peggy. "This Mormon Sunday School Teacher Was Dismissed for Using Church's Own Race Essay in Lesson." *Salt Lake Tribune*, May 5, 2015. https://archive.sltrib.com/article.php?id=2475803&itype=CMSID.

Foster, Lawrence. "From Frontier Activism to Neo-Victorian Domesticity: Mormon Women in the Nineteenth and Twentieth Centuries." *Journal of Mormon History* 6 (1979): 3–21.

Foucault, Michel. *The History of Sexuality*. Vol. 1. New York: Penguin, 1990.

Freud, Sigmund. *The Uncanny*. Translated by David McClintock. London: Penguin Books, 2003.

Frias, Lauren. "Mormon-Church-Linked Investment Fund Amassed $100 Billion in Tax-Free Money and Claimed It Was Being Stored in Preparation for 'the Second Coming of Christ,' According to a Whistleblower Complaint." *Business Insider*, December 17, 2019. https://www.insider.com/mormon-church-ensign-100-billion-in-tax-exempt-accounts-whistleblower-2019-12.

Friend Harding, Susan. *The Book of Jerry Falwell: Fundamentalist Language and Politics*. Princeton University Press, 2000.

Fung, Archon. "Infotopia: Unleashing the Democratic Power of Transparency." *Politics and Society* 41, no. 2 (2013): 183–212.

Ganzevoort, R. Ruard. "Religious Coping Reconsidered, Part Two: A Narrative Reformation." *Journal of Psychology and Theology* 26, no. 3 (1998): 276–86.

Garr, Arnold K. "Joseph Smith: Campaign for President of the United States." *Ensign* (February 2009). https://www.churchofjesuschrist.org/study/ensign/2009/02/joseph-smith-campaign-for-president-of-the-united-states.

Geertz, Clifford. *Interpretation of Cultures*. New York: Basic Books, 1966.

Giddens, Anthony. *Modernity and Self-Identity: Self and Society in the Late Modern Age*. Stanford University Press, 1991.

Givens, Terryl L. *People of Paradox: A History of Mormon Culture*. New York: Oxford University Press, 2007.

Givens, Terryl L. *The Viper on the Hearth: Mormons, Myths, and the Construction of Heresy*. New York: Oxford University Press, 1997.

Glaser, Barney, and Anselm Strauss. *The Discovery of Grounded Theory: Strategies for Qualitative Research*. New York: Aldine, 1967.

Goffman, Erving. *Interaction Ritual: Essays on Face-to-Face Behavior*. New York: Anchor Books, 1967.

Goffman, Erving. *The Presentation of Self in Everyday Life*. New York: Doubleday, 1959.

Gooren, Henri. "De expanderende mormoonse kerk in Latijns Amerika: Schetsen uit een wijk in San José, Costa Rica." Master's thesis, University of Utrecht, 1991.

Gooren, Henri. "The Mormons of the World: The Meaning of LDS Membership in Central America." Glenn M. Vernon Lecture, Mormon Social Science Association, Fall 2007. https://www.mormonsocialscience.org/wp-content/uploads/2009/11/28-2-Fall2007.pdf.

Gordon, Scott. "Journeys of Faith on the Internet." Panel discussion, Mormonism and the Internet Conference, Utah Valley University, Orem, March 29, 2012.

Graff, Stephanie. "'No Demand' for Caffeine at BYU?" *Digital Universe*, September 11, 2012. https://universe.byu.edu/2012/09/11/no-demand-for-caffeine-at-byu/.

Green-Miner, Brittany, and Ashton Goodell. "Mormon Women Wear Pants to Church." FOX 13 News (broadcast television). Salt Lake City, December 16, 2012. https://www.fox13now.com/2012/12/16/mormon-women-wear-pants-to-church-for-equality.

Grover, Mark L. "The Mormon Priesthood Revelation and the São Paulo, Brazil Temple." *Dialogue* 23, no. 1 (1990): 39–53.

Gumperz, John. *Discourse Strategies*. London: Cambridge University Press, 1982.

Habermas, Jürgen. *The Structural Transformation of the Public Sphere: An Inquiry into a Category of Bourgeois Society*. Translated by Thomas Burger. Cambridge, MA: MIT Press, 1991.

Haglund, Kristine. "What the 'Mormon Moment' Actually Accomplished." *Slate*, December 1, 2014. https://slate.com/human-interest/2014/12/mormon-moment-is-over-but-it-changed-mormon-culture-for-good.html.

Hall, Stuart. "Encoding/Decoding." In *Media and Cultural Studies*, edited by Meenakshi Gigi Durham and Douglas M. Kellner, 163–73. Malden, MA: Blackwell, 2001.

Hall, Stuart. "Who Needs Identity?" In *Questions of Cultural Identity*, edited by Stuart Hall and Paul du Gay, 1–17. London: Sage, 1996.

hannahwheelwright. "Pantsgate 2012." *Young Mormon Feminists* (blog), December 13, 2012. https://youngmormonfeminists.org/2012/12/13/pantsgate-2012/.

Haws, J. B. *The Mormon Image in the American Mind: Fifty Years of Public Perception*. Oxford University Press, 2013.

Heilman, Samuel. *The People of the Book: Drama, Fellowship, and Religion*. Livingston, NJ: Transaction, 2001.

Henderson, Peter, and Kristina Cooke. "Special Report: Mormonism Besieged by the Modern Age." Reuters, January 31, 2012. https://www.reuters.com/article/2012/01/31/us-mormonchurch-idUSTRE80T1CM20120131/.

Hilton Sheldon, Carrel. "Launching Exponent II." *Exponent II* 22, no. 4 (Summer 1999). https://exponentii.org/history/.

Hinckley, Gordon B. Interview by Larry King. *Larry King Live*, CNN, December 26, 2004.

Hine, Christine. *Virtual Ethnography*. London: Sage, 2000.

Hirschman, Albert O. *Exit, Voice, and Loyalty: Responses to Decline in Firms, Organizations, and States*. Cambridge, MA: Harvard University Press, 1970.

Hitchens, Christopher. "Mitt Romney and the Weird and Sinister Beliefs of Mormonism." *Slate*, October 17, 2011. https://slate.com/news-and-politics/2011/10/is-mormonism-a-cult-who-cares-its-their-weird-and-sinister-beliefs-we-should-be-worried-about.html.

Holquist, Michael. *Dialogism: Bakhtin and His World*. 2nd ed. New York: Routledge, 2002.

Hoover, Stewart. *Religion in the Media Age*. New York: Routledge, 2006.

Horowitz, Jason. "The Genesis of a Church's Stand on Race." *Washington Post*, February 28, 2012. https://www.washingtonpost.com/politics/the-genesis-of-a-churchs-stand-on-race/2012/02/22/gIQAQZXyfR_story.html.

Hoyt, Amy, and Sara Patterson. "Mormon Masculinity: Changing Gender Expectations in the Era of Transition from Polygamy to Monogamy, 1890–1920." *Gender & History* 23, no. 1 (April 2011): 72–91.

Hudson Cassler, Valerie. "I Am a Mormon Because I Am a Feminist." FAIR, September 2010. https://www.fairlatterdaysaints.org/testimonies/scholars/valerie-hudson-cassler.

Hughes, Richard T. "The Mormon Faith and the Romney Doctrine of American Exceptionalism." *Huffington Post Blog*, September 12, 2012. https://www.huffpost.com/entry/mormon-faith-and-the-romney-doctrine-of-american-exceptionalism_b_1874881?utm_hp_ref=religion.

Hunter, Howard W. "Your Temple Recommend." *New Era* (April 1995). https://www.churchofjesuschrist.org/study/new-era/1995/04/your-temple-recommend.

Hurst, Alan. "Of Caffeine and Covenants." *Peculiar People* (blog), September 19, 2012. https://www.patheos.com/blogs/peculiarpeople/2012/09/of-caffeine-and-covenants/.

I'm a Mormon Feminist. "Home." 2013. https://mormonfeminist.org/.

Iversen, Joan. "Feminist Implications of Mormon Polygyny." *Feminist Studies* 10, no. 3 (1984): 505–22.

Jackson, Kent P. "Book Review: Richard Lyman Bushman, Joseph Smith: Rough Stone Rolling." *Mormon Historical Studies* 7, no. 2 (2006): 133–47.

Jeffress, Robert. "Video of Pastor Robert Jeffress at Values Voter Summit." *Deseret News*, October 8, 2011. https://www.deseret.com/2011/10/8/20221616/video-of-pastor-robert-jeffress-at-values-voters-summit.

Jentsch, Ernst Anton. *On the Psychology of the Uncanny*. Translated and edited by Roy Sellars. Basingstoke: Palgrave Macmillan, 2009.

Jeppsen, Catherine. "Mormon Women Wearing Pants Love the Gospel." *OnFaith* (blog), December 14, 2012. Retrieved via Internet Archive at https://web.archive.org/web/20140611011241/http://www.faithstreet.com/onfaith/2012/12/14/mormon-women-wearing-pants-love-the-gospel/11140.

Jillette, Penn. "Mitt's Magical Mormon Undies: Penn Jillette's Rant Redux." Big Think, September 18, 2012. https://www.youtube.com/watch?v=_qJDd-2tM-A.

Jiménez-Martínez, César, and Lee Edwards. "The Promotional Regime of Visibility: Ambivalence and Contradiction in Strategies of Dominance and Resistance." *Communication and the Public* 8, no. 1 (2022): 14–28.

Johnson, Eric. "The Mormon Taqiyya." *Mormonism Researched*, July–August 2013. https://www.mrm.org/lying-for-lord.

Johnson, Sonia. *From Housewife to Heretic*. New York: Doubleday, 1981.

Kaleem, Jaweed. "Hundreds of Mormon Ads Launched in New York City." Huffington Post, June 22, 2011. https://www.huffpost.com/entry/mormon-ads-new-york_n_881834.

Kanter, Rosabeth M. *Commitment and Community: Communes and Utopias in Sociological Perspective*. Cambridge, MA: Harvard University Press, 1972.

Kanter, Rosabeth M. "Commitment and Social Organization: A Study of Commitment Mechanisms in Utopian Communities." *American Sociological Review* 33 (1968): 499–517.

Kaplan, Cora. "Aurora Leigh." In *Feminist Criticism and Social Change*, edited by Judith Newton and Deborah Rosenfelt, 134–64. New York: Routledge, 1985.

Katz, Elihu, Jay G. Blumler, and Michael Gurevitch. "Uses and Gratifications Research." *Public Opinion Quarterly* 37, no. 4 (1974): 509–23.

Kauffman, B. J. "Feminist Facts: Interview Strategies and Political Subjects in Ethnography." *Communication Theory* 2, no. 3 (1992): 187–206.

Keck, Kristi. "Romney Takes Leap of Faith with Religion Speech." CNN Politics, December 6, 2007. https://www.cnn.com/2007/POLITICS/12/05/romney.speech/.

Kim, Susanna. "Is the Word 'Mormon' Really Trademarked?" ABC News, June 4, 2014. https://abcnews.go.com/Business/church-day-saints-trademark-word-mormon/story?id=23988596.

Kimberly. "Keep Busy in the Face of Discouragement." *Feminist Mormon Housewives* (blog), January 21, 2013. https://www.feministmormonhousewives.org/2013/01/keep-busy-in-the-face-of-discouragement/.

King, Robert R., and Kay A. King. "The Effect of Mormon Organizational Boundaries on Group Cohesion." *Dialogue* 7, no. 1 (1972): 60–75.

King Newell, Linda. "A Gift Given, a Gift Taken: Washing, Anointing, and Blessing the Sick among Mormon Women." *Sunstone* 29 (1981). https://ldsseminary.files.wordpress.com/2018/02/a-gift-given-a-gift-taken-linda-newell.pdf.

King Newell, Linda. "The Historical Relationship of Mormon Women and Priesthood." *Dialogue: A Journal of Mormon Thought* 18, no. 3 (1985). https://www.dialoguejournal.com/wp-content/uploads/sbi/articles/Dialogue_V18N03_23.pdf.

Kinnvall, Catarina. "Globalization and Religious Nationalism: Self, Identity, and the Search for Ontological Security." *Political Psychology* 25, no. 5 (2004): 741–67.

Kirn, Walter. "The Mormon Moment." *Newsweek*, June 5, 2011. https://www.newsweek.com/mormon-moment-67951.

Kline, Caroline. "Good Mormon Feminists vs. Bad Mormon Feminists: The Dividing Line." *Feminism and Religion* (blog), July 4, 2011. https://feminismandreligion.com/2011/07/04/good-mormon-feminists-vs-bad-mormon-feminists-the-dividing-line/.

Knoll, Benjamin, and Jana Riess. "'Infected with Doubt': An Empirical Overview of Belief and Non-belief in Contemporary American Mormonism." *Dialogue: A Journal of Mormon Thought* 50, no. 3 (2017): 1–38.

Knowlton, David. "On Mormon Masculinity." *Sunstone* 88 (1992), 19–31. https://sunstone.org/wp-content/uploads/sbi/articles/088-19-31.pdf.

Kofford, Cree-L. "Marriage in the Lord's Way, Part One." *Ensign* (June 1998). https://www.churchofjesuschrist.org/study/ensign/1998/06/marriage-in-the-lords-way-part-one.

Krotoski, Aleks. "What Effect Has the Internet Had on Religion?" *Guardian*, April 16, 2011. https://www.theguardian.com/technology/2011/apr/17/untangling-web-aleks-krotoski-religion.

Lamb, Christina. "Gloves Are off as Obama Hits at 'Weird' Mitt; a Worried Presidential

Team Has Seized on the Mormon Faith of His Biggest Republican Rival." *Sunday Times* (London), October 23, 2011, 36.

Larsen, Dean L. "Marriage and the Patriarchal Order." *Ensign* (September 1982). https://www.churchofjesuschrist.org/study/ensign/1982/09/marriage-and-the-patriarchal-order.

Larsen, Kent. "The Bott Gaffe: A Chronology." *Times and Seasons* (blog), March 6, 2012. http://archive.timesandseasons.org/2012/03/the-bott-gaffe-a-chronology/.

Larsen, Richard. "Comparing Obama, Romney on Religion." *Idaho State Journal*, March 22, 2008.

Lauritzen, Stephanie. "The Dignity of Your Womanhood." *Mormon Child Bride* (blog), December 5, 2012. https://mormonchildbride.blogspot.com/2012/12/the-dignity-of-your-womanhood.html.

Lauritzen, Stephanie. "It Feels Right." *Mormon Child Bride* (blog), April 4, 2012. https://mormonchildbride.blogspot.com/2012/04/it-feels-right.html.

Lawrence, Gary C. *How Americans View Mormonism: Seven Steps to Improve Our Image.* Orange, CA: Parameter Foundation, 2008.

Lawrence, Jill. "Will Mormon Faith Hurt Bid for White House? Mitt Romney Says His Religion Isn't a Factor, but Some Voters Say It Is." *USA Today*, February 13, 2007, 1A.

LDS. "About Patriarchal Blessings." *New Era* (March 2004). https://www.churchofjesuschrist.org/study/new-era/2004/03/about-patriarchal-blessings.

LDS. "Are 'Mormons' Christian?" Gospel Topics. Church of Jesus Christ of Latter-day Saints, November 20, 2013. Retrieved via Internet Archive at https://web.archive.org/web/20131213140552/http://www.lds.org/topics/christians.

LDS. "Christmas." Gospel Topics. Church of Jesus Christ of Latter-day Saints, November 20, 2013. Retrieved via Internet Archive at https://web.archive.org/web/20131223193230/http://www.lds.org/topics/christmas.

LDS. "The Family: A Proclamation to the World." Church of Jesus Christ of Latter-day Saints, 1995. https://www.lds.org/topics/family-proclamation.

LDS. "FARMS Becomes Part of BYU." *Ensign* (January 1998). https://www.lds.org/ensign/1998/01/news-of-the-church/farms-becomes-part-of-byu.

LDS. "First Vision Accounts." Gospel Topics. Church of Jesus Christ of Latter-day Saints, November 20, 2013. Retrieved via Internet Archive at https://web.archive.org/web/20131206175257/http://www.lds.org/topics/first-vision-accounts.

LDS. "General Authorities and General Officers of the Church of Jesus Christ of Latter-day Saints." Church of Jesus Christ of Latter-day Saints, October 2023. https://assets.churchofjesuschrist.org/09/80/0980519967b511ee882feeeeac1e6623c39e93bf/general_authority_chart_november_2023_eng.pdf.

LDS. "Gospel Learning." Gospel Topics. Church of Jesus Christ of Latter-day Saints, November 20, 2013. Retrieved via Internet Archive at https://web.archive.org/web/20131222032903/http://www.lds.org/topics/gospel-study.

LDS. "Growth into a Worldwide Church." In *Church History in the Fulness of Times: Student Manual*, chapter 42. Salt Lake City: Church of Jesus Christ of Latter-day Saints, 2002. https://www.churchofjesuschrist.org/study/manual/church-history-in-the-fulness-of-times/chapter-forty-two.

LDS. "How Does the Church Define Gender?" Church of Jesus Christ of Latter-day Saints, 2021. https://www.churchofjesuschrist.org/topics/transgender/understanding.

LDS. "Internet." In *Handbook 2: Administering the Church*. 21.1.22, p. 183. Salt Lake City: Church of Jesus Christ of Latter-day Saints, 2010. https://www.churchofjesuschrist.org/bc/content/shared/content/english/pdf/language-materials/08702_eng.pdf?lang=eng.

LDS. "Jesus Christ." Gospel Topics. Church of Jesus Christ of Latter-day Saints, November 2013. Retrieved via Internet Archive at https://web.archive.org/web/20131204200008/http://www.lds.org/topics/jesus-christ.

LDS. *Latter-day Saint Woman*. Vol. 1. Salt Lake City: Church of Jesus Christ of Latter-day Saints, 2000.

LDS. "A Mormon Moment," September 9, 2001. https://www.newsweek.com/mormon-moment-152121.

LDS. "Peace and Violence among 19th-Century Latter-day Saints." Gospel Topics. Church of Jesus Christ of Latter-day Saints, 2014. https://www.churchofjesuschrist.org/study/manual/gospel-topics-essays/peace-and-violence-among-19th-century-latter-day-saints.

LDS. "People and Places." *New Era* (August 1971). https://www.churchofjesuschrist.org/study/new-era/1971/08/people-and-places.

LDS. "Plural Marriage in the Church of Jesus Christ of Latter-day Saints." Gospel Topics. Church of Jesus Christ of Latter-day Saints, 2014. https://www.churchofjesuschrist.org/study/manual/gospel-topics-essays/plural-marriage-in-the-church-of-jesus-christ-of-latter-day-saints.

LDS. "Policies and Procedures." *New Era* (August 1971). https://www.churchofjesuschrist.org/study/new-era/1971/08/policies-and-procedures.

LDS. "Programs and Policies Newsletter." *New Era* (July 1971). https://www.churchofjesuschrist.org/study/ensign/1971/03/programs-and-policies-newsletter.

LDS. "Prophet, Seer, and Revelator." Church of Jesus Christ of Latter-day Saints, n.d., https://history.churchofjesuschrist.org/content/prophet-seer-and-revelator.

LDS. "Race and the Priesthood." Gospel Topics. Church of Jesus Christ of Latter-day Saints, December 6, 2013. Retrieved via Internet Archive at https://web.archive.org/web/20131216073826/http://www.lds.org/topics/race-and-the-priesthood.

LDS. *Saints: The Story of the Church of Jesus Christ in the Latter Days*. Vol. 3, *Boldly, Nobly, and Independent, 1893–1955*. Salt Lake City: Church of Jesus Christ of Latter-day Saints, 2022.

LDS. "Transgender Individuals." In *General Handbook*. 38.6.23. Salt Lake City: Church of Jesus Christ of Latter-day Saints, 2021. https://www.churchofjesuschrist.org/study/manual/general-handbook/38-church-policies-and-guidelines.

LDS. "250: We Are All Enlisted." *Hymns of the Church of Jesus Christ of Latter-day Saints*. Salt Lake City: Church of Jesus Christ of Latter-day Saints, 2002. https://www.churchofjesuschrist.org/music/library/hymns/we-are-all-enlisted.

LDS. *Young Women Manual 1*. Salt Lake City: Church of Jesus Christ of Latter-day Saints, 2002.

LDSLiving. "Professor, LDS Convert: Mormonism Is the Most Feminist of All the Christianities." *LDSLiving*, March 25, 2016. https://www.ldsliving.com/professor-lds-convert-mormonism-is-the-most-feminist-of-all-the-christianities/s/84907.

Lévy, Pierre. *Becoming Virtual: Reality in the Digital Age*. Translated by Robert Bononno. Boston: Da Capo Press, 1998.

Lincoln, Bruce. "Mythic Narrative and Cultural Diversity in American Society." In *Myth and Method*, edited by Laurie L. Patton and Wendy Doniger, 163–76. Charlottesville: University Press of Virginia, 1996.

Ludlow, Daniel H. "Of the House of Israel." *Ensign* (January 1991).

Lythgoe, Dennis L. "The Changing Image of Mormonism." *Dialogue: A Journal of Mormon Thought* 3, no. 4 (1968): 45–58.

Mark. "Mitt Romney's Faithful Life." *Get Religion* (blog), November 13, 2011. https://www.getreligion.org/getreligion/2011/11/mitt-romneys-faithful-life.

Mattingly, Carol. *Appropriate[ing] Dress: Women's Rhetorical Style in Nineteenth-Century America*. Carbondale: Southern Illinois University Press, 2002.

Mauss, Armand. *The Angel and the Beehive: The Mormon Struggle with Assimilation*. Chicago: University of Illinois Press, 1994.

Maxwell, Neal A. "Becometh as a Child." General Conference address. Church of Jesus Christ of Latter-day Saints, April 1996. https://www.churchofjesuschrist.org/study/general-conference/1996/04/becometh-as-a-child.

Maxwell, Neal A. "The Net Gathers of Every Kind." General Conference address. Church of Jesus Christ of Latter-day Saints, October 1980. https://www.churchofjesuschrist.org/study/general-conference/1980/10/the-net-gathers-of-every-kind.

Maxwell, Neal A. "Remember How Merciful the Lord Hath Been." General Conference address. Church of Jesus Christ of Latter-day Saints, April 2004. https://www.churchofjesuschrist.org/study/general-conference/2004/04/remember-how-merciful-the-lord-hath-been.

McBaine, Neylan. *Women at Church: Magnifying LDS Women's Local Impact*. Draper, UT: Greg Kofford Books, 2014.

McBride, Erin Ann. "Pants in Church: A Feminist Movement." *The Church* (blog). Meridian Magazine, December 13, 2012. https://latterdaysaintmag.com/article-1-11915/.

McConkie, Joseph Fielding, and Craig J. Ostler. *Revelations of the Restoration: A Commentary on the Doctrine and Covenants and Other Modern Revelations*. Salt Lake City: Deseret Books, 1964.

McKitrick, Cathy. "Mormon Women Wear Pants to Church despite Objections." *Salt Lake Tribune*, December 17, 2012. https://archive.sltrib.com/article.php?id=55477393&itype=cmsid.

McLuhan, Marshall. *Understanding Media: The Extensions of Man*. New York: McGraw-Hill, 1964.

Miller, Lisa. "Mitt Romney's Hard-Hearted Twist on the Mormon Work Ethic." *Washington Post*, September 20, 2012, B02.

Miller, Lisa. "Romney Preaches the Gospel of Success." *Washington Post*, September 1, 2012, B02.

Mills, Austin. "Offer Caffeinated Beverages on Campus." Change.org (petition), October 11, 2016. https://www.change.org/p/brigham-young-university-offer-caffeinated-beverages-on-campus.

Moore, Carrie A. "New LDS Ad Campaign Touts the 'Truth Restored.'" *Deseret News*, April

4, 2008. https://www.thechurchnews.com/2008/4/4/23231915/new-lds-ad-campaign-touts-the-truth-restored.

Morgan, Mandy. "BYU Students Energized by Alum Mitt Romney's Presidential Bid." *Deseret News*, November 6, 2012. https://www.deseret.com/2012/11/6/20509346/byu-students-energized-by-alum-mitt-romney-s-presidential-bid.

Moslener, Sara. *Virgin Nation: Sexual Purity and American Adolescence*. New York: Oxford University Press, 2015.

Mountford, Roxanne. *The Gendered Pulpit: Preaching in American Protestant Spaces*. Carbondale: Southern Illinois University Press, 2003.

Murphy, Thomas W., and Angelo Baca. "Rejecting Racism in Any Form: Latter-day Saint Rhetoric, Religion, and Repatriation." *Open Theology* 2, no. 1 (2016): 700–725. https://doi.org/10.1515/opth-2016-0054.

Myler, Crystal. "Caffeine Protest Stopped on BYU's Brigham Square." *Digital Universe*, September 14, 2012, https://universe.byu.edu/2012/09/14/caffeine-policy-protest-stopped-in-brigham-square/.

Neuman, Scott, and Barbara Bradley Hagerty. "Romney Seeks to Allay Concerns about His Faith." NPR, December 6, 2007. https://www.npr.org/2007/12/06/16970082/romney-delivers-speech-on-faith.

Newsroom. "Approaching Latter-day Saint Doctrine." Church of Jesus Christ of Latter-day Saints, May 4, 2007. https://newsroom.churchofjesuschrist.org/article/approaching-mormon-doctrine.

Newsroom. "Bishops See National Trend in Mormon Congregations." Church of Jesus Christ of Latter-day Saints, February 28, 2008. https://newsroom.churchofjesuschrist.org/article/bishops-see-national-trend-in-mormon-congregations.

Newsroom. "Church Asks Activist Group to Reconsider Plans to Protest at General Conference." Church of Jesus Christ of Latter-day Saints, March 17, 2014. Retrieved via Internet Archive at http://web.archive.org/web/20140723033743/http://www.mormonnewsroom.org/article/church-asks-activist-group-to-reconsider-general-conference-protest-plans.

Newsroom. "Church Provides Context for Recent Media Coverage on Gospel Topics Pages." Church of Jesus Christ of Latter-day Saints, 2014. https://newsroom.churchofjesuschrist.org/article/church-provides-context-gospel-topics-pages.

Newsroom. "Church Statement regarding 'Washington Post' Article on Race and the Church." Church of Jesus Christ of Latter-day Saints, February 29, 2012. https://newsroom.churchofjesuschrist.org/article/racial-remarks-in-washington-post-article.

Newsroom. "Facts and Statistics." Church of Jesus Christ of Latter-day Saints, 2022. https://newsroom.churchofjesuschrist.org/facts-and-statistics/.

Newsroom. "'In One Heavenly Family': Scholar Terryl Givens on Proxy Baptism." Church of Jesus Christ of Latter-day Saints, July 31, 2012. https://newsroom.churchofjesuschrist.org/article/proxy-baptism-terryl-givens.

Newsroom. "Mormonism in the News: Getting It Right." Church of Jesus Christ of Latter-day Saints, 29 August 2012. https://newsroom.churchofjesuschrist.org/article/mormonism-news--getting-it-right-august-29.

Newsroom. "The Name of the Church." Church of Jesus Christ of Latter-day Saints, August 16, 2018. https://newsroom.churchofjesuschrist.org/article/name-of-the-church.

Newsroom. "Political Neutrality." Church of Jesus Christ of Latter-day Saints, February 4, 2012. Retrieved via Internet Archive at https://web.archive.org/web/20120204165855/http://www.mormonnewsroom.org/official-statement/political-neutrality.

Newsroom. "Political Neutrality and Participation." Church of Jesus Christ of Latter-day Saints, June 1, 2023. https://newsroom.churchofjesuschrist.org/official-statement/political-neutrality.

Newsroom. "Positioning Church Doctrine—How Church Members See Themselves." Church of Jesus Christ of Latter-day Saints, June 15, 2007. https://newsroom.churchofjesuschrist.org/article/positioning-church-doctrine-how-mormons-see-themselves.

Newsroom. "The Religious Experience of Mormonism." Church of Jesus Christ of Latter-day Saints, June 1, 2008. https://newsroom.churchofjesuschrist.org/article/the-religious-experience-of-mormonism.

Newsroom. "Style Guide—the Name of the Church." Church of Jesus Christ of Latter-day Saints, 2018. https://newsroom.churchofjesuschrist.org/style-guide.

Oaks, Dallin H. "The Divinely Inspired Constitution." *Ensign* (February 1992). https://www.churchofjesuschrist.org/study/ensign/1992/02/the-divinely-inspired-constitution.

O'Dea, Thomas. *The Mormons*. Chicago: University of Chicago Press, 1957.

Ohlheiser, Abby. "Bill Graham Is No Longer Saying Mormonism Is a Cult for Some Reason." *Slate*, October 16, 2012. https://slate.com/news-and-politics/2012/10/billy-graham-website-scrubbed-of-mormonism-cult-reference-after-endorsement.html.

O'Leary, Stephen D., and Brenda E. Brasher. "The Unknown God of the Internet: Religious Communication from the Ancient Agora to the Virtual Forum." In *Philosophical Perspectives on Computer-Mediated Communication*, edited by Charles Ess, 233–69. Albany: State University of New York Press, 1996.

Oppel, Richard A., Jr., and Erik Eckholm. "Prominent Pastor Calls Romney's Church a Cult." *New York Times*, October 7, 2011. https://www.nytimes.com/2011/10/08/us/politics/prominent-pastor-calls-romneys-church-a-cult.html.

Orsi, Robert. *The Madonna of 115th Street: Faith and Community in Italian Harlem*. New Haven, CT: Yale University Press, 1985.

Otterson, Michael. "Anti-Church Material." Interview by Ruth Todd. YouTube video, July 2, 2012. https://www.youtube.com/watch?v=JSUvFTQu5nY.

Otterson, Michael. "Michael Otterson: How Do Mormons Answer 'Not Christian' Claims?" *Deseret News*, October 23, 2011. https://www.deseret.com/2011/10/23/20224969/how-do-mormons-answer-not-christian-claims.

Packer, Boyd K. "All-Church Coordinating Council." Church of Jesus Christ of Latter-day Saints, May 18, 1993. Retrieved via Internet Archive at https://archive.org/details/coordinating_council_1993_boyd_k_packer/page/n3/mode/2up.

Palmer, Lee A., ed. "Ward Teaching." *Improvement Era* 48, no. 6 (1945): 354. http://archive.org/stream/improvementera4806unse#page/n35/mode/2up/search/palmer.

Parker, Mike. "Changes at the Maxwell Institute, and 'Controlling the Narrative.'" *FAIR* (blog), June 23, 2012. https://www.fairlatterdaysaints.org/blog/2012/06/23/changes-at-the-maxwell-institute-and-controlling-the-narrative.

Pavia, Catherine Matthews. "Literacy and Religious Agency: An Ethnographic Study of an Online LDS Women's Group." PhD diss., University of Massachusetts–Amherst, 2009.

Pavia, Catherine Matthews. "The 'My Online Friends' Religious Enclave: Expanding the Definition and Possibilities of Enclaved Discourses." *Rhetoric Review* 39, no. 1 (2020): 88–100.

Pavlik, Steve. "Of Saints and Lamanites: An Analysis of Navajo Mormonism." *Wicazo Sa Review* 8, no. 1 (1992): 21–30.

Pearson, Erika. "All the World Wide Web's a Stage: The Performance of Identity in Online Social Networks." *First Monday* 14, no. 3 (2009). https://firstmonday.org/ojs/index.php/fm/article/view/2162/2127.

Peters, John Durham. "Mormonism and Media." In *Oxford Handbook of Mormonism*, edited by Philip Barlow and Terryl Givens, 407–22. New York: Oxford University Press, 2015.

Peterson, Boyd Jay. *Hugh Nibley: A Consecrated Life*. Draper, UT: Greg Kofford Books, 2002.

Peterson, Eric S. "New Mormon-Feminist Group Lobbies LDS Church." *City Weekly*, September 21, 2010. https://www.cityweekly.net/utah/new-mormon-feminist-group-lobbies-lds-church/Content?oid=2149312.

Peterson, Greg. "The Internet and Christian and Muslim Communities." In *Religion and Popular Culture in America*, edited by Bruce David Forbes and Jeffery H. Mahan, 123–38. Los Angeles: University of California Press, 2000.

Petrey, Taylor. "Issues in Mormon Feminism." *Patheos* (blog), January 7, 2013. https://www.patheos.com/blogs/peculiarpeople/2013/01/issues-in-mormon-feminism/.

Pew Research Center. "Americans Learned Little about the Mormon Faith, but Some Attitudes Have Softened." December 14, 2012. https://www.pewresearch.org/religion/2012/12/14/attitudes-toward-mormon-faith/.

Pew Research Center. "America's Changing Religious Landscape." May 12, 2014. https://www.pewforum.org/2015/05/12/americas-changing-religious-landscape/.

Pew Research Center. "The Media, Religion and the 2012 Campaign for President." December 14, 2012. https://www.pewresearch.org/journalism/2012/12/14/media-religion-and-2012-campaign-president/.

Pew Research Center. "Romney's Mormon Faith Likely a Factor in Primaries, Not in a General Election." November 23, 2011. https://www.pewresearch.org/religion/2011/11/23/romneys-mormon-faith-likely-a-factor-in-primaries-not-in-a-general-election/.

Pixton, Paul B. "Common Consent." In *Encyclopedia of Mormonism*, edited by Daniel H. Ludlow. Macmillan, 1992.

Poe, Marshall T. *A History of Communications: Media and Society from the Evolution of Speech to the Internet*. New York: Cambridge University Press, 2010.

Postman, Neil. *Amusing Ourselves to Death: Public Discourse in the Age of Show Business*. New York: Penguin, 1985.

Postman, Neil. *Technopoly: The Surrender of Culture to Technology*. New York: Knopf, 1992.

Pratt, Timothy. "Mormon Women Set Out to Take a Stand, in Pants." *New York Times*, December 19, 2012. https://www.nytimes.com/2012/12/20/us/19mormon.html.

Prince, Gregory A. "Mitt Romney Is *Not* the Face of Mormonism." *Huffington Post Blog*, September 19, 2012. https://www.huffpost.com/entry/mitt-romney-is-not-the-face-of-mormonism_b_1897404.

Pruden, Wesley. "Then It's Agreed: They're Sorry." *Washington Times*, December 14, 2007. A04.

Pugmire, Genelle. "LDS Church Working on Online Topics Project." *Daily Herald*, January 17, 2014. Retrieved via Internet Archive at https://web.archive.org/web/20140117031250/http://www.heraldextra.com/news/local/lds-church-working-on-online-topics-project/article_4afdfb8d-8cdc-5a4e-8477-7cf21de7d7e7.html.

Qian, Hua, and Craig R. Scott. "Anonymity and Self-Disclosure on Weblogs." *Journal of Computer-Mediated Communication* 12 (2007): 1428–51.

Quinn, D. Michael. *The Mormon Hierarchy: Extensions of Power*. Salt Lake City: Signature, 1997.

Rappaport, Roy. *Ritual and Religion in the Making of Humanity*. New York: Cambridge University Press, 1999.

Rasmussen, Ellis T. *A Latter-day Saint Commentary on the Old Testament*. Salt Lake City: Deseret Book, 2004.

Ravitz, Jessica. "The Making of Mitt Romney: A Look at His Faith Journey." *CNN Belief Blog*, October 27, 2012.

Reeve, W. Paul. *Religion of a Different Color: Race and the Mormon Struggle for Whiteness*. New York: Oxford University Press, 2015.

Reingold, Howard. *The Virtual Community: Homesteading on the Electronic Frontier*. Reading, MA: Addison-Wesley, 1993.

Religious News Service. "Mormon Church Said to Be Keeping Files on Dissenters." *Times-News*, August 13, 1992, 5B.

Reno, Jamie. "Exclusive: Brigham Young's Great-Great-Granddaughter on Mormonism and Mitt Romney." Daily Beast, August 7, 2012. https://www.thedailybeast.com/exclusive-brigham-youngs-great-great-granddaughter-on-mormonism-and-mitt-romney.

Richards, Willard. "Journal, 1842–43: President Joseph Smith's Journal 1843 as Kept by Willard Richards." In *An American Prophet's Record: The Diaries and Journals of Joseph Smith*, edited by Scott Faulring, 256–449. Salt Lake City: Signature Books in Association with Smith Research Associates, 1989.

Riess, Jana. "Mormon Throwdown: Harry Reid Goes Mano-a-Mano with Mitt Romney." *Religion News Service* (blog), September 24, 2012. Retrieved via Internet Archive at https://web.archive.org/web/20140928091649/https://archives.religionnews.com/blogs/jana-riess/mormon-throwdown-harry-reid-goes-mano-a-mano-with-mitt-romney.

Riess, Jana. *The Next Mormons: How Millennials Are Changing the LDS Church*. London: Oxford University Press, 2019.

Roberts, B. H. *Studies of the Book of Mormon*. Edited by Brigham D. Madsen. Urbana: University of Illinois Press, 1985.

Romney, Mitt. "Faith in America." Speech, George Bush Presidential Library, College Station, Texas, December 6, 2007. https://www.npr.org/templates/story/story.php?storyId=16969460.

Roof, Wade Clark. *Spiritual Marketplace: Baby Boomers and the Remaking of American Religion*. Princeton University Press, 1999.

Ruchti, Elizabeth. "The Performance of Normativity: Mormons and the Construction of an American Masculinity." *Journal of Men, Masculinities, and Spirituality* 1, no. 2 (2007): 137–54.

Rutten, Tim. "A Religious 'Test' for Mitt Romney." *Los Angeles Times*, June 1, 2011. https://

www.latimes.com/opinion/la-xpm-2011-jun-01-la-oe-0601-rutten-20110601-story.html.

Saad, Lydia. "In U.S., 22% Are Hesitant to Support a Mormon in 2012." Gallup, June 20, 2011. https://news.gallup.com/poll/148100/hesitant-support-mormon-2012.aspx.

Schimmel, Solomon. "The Blogosphere of Resistance: Anonymous Blogging as a Safe Haven for Challenging Religious Authority and Creating Dissident Communities." In *Media, Spiritualities and Social Change*, edited by Stewart M. Hoover and Monica M. Emerich, 147–57. New York: Continuum, 2011.

Schmuhl, Emily. "Valerie Hudson: A Feminist Because of Faith." *Deseret News*, March 11, 2010. https://www.deseret.com/2010/3/11/20101322/valerie-hudson-a-feminist-because-of-faith.

Schudson, Michael. "Dynamics of Distortion in Collective Memory." In *Memory Distortion: How Minds, Brains, and Societies Reconstruct the Past*, edited by Daniel L. Schacter, 346–64. Cambridge, MA: Harvard University Press, 1997.

Schultheis, Emily. "Mormon Church Runs Search Ads on Romney's Name." Politico, November 5, 2012. https://www.politico.com/blogs/burns-haberman/2012/09/mormon-church-runs-search-ads-on-romneys-name-134567.

Scott, Richard G. "The Sanctity of Womanhood." *New Era* (November 2008). https://www.churchofjesuschrist.org/study/new-era/2008/11/the-sanctity-of-womanhood.

Shafovaloff, Aaron. "Mormonism, Officiality, and Plausible Deniability." Mormonism Research Ministry, 2009. https://www.mrm.org/official-doctrine.

Shipps, Jan. *Mormonism: The Story of a New Religious Tradition*. Champaign: University of Illinois Press, 1987.

Shipps, Jan. *Sojourner in the Promised Land: Forty Years among the Mormons*. Urbana: University of Illinois Press, 2000.

Sill, Sterling W. "The Strait Gate." *Ensign* (July 1980). https://www.churchofjesuschrist.org/study/ensign/1980/07/the-strait-gate.

Sitati, Joseph W. "Blessings of the Gospel Available to All." General Conference address. Church of Jesus Christ of Latter-day Saints, October 4, 2009. https://www.churchofjesuschrist.org/study/general-conference/2009/10/blessings-of-the-gospel-available-to-all.

Skinner, Jessica Lynn. "Awareness and Perceptions of Church Advertising: Student Reactions to the Mormon Church's Advertising Campaign." Master's thesis, University of Kansas, 2008. https://www.proquest.com/docview/275671975.

Smith, Daymon Mickel. *The Last Shall Be First and the First Shall Be Last: Discourse and Mormon History (a Dissertation)*. CreateSpace Independent Publishing, 2010.

Smith, Gregory L. "Dubious 'Mormon' Stories: A Twenty-First Century Construction of Exit Narratives." *Interpreter: A Journal of Mormon Thought*, February 23, 2013. https://journal.interpreterfoundation.org/wp-content/uploads/2013/02/SMITH1-Review-Mormon-Stories.pdf.

Smith, Gregory L. "Introduction." In *An Open Letter to Dr. Michael Coe*. Foundation for Apologetic Information and Research, 2011. https://www.fairlatterdaysaints.org/archive/publications/an-open-letter-to-dr-michael-coe.

Smith, Gregory L. "Polygamy, Prophets, and Prevarication: Frequently and Rarely Asked

Questions about the Initiation, Practice, and Cessation of Plural Marriage in the Church of Jesus Christ of Latter-day Saints." Foundation for Apologetic Information and Research, 2005. https://www.fairlatterdaysaints.org/archive/publications/polygamy-prophets-and-prevarication.

Smith, Gregory L. "Shattered Glass: The Traditions of Mormon Same-Sex Marriage Advocates Encounter Boyd K. Packer." *Mormon Studies Review* 23, no. 1 (2011): 61–85. https://scholarsarchive.byu.edu/cgi/viewcontent.cgi?article=1835&context=msr.

Smith, Hyrum. "The Word of Wisdom." *Times and Seasons* 3, no. 15 (June 1, 1842): 799–814. https://www.josephsmithpapers.org/paper-summary/times-and-seasons-1-june-1842/2.

Smith, Joseph. *An American Prophet's Record: The Diaries and Journals of Joseph Smith*. Edited by Scott Faulring. Salt Lake City: Signature Books in association with Smith Research Associates, 1989.

Solie, Stacey. "Jim Lehrer: Ask Mitt Romney If He Stands by Mormonism's Views of Women." Daily Beast, October 2, 2012. https://www.thedailybeast.com/jim-lehrer-ask-mitt-romney-if-he-stands-by-mormonisms-views-of-women.

Sorenson, Kim Crenshaw. "A Latter-day Father's Guidebook." *Ensign* (February 1995). Salt Lake City: Church of Jesus Christ of Latter-day Saints. https://www.churchofjesuschrist.org/study/ensign/1995/02/a-latter-day-fathers-guidebook.

Stacey, Judith. "Can There Be a Feminist Ethnography?" *Women's Studies International Forum* 11, no. 1 (1988): 21–27.

Stark, Rodney. "Why Religious Movements Succeed or Fail: A Revised General Model." *Journal of Contemporary Religion* 11, no. 2 (1996): 133–46.

Stewart, D. Michael. "I Have a Question: What Do We Know about the Purported Statement of Joseph Smith That the Constitution Would Hang by a Thread and That the Elders Would Save It?" *Ensign* (June 1976). https://www.churchofjesuschrist.org/study/ensign/1976/06/i-have-a-question/did-joseph-smith-say-that-the-constitution-would-hang-by-a-thread-and-that-the-elders-would-save-it?

Stewart, John J., and William E. Berrett. *Mormonism and the Negro*. Orem, UT: Bookmark, 1967.

Stolberg, Sheryl Gay. "For Romney, a Role of Faith and Authority." *New York Times*, October 15, 2011. https://www.nytimes.com/2011/10/16/us/politics/for-romney-a-role-of-faith-and-authority.html.

Sullivan, Amy. "The De Facto Religious Test in Presidential Politics." *Time*, October 21, 2011. https://swampland.time.com/2011/10/21/the-de-facto-religious-test-in-presidential-politics/.

Sullivan, Amy. "Mitt Romney's Evangelical Problem." *Washington Monthly*, September 2005. https://washingtonmonthly.com/2005/09/01/mitt-romneys-evangelical-problem/.

Tanner, Jerald, and Sandra Tanner. *Evolution of the Mormon Temple Ceremony: 1842–1990*. Salt Lake City: Utah Lighthouse Ministry, 1990.

Tanner, Jerald, and Sandra Tanner. *Mormonism: Shadow or Reality?* Modern Microfilm, 1964.

Taylor, Charles. *Modern Social Imaginaries*. Durham: Duke University Press, 2003.

Taylor, Scott. "Mormons & Media: A Presidential Spin, Thanks to Romney, Huntsman." *Deseret Morning News*, February 1, 2011. https://www.deseret.com/2011/2/1/20170901/mormons-media-a-presidential-spin-thanks-to-romney-huntsman.

Telushkin, Shira. "The Facebook of Mormon." *Atlantic*, January 31, 2014. https://www.theatlantic.com/technology/archive/2014/01/the-facebook-of-mormon/283467/.

Thomas, William I., and Dorothy Thomas. *The Child in America*. 2nd ed. New York: Alfred Knopf, 1929.

Tippett, Krista. "Mormon Demystified: Interview with Joanna Brooks." *On Being*, National Public Radio, October 20, 2011.

Turkle, Sherry. *Life on the Screen: Identity in the Age of the Internet*. New York: Simon & Schuster, 1995.

Turner, Victor. *The Ritual Process: Structure and Anti-Structure*. New York: Aldine, 1969.

Twain, Mark. *Roughing It*. Hartford, CT: American Publishing Company, 1872.

Uchtdorf, Dieter F. "A Matter of a Few Degrees." General Conference address. Church of Jesus Christ of Latter-day Saints, April 5, 2008. https://www.churchofjesuschrist.org/study/ensign/2008/05/a-matter-of-a-few-degrees.

Uchtdorf, Dieter F. "O How Great the Plan of Our God!" General Conference address. Church of Jesus Christ of Latter-day Saints, October 2016. https://www.churchofjesuschrist.org/study/general-conference/2016/10/o-how-great-the-plan-of-our-god.

van Biema, David. "Kingdom Come." *Time*, August 4, 1997. https://content.time.com/time/subscriber/article/0,33009,986794-7,00.html.

van Dijk, Teun Adrianus. "Critical Discourse Analysis." In *Handbook of Discourse Analysis*, edited by Teun Adrianus van Dijk, 466–85. New York: Harcourt, 1985.

Wadsworth, Nathaniel Hinckley. "Copyright Laws and the 1830 Book of Mormon." *BYU Studies* 45, no. 3 (2006): 77–95.

Walch, Tad. "Ordain Women Founder's Recruitment Efforts Result in Excommunication from LDS Church." *Deseret News*, June 23, 2014. https://www.deseret.com/2014/6/23/20543750/ordain-women-founder-s-recruitment-efforts-result-in-excommunication-from-lds-church.

Walch, Tad. "Polygamy Essays Provide Information about Early LDS Church—and Current Leadership." *Deseret News*, October 25, 2014. https://www.deseret.com/2014/10/25/20551279/polygamy-essays-provide-information-about-early-lds-church-and-current-leadership.

Wear Pants to Church Day. Community page. Facebook. 2012. https://www.facebook.com/WearPantsToChurchDay.

Wear Pants to Church Day. Event page. Facebook. 2012. https://www.facebook.com/events/144815455666087/.

Weaver, Sarah Jane. "Share More Gospel Messages on Social Media, Elder Bednar Says." *Church News*. Salt Lake City: Church of Jesus Christ of Latter-day Saints, August 19, 2014. https://www.lds.org/church/news/share-more-gospel-messages-on-social-media-elder-bednar-says.

Welch, Rosalynde. "The Odd Couple: Story and Community." *Patheos* (blog), June 28, 2012. https://www.patheos.com/latter-day-saint/odd-couple-rosalynde-welch-06-29-2012.

What Women Know. "All Are Alike Unto God." 2012. http://whatwomenknow.org/all_are_alike/.

Whitelocks, Sadie. "'I Hadn't Worn Pants to Church for 37 Years': Mormon Women Ditch

Strict Dress Code in Push for Gender Equality." *Daily Mail*, December 17, 2012. https://www.dailymail.co.uk/femail/article-2249477/I-hadnt-worn-pants-church-37-years-Mormon-women-ditch-strict-dress-code-push-gender-equality.html.

Whitelocks, Sadie. "Mormon Women Launch 'Wear Pants to Church Day' in Backlash over Strict Dress Code." *Daily Mail*, December 13, 2012. https://www.dailymail.co.uk/femail/article-2247550/Mormon-women-launch-wear-pants-church-day-backlash-strict-dress-code.html.

Wilcox, Clyde, and Carin Robinson. *Onward Christian Soldiers? The Religious Right in American Politics*. 4th ed. Boulder: Westview, 2010.

Wilcox, Linda P. "The Imperfect Science: Brigham Young on Medical Doctors." *Dialogue: A Journal of Mormon Thought* 12 (1979): 26–36.

Williams, Lane. "Mormon Media Observer: Time to End the Secrecy Allegation against Mormons." *Deseret News*, August 27, 2012. https://www.deseret.com/2012/8/27/20505941/mormon-media-observer-time-to-end-the-secrecy-allegation-against-mormons/.

Williams, Lane. "Mormon Media Observer: What Mitt Might Have Said." *Deseret News*, September 4, 2012. https://www.deseret.com/2012/9/4/20506233/mormon-media-observer-what-mitt-might-have-said.

Wilson, Jonathan Max. "Announcing the 1st Semiannual LDS Friends & Foes Rendezvous." *Millennial Star* (blog), February 13, 2014. https://www.millennialstar.org/announcing-the-1st-semiannual-lds-friends-foes-rendezvous/.

Wilson, Ron. "'I'm a Mormon' Media Campaign." Interview by Brooke Gladstone. *On the Media* podcast, October 14, 2011, https://www.wnycstudios.org/podcasts/otm/segments/164767-im-mormon-media-campaign.

Winslow, Ben. "BYU Caffeine Movement Fizzles." FOX 13 Online News, September 13, 2012. https://www.fox13now.com/2012/09/13/byu-caffeine-movement-fizzles.

Winslow, Ben. "LDS Church Clarifies Caffeine Use for Faithful." FOX 13 Online News, August 30, 2012. https://www.fox13now.com/2012/08/30/lds-blog-post-says-caffeine-ok-for-mormons.

Winter, Caroline. "How the Mormons Make Money." *Businessweek*, July 18, 2012. http://www.businessweek.com/articles/2012-07-10/how-the-mormons-make-money.

Woodford, Robert J. "Doctrine and Covenants Editions." In *Encyclopedia of Mormonism*, edited by Daniel H. Ludlow. Macmillan, 1992.

Woodger, Mary Jane. "Elaine Anderson Cannon, Young Women General President: Innovations, Inspiration, and Implementations." *Journal of Mormon History* 40, no. 4 (2014): 192.

Young, Brigham. "The Persecution of the Saints, Etc." In *Journal of Discourses*, vol. 10, no. 25. Salt Lake City: Deseret Book, 1974, 1863.

Zickuhr, Kathryn, and Aaron Smith. "Digital Differences." Pew Research Center, April 13, 2012. https://www.pewresearch.org/internet/2012/04/13/digital-differences/.

Index

Italicized page numbers indicate material in the front matter.